General Principles of
Sacramental Theology

General Principles of Sacramental Theology

Roger W. Nutt

The Catholic University of America Press
Washington, D.C.

The paper used in this publication meets the minimum requirements of
American National Standards for Information Science — Permanence of
Paper for Printed Library Materials, ANSI Z39.48-1984.

∞

Library of Congress Cataloging-in-Publication Data
Names: Nutt, Roger W., author.
Title: General principles of sacramental theology / Roger W. Nutt.
Description: Washington, D.C. : The Catholic University of America Press,
2017. | Includes bibliographical references and index.
Identifiers: LCCN 2016050355 | ISBN 9780813229386 (pbk. : alk. paper)
Subjects: LCSH: Sacraments — Catholic Church. | Sacraments — History
of doctrines.
Classification: LCC BX2200 .N88 2017 | DDC 234/.16 — dc23
LC record available at https://lccn.loc.gov/2016050355

Contents

Book provides structure for understanding.

Acknowledgments

This project, like my entire life, was worked out within a manifold web of dependency. Due to the generous support of the administration and the board of trustees of Ave Maria University, I recently enjoyed the benefit of a semester-long sabbatical. This book is the product of that sabbatical, for which I owe special thanks to my (then) department chairman, Gregory Vall, and several other administrators and trustees who blessed the proposal with their support at the various stages of approval, especially Seana Sugrue, Michael Dauphinais, H. James Towey, Robert Kennedy, and Michael T. O. Timmis. Ave Maria University's founder and principal benefactor, Thomas Monaghan, deserves a special note of thanks for all that he has done to make our work at Ave Maria possible.

I owe a special debt of gratitude to the staff of Canizaro Library of Ave Maria University for their tireless and timely support of my work, especially Jennifer Nodes, Sarah DeVille, Stan Smolinski, Carianne Wilson, and William Szwagiel.

For any merit that may be found in these pages, I am deeply indebted to Jeffrey Froula, Sr. Albert Marie Surmanski, OP, Reginald Lynch, OP, Paul Keller, OP, Katie Froula, and Matthew Levering. These six generous scholars read and commented on the manuscript at different stages of its development. Each offered penetrating, insightful, and charitably honest feedback, without which this work would have never seen the light of day. To the very best of my ability, I incorporated these suggestions into the revision of the work, but I recognize that while the final product is vastly improved due to the feedback of these readers, it nevertheless contains imperfections that are the product of my own shortcomings alone. The comments of two anonymous reviewers were also of inestimable value – even though I can't thank you each by name, I recognize your unmerited kindness to me. Mrs. Kelsey Wanless and Mrs. Anna Reynolds provided gracious and impeccable help in preparing the manuscript for publication.

John Martino of the Catholic University of America Press provided support and encouragement that went well beyond the call of duty. I shall not forget the depth of his professionalism or the acuteness of his most helpful judgments. Susan Needham's editorial work provided an added layer of precision; fortunately for me, only she knows just how much she contributed to this book!

My childhood friend Chris Specht passed away from cancer as I was nearing the completion of this manuscript. We became friends through the joys of little league baseball – his dad, Ron, lovingly and patiently coached and mentored us as if we were all his sons. Sadly, Chris left behind a charming wife, Monica, and two precious young children, Cullen and Ayla. The latter stages of his battle overlapped with much of my work on this volume. He asked me about the content and my progress regularly, and the book become a source of many memorable conversations with him. He looked forward to seeing the book in print. I will always fondly associate this material with his memory; may he rest in peace!

I owe the deepest gratitude to those closest to me: John Lawrence Nelson for his prayers; Fr. Matthew L. Lamb for his friendship; Ralph and Ann Van Vickle and Julie Van Vickle for their support and encouragement over the years; my loving parents, Roger and Dianne Nutt, and my sister, Kristen Payton, for a lifetime of unmerited blessings; and Dr. Anthony Buhl for his mentoring guidance.

I dedicate this volume to my wife, Susan, and our son, Timothy. They both made significant sacrifices to ensure the productivity of my sabbatical. The satisfaction of bringing this volume to fruition belongs to us all.

General Principles of
Sacramental Theology

Introduction

In John 15:15 Jesus refers to his followers as "friends." St. Thomas frequently took up this teaching of Christ to indicate the spiritual significance of the sacraments of the Church. Because, Thomas teaches, "it is the special feature of friendship to live together with friends," it was most fitting that Christ should leave the Church the gift of his presence in the Eucharist. At a time in which sacramental rites and ecclesial institutions are viewed with suspicion and in an impersonal and juridical fashion, it is important to recall that for Christ and his followers, the Church and her sacraments are fundamentally sources of communion among friends.[1]

This book stands within the division of labor of systematic theology as a work *de Sacramentis in Genere*, or a work on the principles that are common to all of the seven sacraments. (In English this material is often called "the sacraments in common" or "general sacramental theology.") As such, the book does not offer a developed

1. More will be said below about Aquinas's teaching on friendship in relation to the sacraments, especially the Eucharist. For a treatment of this theme with special consideration of the relation between Christian charity and friendship, see John-Pierre Torrell, OP, "Charity as Friendship in St. Thomas Aquinas," in *Christ and Spirituality in St. Thomas Aquinas*, trans. Bernhard Blankenhorn, OP (Washington, D.C.: The Catholic University of America Press, 2011), 45–64. For a more general treatment of friendship in Aquinas, see Daniel Schwartz, *Aquinas on Friendship*, Oxford Philosophical Monographs (Oxford: Oxford University Press, 2007). For excerpts on friendship in Plato, Aristotle, Cicero, Seneca, Aelred, Aquinas, Montaigne, Bacon, Kant, Emerson, Kierkegaard, and Telfer, see Michael Pakaluk, ed., *Other Selves: Philosophers on Friendship* (Indianapolis, Ind.: Hackett Publishing Company, Inc., 1991).

treatment of any one, let alone all, of the seven sacraments of the Catholic Church, though references to them are made throughout the work, where relevant. Rather, general sacramental theology covers those basic topics and principles — such as the nature of the sacraments, sacramental grace, sacramental character, sacramental causality, the necessity and number of the sacraments, sacramental matter and form, *inter alia* — which apply to all seven. An understanding of these topics and principles is necessary and important for an appreciation of each of the seven sacraments and the sevenfold sacramental system as a whole.

The work is composed and organized in such a way that it can be used for personal study or as a course text, serving as a component of a larger course on the seven sacraments, or even as a foundational outline of a course on the principles of general sacramental theology that could be augmented by the reading of primary texts. The goal of the book is to assist the reader and student of Catholic theology in achieving broad-based competency in the general principles of Catholic sacramental theology. The attempt to reach this goal required judgments about just how much detail to present, especially at the historical level. It is not a narrative historical introduction to the topics normally covered within general sacramental theology, although it includes many references to the so-called historical sources, especially the teaching of the Magisterium. The book provides a running argument in defense of the intelligibility of Catholic teaching in this area, with special advertence to the theology of St. Thomas Aquinas.

This work also addresses a current lacuna in English-language theological literature. Bernard Leeming's highly respected book *Principles of Sacramental Theology* was published more than sixty years ago. Since that time, there has been a noted decrease, especially in English-language sacramental theology, in treatments of the general principles of sacramental theology.

This trend is the result of a long series of factors in Western thought and culture. Shortly after Aquinas's death, some medieval authors began to construe philosophical knowledge in a new way that set the stage for the Enlightenment's discomfort with classical metaphysics. The *via moderna*, as historians of philosophy call it, denies that we can know fundamental aspects of reality that were presented in the metaphysics of the *via antiqua* as exemplified in the works of theologians like Albert the Great, Aquinas, and Bonaventure and philosophers like Aristotle. Without recourse to the auxiliary language of classical metaphysics as a patrimony of true knowledge about the foundational order of reality — a patrimony that can be drawn upon for the systematic presentation of revealed knowledge — theologians turned to other tools for the articulation of revealed doctrine. Within the more narrow confines of this new view of reality, the sacramental symbols and gestures are commonly presented from the perspective of human experience and studied and explained according to the methods of scientific history.[2] This historical approach to the Christian sacraments displaces the centrality of the theological realities that ground and order the Church's sacramental worship, namely, the triune God, Christ, and Christ's priestly activity within the Church.[3] So a metaphysically agnostic approach to sacramental worship has come to outweigh studies of the principles of sacramental theology, with the result that, at least according to Romanus Cessario, "the study of sacramental theology [today] remains almost exclusively subordinated to the programs in liturgical studies."[4]

2. For a comparison of the uses and understanding of "sign" in Albert the Great and "symbol" in the more experiential, post-Rahnerian sacramental theologians, especially Louis-Marie Chauvet, see Sr. Albert Marie Surmanski, OP, "Sign and Symbol: Sacramental Experience in Albert's *De corpore domini*," *New Blackfriars* 97 (2016): 479–91.

3. A radical example of this trend is found in Siobhan Garrigan's *Beyond Ritual: Sacramental Theology after Habermas* (Burlington, Vt.: Ashgate, 2004). Garrigan advocates a separation of sacramental theology from Church doctrine, and the replacement of doctrine with "the practical meaning of the Christian message by articulating a new sense of inclusiveness in terms of both language and experience, particularly as is manifest at the margins of the Church" (Garrigan, p. 1).

4. Romanus Cessario, OP, "The Sacraments of the Church," in *Vatican II: Renewal Within Tradition*, ed. Matthew Lamb and Matthew Levering (Oxford: Oxford University Press, 2008), 140. For a creative and theologically rich presentation of liturgical theology

In their purest forms, of course, liturgical, ritual, and sacramental theology each help to illumine the richness of the sacramental life of the Church.[5] In fact, in its remote origins, the liturgical movement in the Catholic Church aimed to foster deeper spiritual and prayerful participation in the sacraments, and many fine liturgists have provided excellent theological material supporting this end, without subordinating the sacraments to categories of experience and historical research.[6] Pius XII's 1947 encyclical letter, *Mediator Dei*, is, to a large degree, the fruit of the positive aspects of this movement. Cyprian Vagaggini (perhaps the most accomplished liturgical theologian of the conciliar period) observed that "it became [in liturgical theology] the practice to give all this material a predominantly historical treatment."[7] He argued that the ideal of these studies shifted from the concern for the spiritual fruitfulness of the Church's worship to that of "tracing the historical development of the objects ... which constitute the liturgy, from their origin to the present day, and this, if possible, not only in the Roman liturgy but in all liturgies, obsolete or current."[8]

It is not difficult to demonstrate the important connections that exist between the holiness of the Church, the pursuit of holiness by the faithful, and the importance of the sacraments as causes of grace. The Universal Call to Holiness that is so central to Vatican II's teaching on the Church cannot be realized if the faithful do not understand and appreciate the irreplaceable role that the sacraments have

---

that includes substantive engagement with the Christian East, see David W. Fagerberg, *Theologia Prima: What Is Liturgical Theology?* (Chicago/Mundelein: Hillenbrand Books, 2004).

5. Vagaggini points out that prior to the liturgical movement in the Catholic Church most liturgical topics were treated solely in a canonical fashion. See Cyprian Vagaggini, *Theological Dimensions of the Liturgy: A General Treatise on the Theology of the Liturgy*, trans. Leonard J. Doyle and W. A. Jurgens (Collegeville, Minn.: Liturgical Press, 1976), xx.

6. The work of Joseph Jungmann, Louis Bouyer, Cyprian Vagaggini, Romano Guardini, and Joseph Ratzinger, to name just a handful of authors, indicates the light that liturgical theology can shed on sacramental worship.

7. Vagaggini, *Theological Dimensions of the Liturgy*, xx.

8. Ibid.

within the Christian moral and spiritual life. The sacraments bestow and nourish the personal communion with Jesus Christ that is the true source of human happiness — hence, the motivation behind this book: to present a vibrant alternative to some of the more dominant strands of scholarship by exploring the areas in which recourse to St. Thomas's teaching can help to highlight the sacraments and their significance within the plan of salvation.

Some explanation should be given to the methodology of the book, which can be summarized by the words "ecclesial" and "Thomistic." The term "ecclesial" signifies more than the use of sources that are Christian in nature. As much as possible, the substantive magisterial teaching of the Church on the particular topics considered below is quoted and developed as a positive theological source and point of reference.

Why, however, include the word "Thomistic" in reference to the methodology of this book? There are many reasons for this. The magisterial teaching of the Church is not to be conflated with the doctrine of any one thinker in the tradition. Nevertheless, in contemplating, preaching, teaching, and developing the magisterial patrimony, Aquinas's theology of the sacraments is particularly helpful. The Council Fathers commend Aquinas to students of theology as follows:

> ... [I]n order that they may illumine the mysteries of salvation as completely as possible, the students should learn to penetrate them more deeply with the help of speculation, *under the guidance of St. Thomas*, and to perceive their interconnections. They should be taught to recognize these same mysteries as present and working in liturgical actions and in the entire life of the Church. They should learn to seek the solutions to human problems under the light of revelation, to apply the eternal truths of revelation to the changeable conditions of human affairs and to communicate them in a way suited to men of our day.[9]

The perception of the "interconnections" of the mysteries of faith, from the theology of the Trinitarian missions to the concrete

9. Decree on Priestly Formation: *Optatam Totius* 16, §3 (October 28, 1965). Available on the Vatican website.

unfolding of these missions in the bestowal of grace through the sacraments, is something that Aquinas's guidance makes particularly fruitful.[10] This does not mean that other Christian thinkers and resources are not presented here and taken seriously. But it does mean that Aquinas's teaching on these topics is especially helpful in providing a renewed exposition of the profundity and intelligibility of the ecclesial doctrines. In particular, questions 60–65 of the Third Part of the *Summa theologiae* offer a veritable thesaurus of wisdom and penetration into the principles of general sacramental theology, as well as into problems and challenges that confront the Church today.

Recourse to Aquinas's saintly wisdom, therefore, is not included as a kind of archeological relic meant to indicate the decadent thought of some good old days, long past but intriguing to reminisce about. Rather, Aquinas's sacramental doctrine, as the fruit of a saint, scholar-doctor, and *avant garde* man of his age, helps to locate the heartbeat of the mystical body. The metaphor of the heart is central to the Christian articulation of the renewal and transformation that the gift of grace effects in each soul justified in Christ. In their commentary on John 6, Francis Martin and William Wright offer the following reflection in conjunction with the causal efficacy of the Eucharist:

> If the Holy Spirit is the soul of the Church, the Eucharist is its beating heart, pumping Christ's blood through the members of his body, the Church. If we are to grow in holiness and love, we must make the Eucharist the center of our lives, because in doing so we make Christ the center of our lives. If we receive Christ worthily in the Eucharist and worship him in Eucharistic adoration, he will fill us with his grace and enlarge our hearts to love and serve more perfectly.[11]

This book argues that a vital sacramental spirituality constitutes the very heartbeat of the Church. Before we can come, though, to an

---

10. For a fuller development of the relationship between Aquinas's theology and the theological renewal called for by Vatican II, see Roger W. Nutt, "From within the Mediation of Christ: The Place of Christ in the Christian Moral and Sacramental Life According to St. Thomas Aquinas," *Nova et Vetera*, English Edition, 5 (2007): 817–42.

11. Francis Martin and William Wright IV, *The Gospel of John* (Grand Rapids, Mich.: Baker Academic, 2015), 131.

appreciation of the significance in Christian life of each of the seven sacraments as the divinely willed means of communion and friendship between God and humanity, we must first lay a sound foundation in the general principles of sacramental theology.

The parts and chapters of this book are meant to follow and build logically upon each other. This structure is not merely pedagogical in nature, though it has that advantage. Rather, there is what medieval theologians called an *ordo* that is intrinsic to the mysteries of faith. Following this *ordo* more readily facilitates comprehension of the material.

Part I presents a methodological and doctrinal foundation so that the theology of the principles of sacramental theology and the seven sacraments themselves can be appreciated in their proper theological context and order. Building on this doctrinal foundation, Part II considers the basic nature of the sacraments. This includes all the aspects that are needed to bring about a sacrament, as well as the doctrine of the necessity of the sacraments. Part III includes chapters on sacramental causality, grace, and character, as well as some material that is organically connected to these topics. Finally, the conclusion is crafted so as to open the reader to the spiritual implications of the principles of the preceding pages.

This work is offered as a source of hope to those seeking deeper intimacy with God amidst the confusion, alienation, and disappointment that accompanies life in a fallen world. Nietzsche's famous "madman" ran wildly through the marketplace "looking for God," ultimately declaring him dead.[12] The general principles of sacramental theology remind Christians that God is not lost, but readily available and willing to pour himself into their hearts through the sacraments of the Church. St. John of the Cross reminds one of his followers that "it should be known that if anyone is seeking God, the Beloved is seeking that person much more."[13] While it is true

12. The "Parable of the Madman" is in Nietzsche's *The Gay Science*, ed. Walter Kaufmann (New York: Vintage, 1974), 181–82.

13. *The Living Flame of Love*, stanza 3, §28. In *The Collected Works of John of the Cross*,

that God is present, in some way at least, everywhere in the created order, the sacraments are the privileged points in which the transformative friendship between God and humanity is realized. It is the work of theologians, pastors, and catechists of this generation to explain again, with renewed intensity, this truth to God's faithful.

---

trans. Kieran Kavanaugh, OCD, and Otilio Rodriguez, OCD (Washington, D.C.: ICS Publications, 1991), 684.

PART I

Methodological and Doctrinal Considerations for a Theology of the Sacraments

.

ONE

The Sacraments as Theology
Wisdom and Theological Method

The purpose of this chapter is to map out a foundational approach to sacramental theology that is open to the breadth of wisdom that emerges from the teaching of Scripture and of the Fathers, Doctors, and Magisterium of the Church. As noted above, in many of its branches, schools, and accepted articulations, Christian theology today has lost its ties to its foundation in metaphysical and theological wisdom and, as a result, it stands cut off from its most profound dimensions. This is the case in sacramental theology, too.

The Pursuit of Wisdom and Sacramental Theology

Perhaps the single characteristic that most differentiates the *via moderna* from the view of the pre-Enlightenment Christians (and ancients) is the abandonment by modernity of the pursuit of wisdom as the aim of both profane and sacred learning. A significant factor to note in this drift away from the pursuit of wisdom, which has many cultural, political, and intellectual components, is that shortly after Aquinas's death in 1274/5 some authors began to construe the nature of philosophical knowledge in a new way.[1] This new presentation of philosophical knowledge gave birth to an understanding of the nature and order of reality that called into question the status of many basic tenets of the Christian faith and metaphysical patrimony. Speaking of the challenges that these trends pose in the context of the sacramental liturgy of the Church, Joseph Ratzinger observed, "The whole problem of knowledge in the modern world is present. If an interior opening-up does not occur in man that enables him to see more than what can be measured and weighed, to perceive the reflection of divine glory in creation, then God remains excluded from our field of vision."[2]

It is beyond the scope of this chapter and book to provide a detailed historical presentation of the problem of knowledge in the modern world; what follows is merely a sketch of broad themes that merit closer inspection in another format. The *via moderna* has at least three basic, interrelated tenets that pose particular challenges for sacramental theologians today.[3] First, there is a new emphasis on the practical and productive forms of knowledge, which displace the contemplative and speculative dimensions of classical and Christian thought.[4] Second, there is the reduction of reality to the empirical and spatial realm.[5] Third, causality and knowledge of being through

1. For a helpful presentation of Aquinas's teaching on wisdom in its many aspects, which has also sections on wisdom in pre-Aristotelian thought, in Aristotle, the Old and New Testaments, and St. Augustine, see Kieran Conley, *A Theology of Wisdom: A Study in St. Thomas* (Dubuque, Iowa: The Priory Press, 1963).

2. Joseph Cardinal Ratzinger, *The Spirit of the Liturgy*, trans. John Saward (San Francisco: Ignatius Press, 2000), 122.

3. For a helpful application of how some of these tenets affected Eucharistic theology after Aquinas, see Marilyn McCord Adams, *Some Later Medieval Theories of the Eucharist: Thomas Aquinas, Giles of Rome, Duns Scotus, and William of Ockham* (Oxford: Oxford University Press, 2010), 4–28. For a discussion of Ockham's (†1347) break with the prior reception of Aristotle's categories, see Armand Maurer, *The Philosophy of William of Ockham in the Light of its Principles* (Toronto: Pontifical Institute of Mediaeval Studies, 1999), 40.

4. In the "aphorisms" of his *The New Organon*, Bacon (†1626) famously declared that "Knowledge is power." See Francis Bacon, *The New Organon and Related Writings* (Indianapolis, Ind.: The Bobbs-Merrill Company, Inc., 1960), 39 [aphorism III].

5. Descartes's proclivity for mathematics gave him a decided preference for geometrical models of reality. "Most of all," Descartes (†1650) explains in his "Discourse on

causes are reduced to the a priori categories of the mind, which are imposed on experience but not derived from it.[6] These tenets progressively moved Western thought into a more practically focused, empirically and spatially circumscribed, and subjectively reliant mode of thought and view of the world.

The focus on production and the material order, and the rejection of a metaphysics of causation, make more difficult the necessary "interior opening-up" that Ratzinger describes. A reappropriation of the wisdom tradition can serve as an avenue for an intellectual and spiritual renewal in the face of these challenges. For Christians and the ancients, by contrast, the pursuit of wisdom corresponds to a whole way of life — a most fully human form of life.

The great schoolmen of the Middle Ages, especially Thomas Aquinas (1225–1274), loved quoting the ancient Greek philosopher Aristotle (ca. 350 B.C.), about the nature of wisdom. "Among other things" about what constitutes a wise man, Aquinas explains that Aristotle "includes the notion that 'it belongs to the wise man to

---

Method," "was I delighted with mathematics because of the certainty of its demonstrations and the evidence of its reasoning; but I did not yet understand its true use, and, believing that it was of service only in the mechanical arts, I was astonished that, seeing how firm and solid was its basis, no loftier edifice had been reared thereupon." See *Discourse on the Method of Rightly Conducting the Reason and Seeking for Truth in the Sciences*, in *Descartes: Key Philosophical Writings*, trans. Elizabeth Haldane and G. R. T. Ross (Hertfordshire: Wordsworth Editions, 1997), 75 [Part I, §8]. For a helpful presentation of the movement to a quantitative and material understanding of reality from Ockham to Descartes, see Matthew R. McWhorter, "The Real Distinction of Substance and Quantity: John of St. Thomas in Contrast to Ockham and Descartes," *The Modern Schoolman* 85 (2008): 225–45.

6. At the apex of the Enlightenment, Immanuel Kant's (†1804) critique of the range of metaphysical knowledge asserted that the mind could not know things in themselves. The metaphysical study of being with recourse to causal knowledge derived from the observation of change in the material world gives way under Kant's critique to the study of appearances (phenomena) as experienced in the mind of the knower. "Kant," Avery Dulles explains, "made room for faith by redefining it, no longer as belief accepted on external authority, but rather as belief resting on motives that are subjectively sufficient and objectively insufficient." See Avery Dulles, *The Assurance of Things Hoped For: A Theology of Christian Faith* (Oxford: Oxford University Press, 1994), 70. For a critical outline of Kant's thought as it relates to Catholic theology, see Giovanni Sala, "What Use Is Kant for Theology?" in *Wisdom and Holiness, Science and Scholarship: Essays in Honor of Matthew L. Lamb*, ed. Michael Dauphinais and Matthew Levering (Ave Maria, Fla.: Sapientia Press, 2007), 293–314.

order.'"[7] How is true wisdom related to ordering or governing? Aquinas explains that what guides the wise ordering of things is the end or purpose. "Since the end of each thing," Aquinas explains, "is its good, a thing is then best disposed when it is fittingly ordered to its end."[8]

What is the highest good or purpose of humanity; what is the ultimate thing for which it is created? Because man is a rational creature, his highest or ultimate good, Aquinas argues, is truth. Aquinas takes this argument to be more than a philosophical conclusion. Truth as humanity's end corresponds to the very mission and purpose of Jesus Christ. "Divine Wisdom testifies," Aquinas notes, "that He has assumed flesh and come into the world in order to make known the truth: 'For this was I born, and for this I came into the world, that I should give testimony to the truth' (John 18:37)."[9]

What does all of this have to do with a book on general sacramental theology? Our "technocratic" mindset (as Pope Francis terms it), which reduces knowledge to production and the nature of reality itself to the spatial-empirical order, makes it all the more difficult to appreciate the spiritual and supernatural significance of the sacraments. Spirituality is seen as another "technique" to master with appropriate reading or training, rather than the discovery and following of the ordering principle of human life. But by his mission, by his life, death, and Resurrection, Christ orders humanity to the truth itself, the truth of human existence, and the true way of living. In Christ, the goal to which humanity is to direct the entirety of life is brought to light and the source of grace to bring this motion to rest is found. "The counsels of a wise friend are of great use," Aquinas explains, "according to Proverbs 27:9: 'Ointment and perfumes rejoice the heart: and the good counsels of a friend rejoice the soul.' But Christ is our wisest and greatest friend. Therefore His counsels are supremely use-

---

7. Thomas Aquinas, *Summa contra gentiles*, book I, 1, trans. Anton Pegis (Notre Dame, Ind.: University of Notre Dame Press, 1955), 59. Aquinas is citing Aristotle's *Metaphysics*, book I, 2 (982a18).

8. Aquinas, *Summa contra gentiles* (Pegis), 59.

9. Ibid, 60 [2].

ful and becoming."[10] The Christian life, then, is the pursuit of discipleship in the counsels of humanity's "wisest and greatest friend," Jesus Christ. In sacramental worship, likewise, humanity must seek the wise counsel of Christ's word and teaching.

The sources of Christian theology do not reduce the practice of religion to the practical ends of making or technique, nor do they reduce the totality of knowledge to the realm of the senses; rather, the life of faith is unveiled as the ultimate pursuit of wisdom, a pursuit that recognizes life with God as the central ordering principle. A wisdom-based approach to faith (and life) is marked by the recognition that eternal life is not something that can be obtained, made, or produced by the mastery of some technique or self-help program; it is sought, rather, in a life ordered to friendship with God. The Psalmist (a profound representative of the wisdom tradition) declares quite clearly that the happy or "blessed" man is one whose "delight is in the law of the Lord, and on his law he mediates day and night" (Psalm 1:2). Viewed within the order of wisdom, the sacraments orient the faithful to the spiritual and supernatural goal of rational life that lies beyond the horizon of the empirical realm and the human power of production.

For this reason Aquinas considers theology or what he calls "sacred doctrine" to be the highest intellectual pursuit. "Sacred doctrine derives its principles," Aquinas explains, "not from any human knowledge, but from the divine knowledge, through which, as through the highest wisdom, all our knowledge is set in order."[11] The knowledge that is communicated in divine Revelation and received by faith "treats of God viewed as the highest cause," and more importantly, "as far as He is known to Himself alone and revealed to others. Hence sacred doctrine is especially called wisdom."[12]

---

10. *Summa theologiae* I-II, q. 108, a. 4, sed contra. Translations from the *Summa theologiae* are from *Summa theologiae*, Complete set, Latin-English (Lander, Wyo.: The Aquinas Institute, 2012), cited hereafter as *ST*. See also Romanus Cessario's "The Sacramental Mediation of Divine Friendship and Communion," in Romanus Cessario, *Theology and Sanctity* (Ave Maria, Fla.: Sapientia Press, 2014), 34–68.

11. *ST* I, q. 1, a. 6, ad 1.   12. *ST* I, q. 1, a. 6.

Ramifications of Wisdom-based Theology for the Sacraments

Sacred doctrine is distinguished from natural philosophy "because it proceeds from principles established by the light of a higher science [than reason alone], namely, the science of God and the blessed."[13] Aquinas's articulation of the sapiential nature of theology and its unique method of proceeding by way of principles communicated or revealed by God has three important ramifications for a foundational sacramental theology.

First, as theology or sacred doctrine, sacramental theology (and liturgical studies) must have as its measure the knowledge bestowed by divine Revelation, the magisterial interpretation of Revelation by the Church, and the privileged witness of the saints and doctors. This does not mean that historical research into the Church's liturgy or the celebration of a particular sacrament can be dismissed by the theologian. The work of theology requires, in addition to historical and philosophical standards embraced by the academy, accountability to the light of divine Revelation.

Second, and following upon the first point, because Christian theology draws upon the wisdom that is contained in divine Revelation and that thus grants access to the wisdom of God himself, arbitrary reasoning ought not to be posited as a form of authentic theological explanation. This means that there is more to the sacraments than merely an abstract divine command or the caprice of ecclesial authority. The sacraments are the product of divine authority, but this authority is ordered by God's wisdom, which aims to lead us to friendship with himself. Ecclesial governance of the sacraments follows upon the order of wisdom that instituted the sacraments. As noted above, "the office" of the wise is to "order." Christ's fulfillment of the liturgical life of Israel by his priestly sacrifice and the continuation of this fulfillment in the sacraments of the New Law draws those who share in it into God's all-wise plan of salvation.

13. *ST* I, q. 1, a. 2.

It is tempting to read the doctrine of worship through the lens of God's omnipotence without reference to his wisdom and goodness. "Why go to Church on Sunday — God is everywhere, right?" "Why go to confession — at all! — *let alone to a priest? God hears me when I ask for forgiveness, right?*" Such questions, while quite understandable, do not proceed from a docility to the promptings of God's wisdom. The real question for all Christians ought to be, not what, hypothetically, the omnipotent God can do, but rather, what is the actual path that he calls his disciples to follow? Catholics have long recognized that God's power is not constricted by the sacraments. But, a truly wisdom-based approach to theology looks to the knowledge of faith to learn the meaning of each sacramental sign and the place of the sacraments within the divinely ordered life of the Church. God does not thus command sacramental worship simply for the sake exacting obedience from the faithful. Rather, the sacramental system provides acts of worship that relate the faithful to God within a just and orderly pattern of fulfillment that unfolds according to the divine wisdom.

There is a culture that is intrinsic to the unfolding of the divine wisdom with regard to the material elements and verbal formulae used in the sacraments. Bread, for example, is not merely a fare of Mediterranean and Near Eastern origin without any signification beyond its culinary usage. Bread was used in the very first Passover meal by the divine initiative on the night in which the Jews were freed from slavery by God (see Exodus 12:8); bread and wine were the sacrificial offerings of Melchizedek the high priest of Salem (see Genesis 14:8); bread was the divinely provided means of sustenance for the chosen people as they journeyed through the desert (see Exodus 16:4); fresh bread was placed before God each week on the Sabbath (see Exodus 25:30 and Leviticus 24:8); and Christ used bread to feed the multitudes and pique their interest in his identity (see John 6:5ff). The same could be said about the water of the flood, the Red Sea, or the Jordan River. As a result, the bread of the sacrament of the Eucharist and the water of Baptism are not merely expressions of the Church's historico-cultural origins, nor are they merely the preferences of the worshipping community: when used within the Church, the bread and water are signs whose focal meaning is derived from their divine appropriation in the Old Law and by Christ.

The third ramification of the sapiential approach to the sacraments is an extension of the previous point. The sacraments are not products of people's religious longings or paternalistic projections. They are expressive, to be sure, of the faith of the worshipping members of the Church, but the faith expressed in the sacraments flows from the revelation of the divine wisdom and the founding intention of Christ himself as the author of what Aquinas calls the whole "rite of the Christian life."[14] Describing Aquinas's approach to the liturgy and the sacraments, Liam Walsh makes the following helpful observation:

> When he comes to deal with the core of the Church's liturgy, in his discussion of the sacraments towards the end of the *Tertia Pars*, he is not opening up a new tract but simply coming in his own good time to discuss the actual working out of the relationship between God and his creation that has been the subject of his single-minded study from the first questions of the *Prima Pars*. Throughout the *Summa* he is writing theology pure and simple, not the theology of this or that. He does not present a theology of the liturgy but incorporates liturgy in his theology.[15]

The correspondence of (God-centered) theological knowledge rooted in faith with the divine wisdom provides an integrated view of reality that is not possible if a lower, less encompassing object, such as human experience or empirical knowledge, is posited as the starting point. "He who considers absolutely the highest cause of the whole universe," Aquinas argues,

> namely God, is most of all called wise. Hence wisdom is said to be the knowledge of divine things, as Augustine says (De Trin. xii, 14). But sacred doctrine essentially treats of God viewed as the highest cause — not only so

---

14. In *ST* III, q. 63, a. 1. Thomas speaks of sacraments as ordered to "the perfecting of the soul in things pertaining to the Divine worship according to the rite of the Christian life [*secundum ritum Christianae vitae*]."

15. Liam Walsh, "Liturgy in the Theology of St. Thomas," *The Thomist* 38 (1974): 557–83, at 559.

far as He can be known through creatures just as philosophers knew Him — "That which is known of God is manifest in them" (Romans 1:19) — but also as far as He is known to Himself alone and revealed to others. Hence sacred doctrine is especially called wisdom.[16]

When Western philosophers, as briefly noted above, began to construe philosophical knowledge in a more empirically based manner, it became increasingly difficult for theologians to articulate the spiritual and causal aspects of faith meaningfully.[17] Catherine Pickstock explains this difficulty as follows: "[B]y the breakdown of the traditional religious order, space becomes a pseudo-eternity which, unlike genuine eternity, is fully comprehensive to the human gaze, and yet supposedly secure from the ravages of time."[18] This breakdown culminates in what Pickstock names the "spatial illusion" of

16. *ST* I, q. 1, a. 6.

17. One notable attempt to articulate the Church's sacramental doctrine in terms that are more compatible with post-Kantian thought is the theology and ontology of symbol developed by Karl Rahner, SJ (†1984). Rahner's thought was influenced by the engagement with Kant in the early transcendental Thomist Joseph Maréchal and in the philosophy of Martin Heidegger; the work of Kant and the work of Heidegger were both prominent during the years of Rahner's seminary and academic formation. He attended the lectures of the Heidegger in 1934. Rahner advocated rooting the meaning of being in the symbolism of an agent's actions: "all beings are by their nature symbolic, because they necessarily 'express' themselves in order to attain their own nature." Karl Rahner, "The Theology of the Symbol," in *More Recent* Writings, vol. 4 of *Theological Investigations*, trans. Kevin Smith (London: Darton, Longman, and Todd, 1966), 221–52, 224. When applied to the sacraments, this experiential and symbolic understanding of being turns the focus from God's use of the liturgical signs to the symbolic expression of the being of the worshipping community in and through the rites of worship. For Rahner's application of his doctrine of being to the sacraments, see his "Introduction" in Karl Rahner, *Meditations on the Sacraments* (New York: Seabury Press, 1977). For a helpful presentation of Rahner's doctrine of symbol, see Patrick Burke, *Reinterpreting Rahner: A Critical Study of His Major Themes* (New York: Fordham University Press, 2002), passim. For an assessment of Rahner's thought by one of his theological contemporaries, see William A. Van Roo, SJ, "Reflections on Karl Rahner's '*Kirche und Sakramente*,'" *Gregorianum* 44 (1963): 465–500. For a summary and explanation of Rahner's principal ideas and works, see Fergus Kerr, *Twentieth-Century Catholic Theologians: From Neoscholasticism to Nuptial Mysticism* (Oxford: Blackwell Publishing, 2007), 87–104. See also Conor Sweeney, *Sacramental Presence after Heidegger: Ontotheology, Sacraments, and a Mother's Smile* (Cascade Books: Eugene, Ore., 2015).

18. Catherine Pickstock, *After Writing: On the Liturgical Consummation of Philosophy* (Oxford: Blackwell, 1998), 48.

modern and post-modern life, which creates a special challenge for the sacramental and liturgical order. "The illusions which [the spatial illusion] can encourage," Pickstock observes, "are only *legitimized* by an increasing denial of genuine transcendence, understood as doxological reliance upon a donating source which one cannot command. Without eternity, space must be made absolute and the uncertainty of time's source and end be suppressed."[19] This means that elements within the created order, such as experience of the physical world, displace the proper emphasis on the transcendent presence of God within the liturgy.

Aquinas's stress on the importance of wisdom provides his sacramental theology with the tools to remain open to the divine transcendence and, by that openness, to avoid circumscribing the sacramental order within the spatial-empirical and experiential realms. One might legitimately ask if the teaching of divine Revelation calls for this broader, wisdom-based metaphysical view of the world. Attunement to wisdom, however, is what opens and orders humanity to a transcendent field of vision. Following John Paul II's encyclical letter *Fides et Ratio*, Matthew Levering notes:

If dogmatic theology is not informed by metaphysical speculation, it cannot articulate the meaning of Scripture, because the mysteries revealed in Scripture are salvific truths intended for all human beings. Scripture's meaning cannot be conveyed solely by more stories in addition to the stories of Scripture. Rather, the narrative of Scripture requires from the theologian the metaphysical questioning that investigates the revealed mysteries by seeking their "ontological, causal and communicative structures" [*Fides et ratio*, no. 66] and thus enables the theologian to express judgments about the meaning of Scripture's claims about God and human beings.[20]

Biblical Revelation, in short, makes claims that presuppose a metaphysical order without offering an explicit and full-blown philosophical treatment of that order — and the biblical theology of the

19. Ibid., 49.
20. Matthew Levering, *Scripture and Metaphysics: Aquinas and the Renewal of Trinitarian Theology* (Oxford: Blackwell Publishing, 2004), 21.

sacraments is no exception. Questions about the relation of the sacraments to God's causal agency, the status of sacramental grace within the created order, the seating of sacramental character in the soul, all invite a wider, wisdom-based investigation into the sacramental life of the Church. As a result, the pursuit of wisdom by means of recourse to metaphysical contemplation within theological reflection issues from an invitation that is embedded within biblical Revelation itself.

John Henry Newman once asked:

What is the nearest approach in the way of symbols, in this world of sight and sense, to represent to us the glories of that higher world which is beyond our bodily perceptions? What are the truest tokens and promises here, poor though they may be, of what one day we hope to see hereafter, as being beautiful and rare?[21]

The pursuit of an answer to these two well-crafted questions opens the way for a consideration of the foundational principles of Catholic sacramental theology. The seven sacraments are, indeed, the visible tokens of God's action (the higher world) and presence to people, in the world, through the Church. The revealed and magisterial patrimony concerning the sacraments contains positive affirmations and implicit philosophical presuppositions that are simply not compatible with every modern and post-modern intellectual and philosophical project. This work views the challenges facing sacramental theology and spirituality today, in the words of Thomas Joseph White, OP, as an "opportunity to rediscover the true insights of Aquinas"[22] and the ecclesial doctrine of general sacramental theology.

21. From May 31 of Newman's "Meditations on the Litany of Loretto for the Month of May," in John Henry Newman, *Selected Sermons, Prayers, and Devotions*, ed. John F. Thornton and Susan B. Varenne (New York: Vintage Spiritual Classics, 1999), 334.

22. White, *Wisdom in the Face of Modernity: A Study in Thomistic Natural Theology* (Ave Maria, Fla.: Sapientia Press, 2009), 27.

TWO

Sin, Redemption, and the Sacramental Economy of Salvation

The Theological Foundations of the Seven Sacraments

St. Thomas and the Ecclesial Tradition

In the *Summa theologiae* St. Thomas begins his treatment of the general principles of sacramental theology in question 60 of the Third Part, which immediately follows his prolonged meditation on the mystery of the Incarnate Word in questions 1–59. Thomas's stated reason for this ordering is as follows: "After considering those things that concern the mystery of the incarnate Word, we must consider the sacraments of the Church, which derive their efficacy from the Word incarnate himself."[1] This passage, in one broad sweep, identifies the importance and spiritual significance of the sacraments in the life of the Church, about which Thomas will devote many questions to explicate more fully.[2]

---

1. *ST* III, q. 60, prologue.
2. For a detailed examination of the "place of the sacraments in the plan of the *Summa*

On the one hand, the sacraments are derivative from the ministry of the Incarnate Word of God. That is to say, the sacraments follow Christ in the consideration of theology because they are related to and depend on the historical events and glorified life of Jesus Christ. On the other hand, because they are derived from Jesus Christ, the sacraments are efficacious, which means that they bring about (or cause) certain things in the Christian life. The efficacious presence of Christ in the liturgical life of the Church is central to Thomas's theology of the sacraments.

The sacraments, therefore, are rooted in (a) the historical reality of the Word's Incarnation, life, and human action culminating in his death on the cross and (b) the eternal and eschatological significance of his Resurrection and Ascension into heaven.[3] An accurate theology of the sacraments must maintain both of these dimensions. Christ did not come merely to clarify what is "already" and "everywhere" present; he came to redeem mankind from sin. And, Christ's actions are not merely historical (as past events); he is risen and ascended and continues his saving ministry from heaven. It is extremely helpful, therefore, in assimilating the principles of sacramental theology to understand how they fit within the revealed order — how they fit within the unfolding of the divine wisdom in salvation history and the life of the Church.

Creation, the Fall, Redemption, and the Sacraments

In the first article of question 60 of the Third Part of the *Summa theologiae*, Aquinas poses a pedagogical question that is framed in a way that enables him to unearth the essential reality of the sacraments, namely, whether sacraments belong in the category of

---

theologiae of Saint Thomas," see Jean-Philippe Revel, *Traité des sacrements*, I.1 *Baptême et sacramentalité. Origine et signification du baptême* (Paris: Les Éditions du Cerf, 2012), 14–28.

3. For a helpful presentation of the full significance of Christ's Resurrection and Ascension for sacramental theology, especially as developed in the magisterial teaching on the liturgy, see Dominic Langevin, OP, *From Passion to Paschal Mystery: A Recent Magisterial Development Concerning the Christological Foundation of the Sacraments*, Studia Friburgensia (Fribourg, Switzerland: Fribourg Academic Press, 2015).

"sign." Aquinas, of course, following a long tradition of theological reflection, answers in the affirmative. Given that sacraments are not human creations (more will be said about the institution of the sacraments below) but signs instituted and employed by God, the question arises as to why God would institute them as the means of communicating the life of grace and merits of his Son's work. This question goes to the heart of many weighty theological and philosophical matters, including the relation of time and creation to God and eternity, and the end or purpose of temporal human existence and eternal life with God. The sacraments have a special role of theological integration in addressing the implications of these types of questions.

Divine Revelation affirms two seemingly contradictory truths: first, that God is present to his creation and, second, that he transcends creation. As the *Catechism of the Catholic Church* teaches:

God is infinitely greater than all his works: "You have set your glory above the heavens" (Ps 8:2). Indeed, God's "greatness is unsearchable" (Ps 145:3). But because he is the free and sovereign Creator, the first cause of all that exists, God is present to his creatures' inmost being: "In him we live and move and have our being" (Acts 17:28). In the words of St. Augustine, God is "higher than my highest and more inward than my innermost self" (*Confessions*, 3, 6, 11).[4]

The *Catechism* further explains that creation is not merely a past event, with no relevance for the present: "With creation, God does not abandon his creatures to themselves. He not only gives them being and existence, but also, and at every moment, upholds and sustains them in being, enables them to act and brings them to their final end."[5] In his teaching on this doctrine, which he calls "*creatio continua,*" Aquinas compares God's ongoing conferral of being on creatures to the sun's continued illumination of the atmosphere: "The preservation of things by God is a continuation of that action whereby He gives existence, which action is without either motion

---

4. *Catechism of the Catholic Church* §300. Hereafter cited as *CCC*.
5. Ibid., §301.

or time; so also the preservation of light in the air is by the continual influence of the sun."[6]

Rational creatures, furthermore, were not created in a merely natural state in which intimacy with God was something foreign to human existence. The first parents of the human race enjoyed a special intimacy with God that went beyond simply the gift of existence within the natural order. "By the radiance of this grace," the *Catechism* explains, "all dimensions of man's life were confirmed. As long as he remained in the divine intimacy, man would not have to suffer or die."[7]

God's covenant with Israel, the Incarnation of the Word, and the sacramental life of the Church are unintelligible without recourse to the doctrine of original sin and its effects and consequences. God's plan for salvation in Christ is a plan of redemption; the Body of Christ, the Church, is a redeemed society.[8] The *Catechism* explains the place that the doctrine of original sin has in our understanding of Christ and human salvation:

The doctrine of original sin is, so to speak, the "reverse side" of the Good News that Jesus is the Saviour of all men, that all need salvation and that salvation is offered to all through Christ. The Church, which has the mind of Christ, knows very well that we cannot tamper with the revelation of original sin without undermining the mystery of Christ.[9]

St. Paul articulates the scope that the doctrine of original sin has for the whole of humanity in his Letter to the Romans: "as sin came into the world through one man and death through sin, and so death spread to all men because all men sinned ... " (5:12). In the same chapter St. Paul also explains the relationship that exists between original sin (and personal sin) and Christ's mission: "then as one man's trespass led to condemnation for all men, so one man's act of righteousness leads to acquittal and life for all men. For as by one

---

6. *ST* I, q. 104, a. 1, ad 4.   7. *CCC* §301.

8. Engagement with the reality of sin (and redemption in Christ) is rare in many contemporary theologies of the liturgy and sacraments.

9. *CCC* §389.

man's disobedience many were made sinners, so by one man's obedience many will be made righteous" (5:18–20).

Original sin, then, is not merely the personal fault of the first parents. The fault of Adam and Eve changed the original state or condition of life that they enjoyed and were called to pass on to their progeny: "be fruitful and multiply" (Gen 1:28). As the *Catechism* succinctly states, in sinning, "Adam and Eve immediately lose the grace of original holiness."[10]

Prior to the Fall, Adam and Eve possessed integral human natures that were elevated by grace to a state of intimacy with God that the tradition speaks of in terms of original justice and holiness. By turning away from God in committing sin and therefore vitiating the grace of original holiness, Adam and Eve entered a new state of existence that, lacking intimacy with God by grace, consisted in disorder and the loss of the "harmony" that they enjoyed prior to the Fall.[11] What exactly is this state? "It is an inordinate disposition [within each individual]," Aquinas teaches, "arising from the destruction of the harmony which was essential to original justice, even as bodily sickness is an inordinate disposition of the body, by reason of the destruction of that equilibrium which is essential to health. Hence it is that original sin is called the *languor of nature*."[12] It is this condition of languor, the state of original sin, typified by the loss of friendship with God in grace that Adam and Eve transmitted to their progeny.

The Church does not teach that original sin constitutes a "personal fault in any of Adam's descendants."[13] Rather, it is inherited by "the transmission of a human nature deprived of original holiness and justice."[14] The most extreme consequence of the Fall is, of course, death, which results from the fact that the soul deprived of

10. *CCC* §399.
11. "Harmony" is the word used by the *CCC* in §400 to explain the integrity of the state of original justice. This harmony affected the relation of the soul to the body, Adam and Eve to each other, Adam and Eve to creation, and, of course, Adam and Eve's relationship with God. Original sin upsets every element of this harmony.
12. *ST* III, q. 82, a. 1.   13. *CCC* §405.
14. *CCC* §404.

the gift of grace is not able to sustain the body unto eternal life, as Aquinas explains:

Man incurred the necessity of dying [by the defect of original sin]; his soul was no longer able to sustain the body forever by conferring life on it. Thus man became subject to suffering and death, not only in the sense that he was capable of suffering and dying as before, but in the sense that he was now under the necessity of suffering and dying.[15]

Additionally, the wound of original sin affects, but does not destroy, "the natural powers" of human nature, subjecting it to "ignorance, suffering ... [and] an inclination to evil that is called 'concupiscence.'"[16] Sin, therefore, is not reducible merely to poor choices, patterns, or social structures of injustice. Sin is also a universal, existential condition from which each and every human being needs to be redeemed.

The consequences of original sin, so obviously manifest in human history and in each and every life, do not reign over people without there being hope of resolution. As early as Genesis 3, the chapter in which the Fall is narrated, God previews his plan to save man from this calamity. In the so-called Protoevangelium (first gospel), God declares to the serpent, "I will put enmity between you and the woman, and between your seed and her seed; he shall bruise your head, and you shall bruise his heel" (Gen 3:15). This passage is widely known for its cryptic difficulty, but one conclusion is clear: the serpent who "beguiled" Adam and Eve into turning away from their harmonious life with God to seek to "be like God" *will not* claim victory forever and will ultimately be defeated.

The entire history of Israel that is narrated in the Old Testament and brought to fulfillment in Christ can be read as God's faithful, unwavering commitment to place hostility between the serpent and the offspring of Eve, hostility that will culminate in the serpent's ultimate defeat by Christ.

15. *Aquinas's Shorter Summa* [Compendium of Theology] (Manchester, N.H.: Sophia Institute Press, 2002), 223 (ch. 193).

16. *CCC* §405.

The theology of original sin and its consequences establishes several truths that must be kept in mind to appreciate what is revealed about Christ, the Church, the sacraments, and the role that each has within human history and the Christian spiritual life. Sin is not a benign master, nor is it a dungeon from which humanity needs merely to be liberated. Sin (original and personal) is the negation of a well-ordered relationship with God — sin offends God because in choosing to sin the sinners love themselves and created things more than God. Sinning entails living a life focused on temporal goods instead of God.

Redemption, Satisfaction, and Sacrifice

In addition to (or along with) constituting an act of injustice against God, sin also disrupts the temporal order by causing direct harm to others, self, and the good of the community. For example, a child may be easily forgiven for doing some harm to a neighbor's property, say, throwing a ball through a window. But the act of forgiving the child does not fix the broken window — the temporal disorder of the act remains unaddressed even though the spiritual aspect of forgiveness from the one whose property was damaged has been obtained.

Two aspects of sin can thus be identified: the mark or stain and the corresponding punishment that is due to the fault. "[W]e call the 'malum culpae' the stain of sin," Cessario explains, commenting on Aquinas's doctrine of satisfaction,

because it chiefly refers to the culpable alienation from God implied in the Christian notion of sin. Sin sullies the Christian soul. In addition, the metaphor of stain also points to the permanent character of sin or the debt of punishment ("reatus poenae") which describes the abiding condition present in the sinner.[17]

How can a justice before God be obtained which addresses both the stain corresponding to the guilt and the punishment or debt cor-

17. Romanus Cessario, OP, *The Godly Image: Christ and Salvation in Catholic Thought from Anselm to Aquinas* (Petersham, Mass.: St. Bede's Publications, 1990), 87.

responding to the fault? Aquinas finds the answer in his biblical theology of the relationship between the Old Law and the New Law, especially in the meaning of sacrifice.

What is the cause of or reason for the many sacrifices embodied in the ceremonial precepts of the Old Law? Aquinas posits a twofold cause for all of the sacrifices of the Old Law: literal and figurative. At the literal level the reason for the sacrifices of the Old Law was "divine worship." Figuratively these sacrifices were "intended to foreshadow Christ."[18] At the literal level (divine worship) the Old Law sacrifices "represented the directing of the mind to God" such that "in offering up sacrifices man made protestation that God is the first principle of the creation of all things, and their last end."[19]

Of the many gifts that God bestowed after humanity "had fallen away by sin,"[20] "the chief" gift is the giving of the Son by the Father. Christ's sacrifice is, therefore, "the chief sacrifice" for which "all the other sacrifices of the Old Law were offered up in order to foreshadow this one individual and paramount sacrifice — the imperfect forecasting the perfect."[21]

At the literal and at the figurative level, not all of the sacrifices of the Old Law pertained to sin. A "holocaust" offering, Aquinas explains, was a sacrifice "offered to God specially to show reverence to His majesty, and love of His Goodness."[22] The "peace-offering" was a sacrifice "which was offered to God either in thanksgiving, or for the welfare and prosperity of the offerers, in acknowledgment of benefits already received or yet to be received."[23] The sacrifice known as the "sin-offering," Aquinas explains, "was offered to God on account of man's need for the forgiveness of sin: and this typifies the state of penitents in satisfying for sins."[24]

In summary, the sacrifices of the Old Law were aimed at "directing the mind to God" or prefiguring Christ: these sacrificial offer-

18. *ST* I-II, q. 102, a. 3.
20. Ibid.
22. Ibid, ad 8.
24. Ibid.

19. Ibid.
21. Ibid.
23. Ibid.

ings constituted acts of worship through which God's goodness and majesty were reverenced, thanksgiving was made, and satisfaction for sin was obtained.

There is a perfect "sacramental" realization in Christ of this sacrificial spirituality to which God directed Israel. Psalm 51 indicates the ongoing tension intrinsic to the act of offering sacrificial animals that does not proceed from a corresponding interior virtue or disposition. "For thou [God] hast no delight in sacrifice;" the contrite Psalmist declares, "were I to give a burnt offering, thou wouldst not be pleased. The sacrifice acceptable to God is a broken spirit; a broken and contrite heart, O God, thou wilt not despise" (Ps 51:16ff.).

Commenting on this passage from Psalm 51 in *The City of God*, St. Augustine remarks: "A sacrifice as commonly understood, therefore, is the visible sacrament of an invisible sacrifice: that is, it is a sacred symbol."[25] This Augustinian insight was formative in Aquinas's thinking about the efficacy of Christ's priestly sacrifice, in which the external aspect (his suffering and death) was a visible manifestation, or sign, of his interior perfection.

The New Testament clearly situates Christ's death on the cross within this Old Testament theology of sacrifice. The oft-quoted John 3:16 reminds us that God "gave his only Son." Why? "God sent the Son into the world," St. John reveals, "not to condemn the world, but that the world might be saved through him" (Jn 3:17). Understanding Christ in relation to the injustice of sin and the purposes of the sacrifices of the Old Law, St. Paul teaches in Romans that "though all have sinned and fall short of the glory of God, they are justified by his grace as a gift, *through the redemption which is in Christ Jesus, whom God put forward as an expiation by his blood*" (3:23ff.; emphasis added).[26] As a result, Christians are not merely "freed" from the

25. Augustine, *The City of God against the Pagans*, ed. and trans. R. W. Dyson (Cambridge: Cambridge University Press, 1998), 397 [Book X, 5].

26. 1 John 2:2 also speaks of Christ as an expiation for sin: "[Jesus Christ] is the expiation for our sins, and not for ours only but also for the sins of the whole world." And Peter and Paul both use the sacrificial language to speak of Christ's death: "For Christ Jesus also died for sins once for all, the righteous for the unrighteous, that he might bring us to

guilt of sin; indeed Christ expiates for the penalty of sin by offering himself as a sacrificial victim on the cross.

Because of the distance between the Creator and the fallen creature, the reestablishment of the communion between the infinite God and the finite creature requires an initiative on the part of God. The *Catechism* explains this dynamic as follows: "Because of his transcendence, God cannot be seen as he is, unless he himself opens up his mystery to man's immediate contemplation and gives him the capacity for it."[27] The Incarnation of the Word and the sacraments instituted by Christ constitute this opening up by God and the capacitation of humanity for communion with him.

The Letter to the Hebrews is especially important for clarifying the sacrificial nature of Christ's death for sin in relation to the offerings of the Old Law. In the ninth chapter the author mentions the high priest's annual ritual within the holy of holies of the temple on the Day of Atonement to offer blood for his sins and those of the people.[28] The annual, repetitive offering of these "gifts and sacrifices," the author concludes, indicate an arrangement "which cannot perfect the conscience of the worshipper" (v. 9). In contrast:

when Christ appeared as a high priest of the good things that have come, then through the greater and more perfect tent (not made with hands, that is, not of this creation) he entered once for all into the Holy Place, taking not the blood of goats and calves *but his own blood*, thus securing an eternal redemption. For if the sprinkling of defiled persons with the blood of goats and bulls and with the ashes of a heifer sanctifies for the purification of the flesh, *how much more shall the blood of Christ, who through the eternal Spirit offered himself without blemish to God, purify your conscience from dead works to serve the living God.* Therefore he is the mediator of a new covenant, so that those who are called may receive the promised eternal inheritance, since a death has occurred which redeems them from the transgressions under the first covenant. (Heb 9:11–15; emphasis added)

God, being put to death in the flesh but made alive in the spirit" (1 Pet 3:18). "I have been crucified with Christ; it is no longer I who live, but Christ who lives with me; and the life I now live in the flesh I live by faith in the Son of God, who loved me and gave himself for me" (Gal 2:20).

27. *CCC* §1028.   28. See Hebrews 9:7–10.

In his commentary on this passage, Aquinas identifies five things that are revealed about the "more perfect tent" that Christ enters. The fifth of these is "why he entered, that is, for the expiation of sins."[29] This means that Christ entered the "more perfect tent," Aquinas explains,

to offer sacrifice for the ignorance of the people, not for his own, since he did not have any. For the blood of Christ, more than that blood [of goats and bulls], is efficacious for this, since through it he obtained eternal redemption. This is as if to say: Through this blood we have been redeemed, and this forever, because its power is infinite.[30]

It is clear that the New Testament presents Christ's death as an atoning or expiatory sacrifice for sin which draws together, perfects, and brings to fulfillment the sacrificial system of the Old Law. Aquinas concludes that all of the effects associated with the sacrificial offerings of the Old Law are obtained by Christ: "Therefore Christ Himself, as man, was not only priest, but also a perfect victim, being at the same time victim for sin, victim for a peace-offering, and a holocaust."[31]

How does this understanding of Christ's work as both the priest and sacrificial victim of the New Law relate to satisfying for both the stain and the debt of punishment that sin brings about? "Two things are required for the perfect cleansing from sins," Aquinas explains, "corresponding to the two things comprised in sin — namely, the stain of sin and the debt of punishment."[32] Christ's death cleanses from both aspects, Aquinas continues, because, "[T]he stain of sin is, indeed, blotted out by grace, by which the sinner's heart is turned to God: whereas the debt of punishment is entirely removed by the satisfaction that man offers to God." Christ's death on the cross, understood as a priestly sacrifice in which the perfect victim is offered by the perfect priest, is the efficient cause of this perfect cleansing:

29. Thomas Aquinas, *Commentary on the Epistle to the Hebrews*, trans. Chrysostom Baer, OPraem (South Bend, Ind.: St. Augustine's Press, 2006), 185 [436].

30. Ibid., 187 [441].   31. *ST* III, q. 22, a. 2.

32. Ibid., a. 3.

Now the priesthood of Christ produces both these effects. For by its virtue grace is given to us, by which our hearts are turned to God, according to Romans 3:24–25: "Being justified freely by His grace, through the redemption that is in Christ Jesus, Whom God hath proposed to be a propitiation, through faith in His blood." Moreover, He satisfied for us fully, inasmuch as "He hath borne our infirmities and carried our sorrows" (Isaiah 53:4). Wherefore it is clear that the priesthood of Christ has full power to expiate sins.[33]

This means that, despite the offense and disorder before God caused by sin, Christ's sacrifice is received by God as fully atoning for the penal ramifications of all sin. To repeat: the Christian message of salvation in Christ includes the full restoration of the order of justice between God and humanity in Christ, not merely the granting of pardon or liberation without reference to the disorder caused by sin. This is so because Christ, being free from sin, was not subject himself to the penality due to sin — death — but chose freely and out of love to suffer the penalty due to sin and to offer himself to the Father as satisfaction for all those who are subject in justice to the penalty.

The Father receives Christ's offering as a superabundant atonement and expiation for sin because of the perfect religious virtue by which the Son freely and lovingly suffers the punishment of sin without himself being subject in justice to this punishment. "He properly atones for an offense who offers something which the offended one loves equally, or even more than he detested the offense," Aquinas explains, "But by suffering out of love and obedience, Christ gave more to God than was required to compensate for the offense of the whole human race."[34]

How is this the case? "First of all," Aquinas continues, "because of the exceeding charity from which He suffered; secondly, on account of the dignity of His life which He laid down in atonement, for it was the life of one who was God and man; thirdly, on account

33. Ibid.
34. *ST* III, q. 48, a. 2.

of the extent of the Passion, and the greatness of the grief endured."
Thus Aquinas concludes, "And therefore Christ's Passion was not
only a sufficient but a superabundant atonement for the sins of the
human race; according to 1 John 2:2: 'He is the propitiation for our
sins: and not for ours only, but also for those of the whole world.'"[35]

These deeply biblical insights create a number of important connections between the theology of salvation in Christ and the principles of the Church's sacramental life. Contemporary theologians
are frequently dismissive of discussing salvation in terms of satisfaction. Aquinas's theory of satisfaction, however, is not rooted in some
blind, cold, wrathful imposition of the Father's anger onto Christ.
Rather, Aquinas views the causality of Christ's death to be rooted in
his free obedience animated by love. Christ satisfies for sin, according to Aquinas, not because the cold forces of necessity required a
requisite pound of innocent flesh, but rather because Christ wills to
fulfill the precepts of the Old Law through loving obedience. Aquinas reads the profound Christology of the famous hymn in Philip-
pians 2:6–11 as the revelatory foundation of this doctrine. In this
hymn St. Paul famously teaches that:

Christ Jesus, who, though he was in the form of God, did not count equality
with God a thing to be grasped, *but emptied himself, taking the form of a ser-
vant, being born in the likeness of men. And being found in human form he humbled himself and became obedient unto death, even death on a cross.* Therefore
God has highly exalted him and bestowed on him the name which is above
every name, that at the name of Jesus every knee should bow, in heaven and
on earth and under the earth, and every tongue confess that Jesus Christ is
Lord, to the glory of God the Father. (Emphasis added)

Christ's exaltation, St. Paul teaches, is the result of humbling
himself in obedience "unto death." This free act of obedience to accept the penalty of death — a penalty to which he, being free from
sin, was not personally subject — out of love for God and neighbor,
is what enabled his death to bring the Law to fulfillment. Converse-

---

35. Ibid.

ly, the repetitive offerings of the priests under the law could never bring about full justice. Christ, Aquinas teaches, "consummated" (Jn 19:30) all the precepts of the Old Law as follows:

those of the moral order which are founded on the precepts of charity, inasmuch as He suffered both out of love of the Father, according to John 14:31: "That the world may know that I love the Father, and as the Father hath given Me commandment, so do I: arise, let us go hence" – namely, to the place of His Passion: and out of love of His neighbor, according to Galatians 2:20: "He loved me, and delivered Himself up for me." Christ likewise by His Passion fulfilled the ceremonial precepts of the Law, which are chiefly ordained for sacrifices and oblations, in so far as all the ancient sacrifices were figures of that true sacrifice which the dying Christ offered for us. Hence it is written (Colossians 2:16–17): "Let no man judge you in meat or drink, or in respect of a festival day, or of the new moon, or of the sabbaths, which are a shadow of things to come, but the body is Christ's," for the reason that Christ is compared to them as a body is to a shadow. Christ also by His Passion fulfilled the judicial precepts of the Law, which are chiefly ordained for making compensation to them who have suffered wrong, since, as is written Psalm 68:5: He "paid that which" He "took not away," suffering Himself to be fastened to a tree on account of the apple which man had plucked from the tree against God's command.[36]

It is this consummation of the Old Law that is lived and perpetuated in the sacramental liturgy of the Church.[37]

A theology of the liturgy and the sacraments is rendered ineffective if it is unable to articulate how Christ's fulfillment of the Old Law is accessible through the ages down to the present day. In short, for every generation that was not privileged to live during Christ's life, to stand at the foot of the cross as John and Mary did, or to see him risen from the dead, the question of contact or access with God through Christ is of fundamental importance. Did Christ's ascension into heaven, into eternal life, vitiate the possibility of all contact with him?

36. *ST* III, 47, a. 2, ad 1.
37. See Matthew Levering, *Christ's Fulfillment of Torah and Temple: Salvation according to St. Thomas Aquinas* (Notre Dame, Ind.: University of Notre Dame Press, 2002).

Participation in the Divine Life: Sacramental Mediation

In metaphysics the doctrine of participation developed as the answer to the problem of the "one and the many." For those not familiar with the problem, which pre-dates even Socrates, Plato, and Aristotle, John Wippel summarizes it as follows: "[T]his problem arises for anyone who, like Aquinas, acknowledges the intelligibility of being and the unity that follows therefrom, and who also wishes to defend the reality of multiplicity or diversity, that is, of the many."[38] The answer to this problem was developed by the profound speculations of the greatest minds of the Western philosophical and theological tradition.[39]

"The many" finite beings exist individually, not as parts or extensions of the substance of the one, but by participation. Aquinas explains:

> For that which is something in its entirety does not participate in it but is essentially identical with it, whereas that which is not something in its entirety but has this other thing joined to it, is said properly to participate in that thing. Thus, if heat were a self-subsistent heat, it would not be said to participate in heat, because it would contain nothing but heat. But since fire is something other than heat, it is said to participate in heat.[40]

In addition to participation in a finite and created manner in existence, Aquinas identifies three modes of participation that are unique to rational creatures. These modes are consequent upon the participation that the image of God in men and women has in the divine life of God: namely, participation by nature, grace, and glory. "We see that the image of God is in man in three ways," Aquinas explains:

38. John F. Wippel, *The Metaphysical Thought of Thomas Aquinas: From Finite Being to Uncreated Being* (Washington, D.C.: The Catholic University of America Press, 2000), 95.

39. For an insightful theological engagement with the problem of the one and the many, see Marc D. Guerra, "The One, the Many, and the Mystical Body," *The Heythrop Journal* 53 (2012): 904–14.

40. *Commentary on Aristotle's Metaphysics*, trans. John P. Rowan (Notre Dame, Ind.: Dumb Ox Books, 1995), 58 [Book 1, lesson 10, #154].

First, inasmuch as man possesses a natural aptitude for understanding and loving God; and this aptitude consists in the very nature of the mind, which is common to all men. Secondly, inasmuch as man actually and habitually knows and loves God, though imperfectly; and this image consists in the conformity of grace. Thirdly, inasmuch as man knows and loves God perfectly; and this image consists in the likeness of glory.[41]

The *imago Dei* that is a "natural aptitude" for knowing and loving is common to rational creatures by the very nature of the human soul. This natural image is elevated by grace, which joins humanity to God in faith and charity, actually or habitually, and glory, by which men and women know and love God perfectly.

How are men and women — finite creatures wounded by sin — able to enjoy the elevated participations in the eternal life of God that are made possible by grace and glory?

In a question on the effects of Christ's Passion, Aquinas dedicates a series of articles to the manifold benefits derived from Christ's priestly mediation. In an objection to holding that Christ's Passion causes deliverance from sin, Aquinas considers that the requirement of Baptism and Penance for the forgiveness of sins indicates that Christ's Passion alone cannot be viewed as a causal remedy for sin. Aquinas replies to this objection by distinguishing between a universal cause and its application. "[S]ince Christ's passion preceded," Aquinas argues, "as a kind of universal cause of the forgiveness of sins, it needs to be applied to each individual for the cleansing of [particular] sins." This application of the universal cause to each individual is made, Aquinas explains, "by baptism and penance and the other sacraments, which derive their power from Christ's passion."[42]

In addition to the remission of sin, as noted above, Christ's priestly sacrifice also delivers people from the debt of sin (*poena peccati*), and this effect is also applied to them, Aquinas indicates, "through faith and charity and the sacraments of faith."[43]

To be delivered from both the stain of sin and its punishment

41. *ST* I, q. 93, a. 4.   42. *ST* III, q. 49, a. 1, ad 4.
43. Ibid., a. 3, ad 1.

by Christ's Passion, one must be, Aquinas reasons, conformed to Christ.[44] "Now we are likened unto Him sacramentally in Baptism," Aquinas argues, following St. Paul, "according to Romans 6:4 'for we are buried together with Him by Baptism into death.'"[45] This is why no penance for the temporal ramifications of sin is applied to the newly baptized: "Hence no punishment of satisfaction is imposed upon men at their baptism, since they are fully delivered by Christ's satisfaction."[46]

This is all summarized very concisely by St. Paul. In his First Letter to Timothy, St. Paul presents Christ's saving work in one sweeping theological category, that of "mediator": "[God] desires all men to be saved and to come to the knowledge of the truth. *For there is one God, and there is one mediator between God and men*, the man Jesus Christ, who gave himself as a ransom for all" (1 Tim 2:5; emphasis added). What does Paul mean by identifying Christ as *the* mediator between God and man? "The office of a mediator," Thomas explains,

is to join together and unite those between whom he mediates: for extremes are united in the mean [medio]. Now to unite men to God perfectively belongs to Christ, through Whom men are reconciled to God, according to 2 Corinthians 5:19: "God was in Christ reconciling the world to Himself." And, consequently, Christ alone is the perfect Mediator of God and men, inasmuch as, by His death, He reconciled the human race to God.[47]

Furthermore, Christ's priestly sacrifice and mediation are not locked away in the annals of history, accessible now only through psychological sentiment. Christ's exercise of his priestly-mediatorial office is continued and applied to each individual in the sacramental life of the Church. The sacraments make it possible for finite sinners to have communion or participation in the divine life, through the sacramental application to the individual of the merits of Christ's priestly mediation.

44. For a discussion of the role of the sacraments in Aquinas's doctrine of deification, see Daria Spezzano, *The Glory of God's Grace: Deification according to St. Thomas Aquinas* (Ave Maria, Fla.: Sapientia Press, 2015), 308–27.

45. *ST* III, q. 49, a. 3, ad 2.   46. Ibid.

47. *ST* III, q. 26, a. 1.

The application of the effects of Christ's Passion, which is the extension of Christ's priestly mediation through time, causes a deeper participation or conformity by grace to God in Christ. The New Testament articulates this sacramental participation in Christ by means of the Greek word *koinonia*, which is represented by the words *communicatio* and *participatio* in the Latin Bible. St. Paul, for example, describes the unity of the Church as a participation in Christ that is brought about by the Eucharist: "The cup of blessing which we bless, is it not a participation [*koinonia/communicatio*] in the blood of Christ? The bread which we break, is it not a participation [*koinonia/participatio*] in the body of Christ?" (1 Cor 10:16). From the truth that the Eucharist realizes communion between the recipient and Christ by means of his sacramental body and blood, Paul then draws a direct ecclesial conclusion: "Because there is one bread, we who are many are one body, for we all partake [*participamus*] of the one bread" (1 Cor 10:17).

Hence, although Christ's earthly life came to an end with his Ascension into heaven, his presence on earth and exercise of his priestly mediation have by no means ceased. There is a connection, a liturgical and sacramental significance, between Christ's presence in heaven at the right hand of the Father and the sacramental worship that he instituted for the Church during his earthly life. In a passage on the implications of Christ's presence in heaven after the Ascension, Aquinas offers the following insights:

[A]s the high-priest under the Old Testament entered the holy place to stand before God for the people, so also Christ entered heaven "to make intercession for us," as is said in Hebrews 7:25. Because the very showing of Himself in the human nature which He took with Him to heaven is a pleading for us, so that for the very reason that God so exalted human nature in Christ, He may take pity on them for whom the Son of God took human nature.... [T]hat being established in His heavenly seat as God and Lord, He might send down gifts upon men, according to Ephesians 4:10: "He ascended above all the heavens, that He might fill all things," that is, "with His gifts," according to the gloss.[48]

48. *ST* III, q. 57, a. 6.

There is, as a result, an ongoing, organic, and real connection between Christ in heaven and his members on earth: he continues to "intercede" for his followers and "send down gifts" from heaven. This same insight was not far from the minds of the Fathers of the Second Vatican Council, who in the *Constitution on the Sacred Liturgy* underscore the connection between Christ's heavenly ministry and the sanctifying power of the sacramental liturgy:

It is therefore quite right to think of the liturgy as the enacting of the priestly role of Jesus Christ. In the liturgy, the sanctification of human beings is being expressed through signs accessible to the senses, and carried out in a way appropriate to each of them. Furthermore, the mystical body of Jesus Christ, that is the head and the members, is together giving complete and definitive public expression to its worship.

It follows that every liturgical celebration, because it is an action of Christ the Priest and of his Body, which is the Church, is a sacred action surpassing all others. No other action of the Church can equal its efficacy by the same title or to the same degree.[49]

Christ, as head of the Church, is the chief celebrant of the Christian sacraments, acting from heaven. Commenting on this passage, Thomas Weinandy affirms a key point of intersection between Aquinas and Vatican II that is important for understanding the spiritual significance of the sacraments: both the Council and St. Thomas focus our attention on the truth that "the sacraments [are] personal 'acts' of Christ and his body" and that this is what "gives them their inherent dynamism and vitality, and thus their unequalled efficacy."[50]

Christ's Ascension, therefore, did not render his priestly mediation inaccessible to the faithful. He instituted the sacraments as a means of communicating the benefits of his death and the fullness

---

49. *Sacrosanctum Concilium* §7. Translation from *Vatican Council II: The Conciliar and Post Conciliar Documents*, ed. A. Flannery (Wilmington, Del.: Scholarly Resources, 1975).

50. Thomas G. Weinandy, OFM, Cap., *Jesus: Essays in Christology* (Ave Maria, Fla.: Sapientia Press, 2014), 191. In his apostolic letter on the 25th anniversary of *Sacrosanctum Concilium* (*Vicesimus Quintus Annus*), John Paul II repeatedly underscores the importance of Christ's presence in the liturgy.

of his heavenly life to the faithful of all places and times from his location in heaven at the right hand of the Father. "[B]y his resurrection," Aquinas explains, "Christ entered upon an immortal and incorruptible life. But whereas our dwelling-place [on earth] is one of generation and corruption, the heavenly place is one of incorruption."[51]

As a result, although Christ did not receive any additional benefit or grace by ascending into heaven, he did, Aquinas explains, "acquire something as to the fittingness of place, which pertains to the well-being of glory."[52] Even though the Ascension deprives the faithful of Christ's temporal presence on earth, Aquinas recognizes that his Ascension into heaven "was more profitable for us than his bodily presence would have been."[53] One of the reasons that he puts forward in defense of this position is that Christ ascended into heaven, rather than remaining on earth:

in order to direct the fervor of our charity to heavenly things. Hence the Apostle says (Colossians 3:1–2): "Seek the things that are above, where Christ is sitting at the right hand of God. Mind the things that are above, not the things that are upon the earth": for as is said (Matthew 6:21): "Where thy treasure is, there is thy heart also." And since the Holy Ghost is love drawing us up to heavenly things, therefore our Lord said to His disciples (John 16:7): "It is expedient to you that I go; for if I go not, the Paraclete will not come to you; but if I go, I will send Him to you." On which words Augustine says (Tract. xciv super Joan.): "Ye cannot receive the Spirit, so long as ye persist in knowing Christ according to the flesh. But when Christ withdrew in body, not only the Holy Ghost, but both Father and Son were present with them spiritually."[54]

By ascending into heaven Christ, consequently, draws and orders the faithful to beatific life by bestowing the grace of the Holy Spirit upon them through the sacraments. The sacraments, as signs, are thus fitted by God's wisdom to the period between Christ's first and second comings, namely, to the period lived in Christian faith.

51. *ST* III, q. 57, a. 1. 52. Ibid., ad 2.
53. Ibid., ad 3. 54. *ST* III, q. 57, a. 1.

Faith, the Letter to the Hebrews explains, "is the assurance of things hoped for, the conviction of things not seen" (11:1).

Since the faithful do not see God "face to face" in faith, the Lord uses the sacraments to provide visible mediations and facilitate participation with the unseen realities that are hoped for in faith. The life of faith is, in the words of Joseph Ratzinger, "a peculiar kind of 'in-between', and mixture of 'already and not yet'. The empirical conditions of life in this world are still in force, but they have been burst open, in preparation for the final fulfillment already inaugurated in Christ."[55]

By the sacraments, the faithful are drawn closer and closer to the reality for which they have been created by God and redeemed in Christ. "The curtain of the Temple has been torn. Heaven has been opened up," Ratzinger explains,

by the union of the man Jesus, and thus of all human existence, with the living God. But this new openness is only mediated by the signs of salvation. We need mediation. As yet we do not see the Lord "as he is." ... The theology of the liturgy is in a special way "symbolic theology", a theology of symbols, which connects us to what is present but hidden.[56]

It is not difficult to find people who are uncomfortable with the ritualized nature of the sacraments or rites of the Church. These rites are criticized in favor of a "pure," non-ritualized, vision of Christian spirituality. Christ's own institution of the sacraments, which included the use of material elements such as bread and wine (see Mt 26:26ff.), water (see Mt 3:13 and 28:19), and oil (Mk 6:13), ought to raise questions about the presentation of Christianity as a purely "spiritual" religion lacking in any formal rites.

Yet, there is an even deeper problem with the rejection of the liturgical-sacramental worship of Christianity, namely, the reduction of prayer and worship to the status of private spirituality instead of communal belonging and participation. "Spirituality" is deemed attractive and intellectually sophisticated, while ritualized religion

55. Joseph Cardinal Ratzinger, *The Spirit of the Liturgy*, 54.
56. Ibid., 60.

suffers a near universal antipathy. This antipathy strikes hard at the prayerful dimension of the sacraments. The putatively spiritual approach to prayer and Christian worship, however, ends in isolating people from God, and ultimately directing prayer toward one's own likes and sentiments, instead of God himself. "One of the unfortunate outcomes of the contemporary penchant for marketing spiritualities," Romanus Cessario observes,

appears in the commonly held view that prayer serves the personal needs of the one who prays. People develop prayer techniques that help them get through a tough day or a difficult period. Within Catholic theology, scant warrant exists for making prayer this kind of therapeutic or palliative exercise. Because prayer constitutes an act of the virtue of religion, God — not man — becomes the first beneficiary of man's prayer.[57]

Cessario's helpful observation is a reminder that for the ancients and the schoolmen of the Middle Ages, the term "religion" was not used primarily to refer to a juridical code of beliefs. Rather, "religion" identified the relationship that one had to God. Religious practice and action stemmed from an awareness of God and a virtuous desire to present oneself to him in a way that recognizes who he really is.

Can justice be rendered to God without any external "religious" acts that indicate a relationship of love and honor to him? St. Paul instructs the Romans to express their "spiritual worship" by presenting "their bodies as a living sacrifice, holy and acceptable to God" (Rm 12:1). Thomas Aquinas explains that "a thing is perfected by being subject to its superior," and this principle pertains to worship because

the human mind, in order to be united to God, needs to be guided by the sensible world, since "invisible things ... are clearly seen, being understood by the things that are made," as the Apostle says (Romans 1:20). Wherefore in the divine worship it is necessary to make use of corporeal things, that man's mind may be aroused thereby, as by signs, to the spiritual acts by

57. Romanus Cessario, OP, "The Grace St. Dominic Brings to the World," in *Theology and Sanctity*, ed. Cajetan Cuddy, OP (Ave Maria, Fla.: Sapientia Press, 2014), 11.

means of which he is united to God. Therefore the internal acts of religion take precedence of the others and belong to religion essentially, while its external acts are secondary, and subordinate to the internal acts.[58]

As a result, Christ did not institute external rites and forms of worship because God needed these things. Rather, he instituted them, in Thomas's words, to stand "as signs of the internal and spiritual works, which are of themselves acceptable to God."[59]

The sacraments, therefore, do not present a merely cold, external, and institutional side of the Christian faith. To the contrary, they are the divinely instituted means by which humanity is protected, through the mediation of signs that foster participation in Christ's own heavenly worship, from regressing into idolatrous forms of worship. These sacramental signs elevate humanity by leading it through the signification of the sacramental elements to the spiritual and eternal realities in which they participate, which they contain, and which they confer.

The Christian journey to the heavenly homeland is animated by "the introduction, at the very core of [its] morality," explains Jean-Hervé Nicolas, "of a principle which is essentially foreign to all pagan conceptions of human life, namely, the principle of grace."[60] Nicolas points to Romans 11:5: "if it is by grace, it is no longer on the basis of works; otherwise grace would no longer be grace," to highlight the centrality of grace in the Christian life.

The New Law of the gospel promulgated by Christ, Aquinas explains, "consists chiefly in the grace of the Holy Ghost, which is shown forth by faith that worketh through love."[61] Aquinas then underscores why the essence of the New Law, grace, which is a spiritual reality, should come to people through bodily forms of worship and external actions:

---

58. *ST* II-II, q. 81, a. 7.
59. Ibid., ad 2.
60. J.-H. Nicolas, OP, *The Mystery of God's Grace* (London: Bloomsbury, 1960), 9.
61. *ST* I-II, q. 108, a. 1.

men become receivers of this grace through God's Son made man, Whose humanity grace filled first, and thence flowed forth to us. Hence it is written (John 1:14): "The Word was made flesh," and afterwards: "full of grace and truth"; and further on: "Of His fullness we all have received, and grace for grace." Hence it is added that "grace and truth came by Jesus Christ." Consequently it was becoming that the grace which flows from the incarnate Word should be given to us by means of certain external sensible objects; and that from this inward grace, whereby the flesh is subjected to the Spirit, certain external works should ensue.

Accordingly external acts may have a ... connection with grace ... as leading in some way to grace. Such are the sacramental acts which are instituted in the New Law, e.g. Baptism, the Eucharist, and the like.[62]

Christ's institution of the sacraments as a means of bestowing the New Law of grace stemmed from his desire to lead humanity to the deepest possible intimacy with him in the grace of the Holy Spirit, and through this to intimacy with the Father. "Since we cannot of ourselves obtain grace," Aquinas observes,

but through Christ alone, hence Christ of Himself instituted the sacraments whereby we obtain grace: namely, Baptism, Eucharist, Orders of the ministers of the New Law, by the institution of the apostles and seventy-two disciples, Penance, and indissoluble Matrimony. He promised Confirmation through the sending of the Holy Ghost: and we read that by His institution the apostles healed the sick by anointing them with oil (Mark 6:13). These are the sacraments of the New Law.[63]

The sacraments are, as a result, not institutional impediments to friendship and intimacy with God in Christ. They are, rather, the very place that Christ established in which he himself remains with the Church "always, to the close of the age" (Mt 28:20). On this point, Thomas Aquinas argues that, as a natural consequence of his love and friendship for his disciples, Christ is really and substantially present in the Eucharist and not merely figuratively so:

[T]his belongs to Christ's love, out of which for our salvation He assumed a true body of our nature. *And because it is the special feature of friendship to live*

---

62. Ibid.
63. Ibid., a. 2.

together with friends, as the Philosopher says (Ethic. ix), He promises us His bodily presence as a reward, saying (Matthew 24:28): "Where the body is, there shall the eagles be gathered together." Yet meanwhile in our pilgrimage He does not deprive us of His bodily presence; but unites us with Himself in this sacrament through the truth of His body and blood. Hence (John 6:57) he says: "He that eateth My flesh, and drinketh My blood, abideth in Me, and I in him." Hence this sacrament is the sign of supreme charity, and the uplifter of our hope, from such familiar union of Christ with us.[64]

Christ's presence and accessibility to his followers in the Eucharist is an extension of his will to remain with his friends. A similar point could be made about each of the sacraments. Christ's Ascension and reign from heaven have not rendered him absent to his followers on earth. He shares his risen life and draws his followers to heaven by acting in and through the sacramental celebrations that he left to the Church as a gift and means for sustaining it unto eternal life. Christ the mediator continues to effect friendship with men and women through the participatory mediation of the sacraments.

These considerations have seated sacramental theology in relation to sin and redemption in Christ. The sacraments were established by Christ during his earthly life as the means by which he would remain present to the Church on earth from his heavenly throne, bestowing, in the sacraments, healing and participation in his grace and heavenly life.

64. *ST* III, q. 75, a. 1 (emphasis added).

PART II

Understanding the Sacraments as Signs

THREE

The Nature of the Sacraments as Signs

The first two articles in Thomas's treatment of general sacramental theology (*ST* III, qq. 60–65) place the sacraments in their genus (article 1) and species (article 2), respectively. Just as horse, dog, and cat all belong to the general category of animal, so also there is something specific to each that diversifies them within the animal genus. Similarly with the broad category of sign: there is something common to all realities that signify, but within this broad category there is also something that differentiates the various types of signs.

A Definition of the Sacraments

In the first article of question 60, Thomas asks the most general question: "Whether a sacrament is a kind of a sign?" He first clarifies that when a common word is used for diverse realities, it is possible that the diverse realities participate in different ways, analogically, in one thing. So, as a result, the word "sacrament" can be applied to different realities, which, even though they are different, can also really share in some common attribute. Thus, Thomas teaches that something "may be called a 'sacrament'" for two different reasons.

"Either," Thomas explains, "from having a certain hidden sanctity, and in this sense a sacrament is a 'sacred secret,'" or, secondly because something has "some relationship to this sanctity, which may be that of cause, or of a sign or of any other relation."[1]

Thomas's work here is rather modest. His formal definition of "sacrament" in the sense of the seven sacraments is not given until the next article. There are, therefore, two ways in which signs can be called sacraments. First, as Thomas indicates, "from having a certain hidden sanctity," or, second, "from having a certain relationship to this sanctity." The common attribute for all realities that may be called "sacrament" in the Christian sense of the term is, hence, that of sanctity. A sacrament in the most general sense of the term is a sign that possesses a hidden sanctity or bears some relationship to it.

This general definition does not, in itself, highlight what differentiates the seven sacraments from other Christian signs, such as holy water. It merely indicates that, to be the kind of sign that can be called a sacrament in the broadest sense of the term, the sign must either possess sanctity or stand in relation to it.

Why does Thomas begin his consideration of the sacraments by asking whether a sacrament is a kind of sign? Why not merely commence by putting forward a definitive definition? Thomas is situating his understanding of the nature of the sacraments within the biblical and theological tradition of the Church. The first part of Thomas's definition, which underscores that a sacrament must have a "hidden sanctity," dovetails with the biblical use of the Greek word *mystērion*, from which the English word "mystery" is derived.

From *Mystērion* to Sacramental Signs

In the Septuagint version of the Old Testament, the Greek word *mystērion* appears about thirty times, mostly in the later books.[2] It

---

1. *ST* III, q. 60, a. 1.

2. For perhaps the most detailed systematic treatment of the word "sacrament" in its Greek and Latin roots, from the Old Testament through the New Testament, and in classical usage up to Augustine, see Jean-Philippe Revel, *Traité des sacrements*. I.1, *Baptême*

always entails an aspect of hiddenness, especially in relation to the unfolding of God's ultimate plan of salvation. In Wisdom 2:22, for example, the wicked lack knowledge of the "secret purposes of God." Wisdom 6:22 likewise uses the word *mystērion* to describe the profundity of wisdom: "I will tell you what wisdom is and how she came to be, and I will hide no secrets from you." In the second chapter of Daniel the word *mystērion* is used several times in reference to the hidden meaning of King Nebuchadnezzar's cryptic dream (see Dn 2:18–19, 21–22, 28).

In the New Testament, Jesus uses *mystērion* to identify the hidden knowledge of the Kingdom of God that has been disclosed to the disciples but not to those outside: "To you has been given the secret (*mystērion*) of the kingdom of God, but for those outside everything is in parables" (Mk 4:11).

St. Paul uses the word *mystērion* numerous times throughout his writings, especially to identify the way in which God's hidden plan of salvation unfolds in Christ. Perhaps the most pointed example of this is the closing sequence of the hymn in the first chapter of Ephesians: "For he has made known to us in all wisdom and insight the *mystery* of his will, according to his purpose which he set forth in Christ as a plan for the fullness of time, to unite all things in him, things in heaven and things on earth" (1:9–10).

In a very concrete example, St. Paul speaks of the relationship between husband and wife in marriage as a "*mystērion*," which refers to the unbreakable relationship between "Christ and the Church" (Eph 5:32).

Other examples of the use of *mystērion* in the New Testament could be provided, but it is beyond the scope of this work to consider each of them. A basic insight, however, can be identified: namely, that God's hidden or mysterious plan of salvation is unfolded

---

et sacramentalité. Origine et signification de baptême, 380–429. For a helpful presentation of words *mystērion* and *sacramentum* from the Bible through Isidore of Seville, see William A. Van Roo, SJ, *The Christian Sacrament* (Rome: Editrice Pontificia Università Gregoriana, 1992), 27–67.

through events or mysteries that have both a visible and an invisible dimension. This "sacramental economy" or plan of salvation culminates in the visible Incarnation of the Word who is in himself a *mystērion* of the presence of the Kingdom of God on earth.

It is fair, at this juncture, to ask what it is that connects the biblical use of *mystērion* with the seven sacraments of the Church, let alone with Aquinas's placement of the sacraments within the category of sign? First, the Greek word *mystērion* is taken up in the Christian tradition to refer to the sacraments of the Church. So the word itself, because of the visible-invisible nature of the biblical mysteries, is simply one way of saying what is indicated by the word "sacrament." The Latin word *sacramentum* enters into theological language because it is the term used in the Latin Bible to translate some of the instances of the Greek word *mystērion*. The Latin Bible maintains a certain elasticity in relation to *mystērion* by sometimes translating it as *sacramentum* and other times merely transliterating it as *mysterium*. This elasticity is indicated by the proclamation in the Roman Eucharistic liturgy of the phrase "*Mysterium Fidei*" just after the consecration in reference to Christ's presence in the Eucharist.

In the cases cited above, for example, Jesus' use of *mystērion* in Mark is rendered in the Vulgate as *mysterium;* the two passages from Ephesians translate *mystērion* as *sacramentum*.

But there is also an even more fundamental theological reason for the connection between the biblical use of *mystērion-sacramentum* and the seven sacraments of the Church.[3] In Colossians 1:24–29, St. Paul speaks of his office as that of a minister of the Word and, hence, the "mystery" of God's plan. Yet, in this passage Paul extends the meaning of "mystery" to the reality of the Christian's participation "in Christ": "To them that God chose to make known how great among the Gentiles are the riches of the glory of this mystery, which is *Christ in you*, the hope of glory. Him we proclaim, warning

---

3. For a developed treatment of this point, see Antonio Miralles, *I Sacramenti Cristiani: Trattato Generale* (Rome: EDUSC s.r.l, 2008), 23–30.

every man and teaching every man in all wisdom, that we may present every man mature *in Christ*" (vv. 27–28; emphasis added).

The sacraments are the points of contact between the *mystērion* and Christian life *in Christ*, according to St. Paul. Antonio Miralles points to several Pauline texts that underscore this point. Galatians 3:26–27 describes Baptism as the insertion of the Christian into the mystery of Christ: "For *in Christ* Jesus you are all sons of God through faith. For as many of you as were baptized *into Christ* have put on Christ." Baptism, in Paul's teaching, is the locus in which the believer is placed *in Christ*.

Similarly, Paul develops this theme in Eucharistic terms in 1 Corinthians 10:16–17. In this text Paul recognizes that the reality of Christian existence *in Christ* as members of his body is an effect of the participation in Christ received by means of his presence in the Eucharist: "The cup of blessing which we bless, is it not a participation in the blood of Christ? The bread which we break, is it not a participation in the body of Christ? Because there is one bread, we who are many are one body, for we all partake of the one bread."

One final note on the biblical doctrine of signs: there is often an amnesia regarding the sacramental vision of the fourth Gospel.[4] Indeed, the declaration that the "Word was made flesh" is sacramental in a fundamental sense. And, further, St. John orders the narrative of the Incarnate Word's life around seven dynamic miracles, each of which he refers to as "signs": the wedding at Cana, three healings, walking on water, the multiplication of loaves, and the raising of Lazarus.[5] Colman O'Neill likens the power operative in the seven sacraments to that of Jesus' "signs" in John's Gospel and argues that St. John's presentation of the "signs" performed by the Incarnate

---

4. For a balanced treatment of the sacramental theology of the fourth Gospel, with insightful criticisms against Bultmann's rejection of any sacramental reading of the Gospel of John, see Raymond Brown, "The Johannine Sacramentary," in Raymond E. Brown, SS, *New Testament Essays* (New York: Image Books, 1968), 77–107; and Brown's "The Eucharist and Baptism in John," in ibid., 108–31.

5. See John 2:12, 4:43ff., 5:1ff., 61ff., 6:16ff., 9:1ff., 11.

Word helps believers to see the dynamic sacramental connection that exists between the Incarnate Word, the Church, and the sacraments:

> When the person of Christ is placed in this way at the source of the entire sacramental order [as in John's Gospel], and when the church, in turn, is viewed as a general sacrament, subordinate to Christ, of the divine saving mercy, the individual sacraments are freed from their isolation as unconnected rituals. They are taken up as integral parts of an economy of grace in which God becomes immanent in his creation so as to bring it to himself.[6]

The hidden mystery of God's plan of salvation is, therefore, made manifest and brought to completion in Christ. This mystery is extended through history in the Church, in which Christ's members are joined to his saving mystery through the sacraments.[7]

The theological traditions that developed in the Greek language simply adopted *mystērion* as the technical term to be used for the seven sacraments, while the Latin tradition used both *mysterium* and *sacramentum*. It is important to note that for more than a millennium Christians did not use *mystērion-sacramentum* to refer exclusively to the seven sacraments.[8] Many other symbolic actions, rites, and sacramentals within the Church were identified as sacraments. The problem for the Church, therefore, was not in a failure to identify the seven sacraments, but how to indicate what was unique to the seven among the many rites and symbols used by the Church.

For example, in his famous work on the sacraments, *De sacramen-*

---

6. Colman E. O'Neill, OP, *Sacramental Realism: A General Theory of the Sacraments* (Chicago: Midwest Theological Forum, 1998), 52.

7. In relation to Baptism, for example, Liam Walsh argues that Clement of Alexandria and Origen maintain that "the rite concretizes the biblical types proclaimed in the texts and brings them to bear on the life of Christians." See Walsh, *Sacraments of Initiation: A Theology of Life, Word, and Rite* (Chicago: Hillenbrand Books, 2011; 2nd ed.), 18.

8. This does not mean that the earliest systematic theologians in the Church did not use *mystērion-sacramentum* to refer to specific sacraments. They did so, in fact, and very readily. For a detailed list of the use of *mystērion-sacramentum* in reference to specific sacraments by Clement of Alexandria, Origen, Eusebius of Caesarea, Athanasius, and John Chrysostom in the East and Tertullian, Cyprian, and Ambrose in the West, see Miralles, *I Sacramenti Cristiani*, 80–93. See also *Battesimo, purificazione, rinascita*, vol. 6 of *Dizionario di spiritualità biblico-patristica* (Padua: Libreria del Santo, 1993).

tis, Hugh of St. Victor (†1141) catalogs, along with the seven sacraments, several other symbolic realities that he also identifies as sacraments. These include: the Incarnation, the Church, liturgical vessels and vestments, consecrated churches, sacramentals, vows, death and judgment, the eschaton, and eternal life. Hugh's treatment of these under the category of "sacrament" comprises a vast work of systematic theology engaging all the major doctrines of the Christian faith.[9]

This broad understanding of "sacrament" had deep resonance with the elasticity of the biblical use of "mystery"; nor was it a problem that merited the corrective attention of the Church until error about the sacraments caused such ambiguity that definitive clarification became necessary.

A first wave of errors came in two polar opposite forms about the nature of the sacraments as signs. In the ninth century, a monastic theologian named Paschasius Rabertus authored a treatise on the Eucharist in which he affirmed in strictly realist terms an identity between the sacrament of the altar and Christ's body and blood. From this perspective, the sacrament would not be a sign of Christ's body and blood, but the very reality itself. In response to the non-symbolic realism of Paschasius Radbertus, a monk and prolific theologian named Ratramnus argued for the opposite position, explaining the sacrament of the altar in exclusively spiritual terms. According to these opposing positions in the controversy, there is either no distinction between the sacrament and the reality signified in the sacrament (Paschasius Radbertus) or no real connection between the sacramental sign and the signified reality (Ratramnus).[10] After this controversy, another theologian named Berengar (†1088) took a position similar to that of Ratramnus but even more pointedly direct in its claims; his position was viewed by his contemporaries as an outright rejection of the doctrine of Real Presence. Accord-

9. See Hugh of St. Victor, *Hugh of St. Victor on the Sacraments of the Christian Faith*, trans. Roy J. Deferrari (Eugene, Ore.: Wipf and Stock, 2007; reprint), 205–476.

10. See Bernard Leeming, SJ, *Principles of Sacramental Theology* (Westminster, Md.: Newman Press, 1956), 564.

ing to Berengar, as signs, the sacraments are empty, carrying no real participation in the reality that is signified. Therefore, the Eucharist was not the body of Christ, but merely an empty sign of it.[11]

In addition to controversies over the very nature of the sacraments as signs, another wave of error arose which contributed to ambiguity over which ecclesial signs and gestures truly belonged among the official sacraments of Church. This error was amplified by growth of the group known as the Waldensians in the 1170s, who recognized only two sacraments, Baptism and Eucharist. As a result, though lists specifying the seven sacraments had been clarified by 1150 (or so) and clearly affirmed by Peter Lombard in the 1160s in the fourth book of his famous work *The Sentences*,[12] in 1208 Pope Innocent III issued a "Declaration of faith for the Waldensians" affirming each of the seven sacraments in the form of a profession of faith.[13]

What it is that accounts for the special identity of the seven sacraments among the many liturgical signs and gestures used by the Church? And, why did the theologians in the Latin tradition, such as Augustine, Lombard, Hugh of St. Victor, Bonaventure, and Thomas Aquinas, place the seven *sacramenta* of the Church in the category of sign? Understanding the sacraments as a species of the category of sign is immensely important to understanding their basic nature as realities, and likewise it is an important key to avoiding and correcting certain errors, like those of Paschasius Rabertus, Ratramnus, and Berengar, that divide Christians on sacramental grounds. The great authors of the Middle Ages, standing in continuity with Fathers of the first millennium, understood the importance of precision on this point with great clarity.[14]

11. Ibid.

12. See Peter Lombard, *On the Doctrine of Signs*, Book 4 of *The Sentences*, trans. Giulio Silano (Toronto: Pontifical Institute of Mediaeval Studies, 2010), 9 (Distinction II, chap. 1).

13. See Heinrich Denzinger, *Enchiridion symbolorum definitionum et declarationum de rebus fidei et morum — Compendium of Creeds, Definitions, and Declarations on Matters of Faith and Morals*, Latin-English, 43rd ed., ed. Peter Hünermann (San Francisco: Ignatius Press, 2012), 262–65 (§790–97).

14. See Peter Lombard, *On the Doctrine of Signs*, Book 4 of *The Sentences*, especially pages 3–9 (Distinction I).

At face value, viewing the sacraments as signs can seem like an equivocation — an attempt to say simultaneously that the sacraments are real and substantial and that they are merely symbolic. This idea, though, could not be further from the truth.

From Augustine to the Bible and Back Again

In his famous work *De Doctrina Christiana* St. Augustine develops a general doctrine of signs that has rich implications for biblical interpretation and sacramental life.[15] "A sign, after all," Augustine explains,

> is a thing, which besides the impression it conveys to the senses, *also has the effect of making something else come to mind*; as when we see a spoor, we think of the animal whose spoor it is; or when we see smoke, we know there is fire underneath; and when we hear the cry of a living creature, we can tell what its mood is; and when the trumpet sounds, soldiers know that they must advance or retreat, or whatever else the battle requires.[16]

A sign, then, in the patrimony of Augustine, is understood to be a reality that in making itself known also points beyond itself to another reality.[17] Augustine divides signs, which can be sounds, words, sights, gestures, and so on, into two groups: natural and convention-

15. For a summary of Augustine's teaching in *De Doctrina Christiana*, see Matthew Levering, *The Theology of Augustine* (Grand Rapids, Mich.: Baker Academic, 2013), 1–17. For a treatment focused on the doctrine of signs in *De Doctrina Christiana*, see John Deely, *Augustine and Poinsot: The Protosemiotic Development* (Scranton, Penn.: University of Scranton Press, 2009), 27–56. See also William A. Van Roo, *The Christian Sacrament*, 38–43; Miralles, *I Sacramenti Cristiani*, 85–98; Jean-Hervé Nicolas, OP, *Synthèse dogmatique: De la Trinité à la Trinité*, Editions Universitaires Fribourg Suisse (Paris: Beauchesne, 1985), §713. (Because Nicolas's work has been issued in various editions, section numbers instead of page numbers will be used in citing the work.) For twenty different applications of *mysterion/sacramentum* in the ancient world, especially in the thought of St. Augustine, see Joseph Lienhard, SJ, "*Sacramentum* and the Eucharist in St. Augustine," *The Thomist* 77 (2013): 173–92.

16. St. Augustine, *Teaching Christianity (De Doctrina Christiana)*, trans. Edmund Hill, OP (New York: New City Press, 1996), 129 (book II, 1, 1) (emphasis added).

17. Augustine was not the originator of philosophical and theological speculation about signs. His pre-conversion career as a rhetorician, knowledge of Stoic philosophers, and admiration for Cicero, as well as, of course, the symbolism of the Christian Scriptures and sacramental worship all contributed to his rich appreciation for the nature of signs. See John M. Rist, *Augustine* (Cambridge: Cambridge University Press, 1994), 23–40.

al. Signs of both kinds possess the property of "making something else come to mind," but natural signs, such as smoke signifying a fire, do so without "any desire or intention of signifying."[18] The so-called "conventional or given signs [*data signa*]," Augustine explains, differ from natural signs in this way: rational creatures offer these signs to each other "in order to show, as far as they can, their moods and feelings, or to indicate whatever it may be they have sensed or understood." The reason why rational creatures give these signs is, Augustine says, "to bring out and transfer to someone else's mind what we, the givers of the sign, have in mind ourselves."[19]

Some of these signs, furthermore, are sacred because they are given to humanity by God. These include the words and events of sacred Scripture and the sacramental rites of the Church. Augustine refers to these later signs as "sacraments."[20] The normal means of communication used by rational creatures is speech — word. It is also true that the Lord did not rely on words alone to make something known; often in his public ministry he used sensible signs coupled with words for the sake of leading humanity through the signification of the sign to a deeper, hidden reality. "Yes, it is true," Augustine explains, "that the Lord gave some sign through the odor of the ointment which was poured over his feet. And in the sacrament of his body and blood the Lord signified what he wished to through the sense of taste. And when the woman was healed by touching the hem of his cloak, it certainly signified something."[21]

Why does the Christian liturgy have so many fewer signs than the system of worship practiced by ancient Israel? Augustine ascribes this to St. Paul's doctrine of the movement from slavery under

18. Augustine, *Teaching Christianity* (*De Doctrina christiana*), 129 (book II, 2).

19. Ibid. (book II, 2, 3).

20. Augustine's application of *sacramentum* to the sacramental rites of the Church is not novel within the systematic tradition of Latin theology. There are many instances from Tertullian onward of the use of the Latin word *sacramentum* in reference to the Christian sacraments. See, for example, Walsh, *Sacraments of Initiation*, 15ff.

21. *Teaching Christianity* (*De Doctrina christiana*), 130 (book II, 3, 4). For Augustine's presentation of the *sacramenta* as signs, see Revel, *Traité des sacrements. I.1, Baptême et sacramentalité. Origine et signification de baptême*, 429–61.

the Old Law to the liberty enjoyed by Christians in light of the risen Christ's victory over death. "The Lord himself," Augustine argues, and the discipline of the apostles, have handed down to us just a few signs instead of many, and these so easy to perform, and so awesome to understand, and so pure and chaste to celebrate, such as the sacrament of baptism, and the celebration of the Lord's body and blood. When people receive these, they have been so instructed that they can recognize to what sublime realities they are referred, and so they venerate them in a spirit not of carnal slavery, but rather of spiritual freedom.[22]

The word "sacrament," therefore, identifies a sign given by God for a sacred purpose. In a famous passage in *City of God*, Augustine joins "sacrament" and "sacred sign" into an overlapping definition of a common reality: "A visible sacrifice," Augustine explains, is "the *sacramentum* of an invisible sacrifice, that is, a sacred sign (*sacrum signum*)."[23]

It is important not to lose sight of the continuity that can be found in the movement from the biblical notion of "mystery" to the seven sacraments of the Church. In fact, as Miralles points out, many of the Fathers of the Church were careful to refer to specific sacraments as the "mystery of x, y, or z" instead of simply the name of the sacrament alone. This means that each sacrament is a "mystery" in the biblical sense. The force of the phrase "the mystery/sacrament of Baptism" is somewhat lost today. It is intended to communicate that Baptism, and each of the sacraments, continue the visible unfolding of God's hidden plan of salvation in Christ.[24]

Augustine's presentation of signs that are appropriated by God for sacred purposes is not the imposition of his philosophical doctrine of signs onto the Christian tradition. Rather, Augustine learned from the Bible and the practice of the Church that a category of spe-

22. Ibid., 175 (book III, 9, 13).
23. See *De Civitate Dei*, X, 5 (CSEL 40. 452, 18–19). "Sacrificium ergo visibile invisibilis sacrificii sacramentum, id est sacrum signum est."
24. For further discussion of this point, especially in reference to St. Ambrose, see Miralles, *I Sacramenti Cristiani*, 89.

cifically sacred signs had been revealed and that this revealed doctrine was the foundation for the practice of the Church.

Following the biblical and patristic tradition, especially the crucial developments of St. Augustine, Thomas speaks of those signs that God has appropriated for sacred purposes as "sacraments." However, as noted above, the definition that Thomas puts forward in article 1 of question 60 is only a general indicator of the nature of the sacraments; it does not identify what differentiates the seven sacraments from the other sacramentals and symbols used by the Church. Thomas completes this work in article 2 of question 60.

St. Thomas's Definition of the Seven Sacraments

The pedagogical question that emerges naturally from these points is presented by Thomas as the topic of article 2, namely, "Whether every sign of a holy thing is a sacrament?"

Thomas's answer to this question builds upon the doctrine of analogy set forth in the first article. Students of theology often flee frantically when confronted with the Thomistic doctrine of analogy. At its basic level, however, analogy is merely a way of deriving knowledge about diverse realities by establishing the extent to which they can and cannot be truthfully compared to each other.[25] In theology and philosophy (and other disciplines, too, such as poetry) these comparisons are useful, to the degree that they are valid.

The Bible frequently makes analogical comparisons to reveal knowledge of deeper realities, such as with the use of names for God like "Father." Analogical reasoning, however, cannot be used validly when diverse realities are either so different (equivocal) that they share no common attributes or when they are completely the same (univocal). For example, the attribute of life cannot be the foundation of any analogical comparison between a living and a non-living

25. For a brief discussion of the use of analogy in the Third Part of the *Summa*, see Roger W. Nutt, "On Analogy, the Incarnation, and the Sacraments of the Church: Considerations from the *Tertia pars* of the *Summa theologiae*," *Nova et Vetera*, English Edition, 12, no. 3 (2014): 989–1004.

thing. No meaningful truth is derived by trying to compare a rock and a cat with respect to the attribute of life.

The broad term "sacrament," however, which indicates a sign appropriated by God for sacred purposes, is applied to diverse realities sharing the common attribute of being signs. Not all of these signs/sacraments, however, are sacraments in the way that the seven are. Thomas specifies what the primary meaning of sacrament — in the sense of the seven — is: "A sacrament properly so called is that which is the sign of some sacred thing pertaining to man; so that properly speaking a sacrament, as considered by us now, is defined as being the 'sign of a holy thing so far as it makes men holy.'"[26]

Sustained reflection on this terse definition, "sign of a holy thing so far as it makes men holy," is of utmost importance for appreciating the centrality of the sacraments within Christian life. What is unique to the seven sacraments among the other signs and symbols employed within Christianity is that the sacraments "make men holy." Sometimes Thomas's teaching on the sacraments as signs is, accordingly, referred to in terms of causality. For example, insofar as they make men holy, the sacraments are not mere signs or empty symbolic gestures; they are causal signs, effecting the grace or holiness that they signify.[27] Thomas's understanding of the effective side of the sacraments has deep resonances with the magisterial axiom that the sacraments work *ex opere operato*, about which more will be said below.[28]

Thomas's view of the sacraments as signs is related to his understanding of an image and the reality from which the image is derived. When speaking of the sacrificial nature of the Mass, Thomas

26. *ST* III, q. 60, a. 2.
27. For a helpful treatment of Aquinas's coupling of the notions of "sign" and "cause" in his understanding of the sacraments, see Benoît-Dominique de La Soujeole, OP, "The Importance of the Definition of Sacraments as Signs," in *Ressourcement Thomism: Sacred Doctrine, the Sacraments, and the Moral Life*, ed. Reinhard Hütter and Matthew Levering (Washington, D.C.: The Catholic University of America Press, 2010), 127–35.
28. For a discussion of Thomas's coupling of the two terms "sign" and "cause" in his definition of sacrament, see Revel, *Traité des sacrements*. I.1, *Baptême et sacramentalité. Origine et signification de baptême*, 480–93.

describes the Eucharist as an "image representing Christ's passion."[29] Thomas's understanding of "image" is helpful in clarifying the nature of the sacramental reality.[30] For something to qualify as an image for Thomas, a special likeness going beyond generic or common similarity is required. "The nature of an image," Thomas explains, "requires likeness in species" as father to son or at least in the sharing of specific accidents.[31] Hence, an image requires, above generic similarity, real likeness to the origin that is participated in by the image, and that the image be truly derived, as son from father, from the originating source that it signifies.

Several clarifications emerge from Thomas's definition of the sacraments that distinguish the seven from other symbolic gestures employed by the Church. First, the sacraments are not efficacious merely as moral realities. Morally efficacious realities may be conducive to bringing about a certain state of affairs, but they do not "make" the state of affairs. Stop signs, for example, are extremely efficacious in bringing automobiles to a halt, but there is nothing about them that is intrinsic to making cars stop. Stop signs are efficacious because they are good reminders. As a stand-alone category, therefore, moral efficacy is not sufficient to articulate the relation between the sacraments and the conferral of holiness upon their recipients.

Second, and related to the previous point, the sacraments are not simply dispositions to grace. Thomas considers the use of certain sacred signs that dispose things for sanctifying actions, such as the blessing of a religious item with holy water or the consecration of an altar. The sign, in these cases, disposes or sets apart the blessed item or consecrated altar for sacred purposes. Thomas denies that sacraments operate this way in relation to holiness and the conferral

29. *ST* III, q. 83, a. 1.
30. For a fuller development of this point in the context of the Eucharist, see Štěpán Martin Filip, OP, "*Imago Repræsentativa Passionis Christi*: St. Thomas Aquinas on the Essence of the Sacrifice of the Mass," trans. Roger W. Nutt, *Nova et Vetera*, English Edition, 7 (2009): 405–38.
31. See *ST* I, q. 93, a. 2.

of grace. Sacraments do not merely dispose their recipients to grace, they actually make them holy. "Things that signify disposition to holiness," Thomas explains, "are not called sacraments ... only those things are called sacraments which signify the perfection of holiness in man."[32] This is so, Thomas explains, because a "disposition is not an end, whereas a perfection is."[33] A disposition is ordered to something else, but the sacraments effect the end of perfection or holiness in men and women.

Third, the sacraments employ natural realities (e.g., water, wine, oil, bread) but *they are not* natural signs. The sacraments have a divine origin and corresponding purpose or intention for their employment. Thomas is very sensitive to the nuances of Christian anthropology, and his common dictum that "the thing known is in the knower according to the mode of the knower"[34] is certainly applicable to sacramental theology. But the sacraments do not complement Christian anthropology as if they were emanations from human nature. Rather, they complement human nature because God, in his wisdom, knows the best way to lead humanity to himself. "Signs are given to men," Thomas explains, "to whom it is proper to discover the unknown by means of the known."[35]

The subtle point that needs internalization here is that the meaning of the sacraments is not, as some scholars have argued, derived primarily or entirely from what the material elements mean in their natural signification or for the worshipping community at the horizontal level. Kenan Osborne, for example, following the work of Gerard van der Leeuw, suggests that the sacraments "have too often been discussed as a specifically Christian phenomenon, ignoring the many connections that the Christian sacraments have, not only with other religions but also human phenomena."[36] A possible danger with this approach lies not in affirming the deeply human

---

32. *ST* III, q. 60, a. 2, ad 3. 33. Ibid.
34. *ST* I, q. 12, a. 4. 35. *ST* III, q. 60, a. 2.
36. Kenan B. Osborne, OFM, *Christian Sacraments in a Postmodern World: A Theology for the Third Millennium* (Mahwah, N.J.: Paulist Press, 1999), 41.

significance of the Christian sacraments, which is true and unde-
niable, but rather in treating them horizontally in isolation from
their significance as signs given within the providential order of the
divine wisdom. To treat them so reduces their signification to the
natural level and affixes their focal meaning to their anthropological significance. The bread of the Eucharist, for example, does not
derive its primary sign value from fond memories of family dinners
at grandma and grandpa's table, though, to be sure, such sentiments
are not wholly irrelevant either.[37] The problem with this tendency,
at its core, is that the natural and common signification of things is
not related to making men holy, which is the purpose of the sacraments. As signs, therefore, the sacraments ought not to be conflated
with the pan-sacramentality found within the rich and wondrous
texture of nature and human culture.

The exclusive focus on the natural meaning of the food, water,
gestures, and oil employed in the sacraments ends up closing off the
faithful to the divine meaning, intention, and agency that the signs
are employed to communicate. "Sensible creatures signify something holy," Thomas teaches in relation to natural signification,
"namely, Divine wisdom and goodness inasmuch as these are holy
in themselves; but not inasmuch as we are made holy by them."[38]
This is why, St. Thomas explains, the rich symbolism of nature is
not sacramental in the sense employed by the Church to indicate
the exact nature of the seven sacraments. Miralles stresses that such
observations are not "secondary," because, above all, a "sacrament is
an event of sanctification."[39]

37. It is interesting to observe that in his book *The Eucharist*, Edward Schillebeeckx
documents the movement in the twentieth century away from a theology of the real presence expressed in terms of substance to a theology that speaks in terms of "transsignifica-
tion" or "transfinalisation" precisely as a concession to Kant's criticism of a metaphysics of
being and to the claims of modern physics. Instead of the reality of the substance of bread,
what is changed, according to these approaches, is the finality or signification that the
bread (and wine) has for the worshipping community. See Schillebeeckx, *The Eucharist*,
trans. N. D. Smith (New York: Sheed and Ward, 1968), 94–95.

38. *ST* III, q. 60, a. 2, ad 1.

39. Miralles, *I Sacramenti Cristiani*, 111.

To do justice to any or all of the sacraments, students of theology and the faithful must keep in mind that, as realities, the sacraments are always signs. The holiness that they effect is in and through their signification, so to appreciate the sacraments and their sanctifying effects, an awareness that the sacraments are unique signs instituted to confer holiness through their signification must be preserved.

FOUR

Sacramental Matter and Form

The Past, Present, and Future Signification of the Sacraments

The profundity of the holiness of the grace of the Holy Spirit cannot be reduced to a one-dimensional signification. The sacramental signs unify in their signification three related aspects of holiness. The sanctification bestowed by the Holy Spirit in the New Law of grace would not be possible were it not for Christ's suffering, death, and Resurrection. Furthermore, as causal signs, the sacramental rites effect the grace that they signify — in the present. And, finally, Christ's paschal mystery and the grace conferred in the sacraments are ordered to the ultimate end of eternal beatitude. As a result, the sacraments do not signify merely the historical aspect of sanctity (Christ's saving work), or only the present aspect (grace), or simply the future (eternal beatitude). The sacraments integrate these three by conferring in the present what Christ merited in the paschal mystery; this conferral of the grace of Christ in the present orders the faithful to future glory.[1]

---

1. For an exposition of the threefold temporal dimension of the sacraments and their threefold signification, see Revel, *Traité des sacrements.* I.1, *Baptême et sacramentalité. Origine et signification de baptême,* 116–21.

Aquinas summarizes these three aspects of sacramental signification under the categories of cause, form, and end:

the very cause of our sanctification, which is Christ's passion; the form of our sanctification, which is grace and the virtues; and the ultimate end of our sanctification, which is eternal life. And all these are signified by the sacraments. Consequently a sacrament is a sign that is both a reminder of the past, i.e. the passion of Christ; and an indication of that which is effected in us by Christ's passion, i.e. grace; and a prognostic, that is, a foretelling of future glory.[2]

How is it possible that a sacramental reality is able to confer the effect of grace? It can be seen in a few explicit episodes that Christ's institution of the sacraments attaches specific words to specific elements. For example, in the institution of the Eucharist the words "this is my body" are pronounced over bread and the words "this is my blood" are pronounced over the chalice of wine. Likewise, Christ commands that the use of water in Baptism be accompanied by the words "in the name of the Father, and of the Son, and of the Holy Spirit" (Mt 28:19).

The Material Element of the Sacraments

As indicated above, St. Thomas approaches this question with a sensitivity to how "divine wisdom provides for each thing according to its mode" by leading people from what is more known to what is less known.[3] Because, Thomas teaches,

the sacred things which are signified by the sacraments are the spiritual and intelligible goods by means of which man is sanctified, it follows that the sacramental signs consist in sensible things: just as in the Divine Scriptures spiritual things are set before us under the guise of things sensible. And hence it is that sensible things are required for the sacraments.[4]

The material element of the sacraments provides, as it were, the tangible point of mediation in which the grace that is signified is able

---

2. *ST* III, q. 60, a. 3.   3. Ibid., a. 4.
4. Ibid.

to be conferred. But, as was noted above, the seven sacraments are not merely part of the common symbolism that can be attributed to things of nature. Rather, they are instituted by God as participatory images of specific realities so that those signified realities can be communicated to the faithful. Because grace is an effect that depends on the divine initiative, the meaning of the material element of the sacrament is not reducible to that element's use within nature alone. "Sensible things considered in their own nature," Thomas observes, "do not belong to the worship or kingdom of God: but considered only as signs of spiritual things in which the kingdom of God consists."[5]

To use signs to signify realities within the Kingdom of God requires that God himself indicate the specific signs to be employed. Citing John 3:5: "Unless a man be born again of *water and the Holy Ghost*, he cannot enter into the kingdom of God," Aquinas concludes that specified material is required for the celebration of the sacraments.

This point addresses an important question that is relevant for theology today. Given that one reality, say cleansing, can be accomplished by many material elements, it seems somewhat superficial to conclude that the matter employed in a sacrament must be limited and specific. Since bleach, Mr. Clean, and ammonia are all cleansing agents, it appears that any of them could, just as validly as water, be the sign of baptismal cleansing.

The problem with this approach to the sacraments is that it treats the material aspect of the sacramental sign as if it were arbitrarily chosen and could be equally replaced by something else. Thomas views the fixity of the material components of the sacraments to be rooted in the divine wisdom. "In the use of the sacraments," Thomas explains, "two things may be considered, namely, the worship of God and the sanctification of man: the former of which pertains to man as referred to God, and the latter pertains to God in reference to man."[6]

5. Ibid., a. 3.
6. Ibid., a. 4.

Thomas points out that "it is not for anyone to determine that which is in the power of another." To whom, then, does the determination of the sacramental matter belong and why? "Since, therefore, the sanctification of man is in the power of God Who sanctifies," Thomas explains, "it is not for man to decide what things should be used for this sanctification, but this should be determined by Divine institution." Following 1 Corinthians 6:11, which declares of Baptism "you are washed, you are sanctified," Thomas concludes that "we must use those things which are determined by Divine institution."[7]

The matter of each of the sacraments, however, does not constitute the sacramental sign all by itself. This is why the signification of the sacraments is not reducible solely to the material elements.

Sacramental Words: The Formal Element of the Sacraments

As a result, there are always words accompanying the specific matter that is required of each sacrament. Without the words, the matter of the sacraments would not be determined to the purpose of sanctification.

What is it that makes the bread, wine, water, and oil of the sacraments signs in a way that they are not in their common usage? Why is water used for drinking not considered a sacrament? "In order to insure the perfection of sacramental signification," Thomas reasons,

---

7. Ibid. It should be noted, however, that Thomas's understanding of sacramental matter is not materialistic. That is, he does not reduce the sacramental sign to the material element. By matter, Thomas means to indicate the basic potency upon which the sacramental sign is built and without which the sacrament could not be brought into being. In most cases, this matter is a material element, such as bread, wine, water, or oil. In certain cases, however, the sacramental matter is not a tangible element. For example, in the case of Penance, Thomas identifies the three parts of Penance (confession, contrition, and satisfaction) as the "proximate" matter of the sacrament, and the sins that the penitent confesses, manifests contrition for, and does penance for as the "remote" matter of the sacrament. Thus for the sacramental sign to be effected in Penance, the penitent must have sins to confess, actually confess them, be contrite, and perform the assigned penance. See *ST* III, q. 84, a. 2, sed contra.

it was necessary to determine the signification of the sensible things by means of certain words. For water may signify both a cleansing by reason of its humidity, and refreshment by reason of its being cool: but when we say, "I baptize you," it is clear that we use water in baptism in order to signify a spiritual cleansing.[8]

Thomas does not view the use of the specific matter and form of the sacraments as arbitrary impositions of the Church. The specificity of the matter and form of the signs is determined by the divine wisdom as the best means to lead to the spiritual realities that God wishes to share in Christ. It is not merely the natural meaning of the elements that is to be discerned in the rite; rather, it is the divine use of these elements in the history of salvation, which is continued to the present day in the sacramental worship of the Church, that is the focal emphasis of the sacred signs known as sacraments.

The necessary composite of specific matter and words indicates that a sacrament is a true reality whose existence is brought about (assuming the proper minister and intention) by the composition of the material element with the words. The material element alone is not adequately specified to be a sacrament, nor do the words alone adequately constitute the sign through which the effects are caused. The reality of each sacrament is brought about only when the proper matter is coupled with the correct verbal formulation.

Thomas draws an analogy between the composition of the sacraments and his doctrine of hylomorphism.[9] Unlike mind-body dualism, which is unable to account for the overall unity of the human being as a body-soul composite, hylomorphism explains the substantial unity of material substances in terms of the composition of matter and form. Just as a human being is one unified reality composed of a soul and body, so too are sacraments composed of a formal and a material element. "In the sacraments," Thomas teaches, "the words are

---

8. *ST* III, q. 60, a. 6.

9. For a helpful treatment of sacramental hylomorphism, which makes important distinctions between sacraments and material substances, see Nicolas, *Synthèse dogmatique*, §725.

as the form, and sensible things are as the matter."[10] Recourse to this doctrine gives Thomas the ability to explain how it is that the material elements (water, wine, oil, bread, and so on) used in the sacraments are distinguishable from their common usage. When coupled with the sacramental words, the material elements become signs capable of making people holy. Thomas explains this as follows:

Now in all things composed of matter and form, the determining principle is on the part of the form, which is as it were the end and terminus of the matter. Consequently for the being of a thing the need of a determinate form is prior to the need of determinate matter: for determinate matter is needed that it may be adapted to the determinate form. Since, therefore, in the sacraments determinate sensible things are required, which are as the sacramental matter, much more is there need in them of a determinate form of words.[11]

The bread and wine of the Eucharist, for example, are changed and therefore no longer substantially present after the consecration, because when the matter is coupled with the form by a validly ordained priest (with the proper intention) the reality of the sacrament is brought about. Likewise, the regular use of water does not confer the effects of Baptism, because water alone, without the sacramental form, is not the reality of the sacramental sign which contains and confers these effects.

Matter, Form, and Sacramental Validity

What happens, following the principles of sacramental theology, if the matter or form is altered during the celebration of a sacrament, wittingly or unwittingly? The correct answer depends upon the degree to which the alteration tarnishes the nature of the sacramental sign. This question has important implications for the life of the Church, given that the spiritual effects of the sacraments are necessary for the spiritual and moral development of the faithful.

10. *ST* III, q. 60. a. 7.
11. Ibid.

It is possible for an alteration to a sacramental celebration to be so minor that the sign is still brought into being and hence its corresponding effects are conferred. But it is also possible that, through a deficit in the correct matter and/or form, the sign is not brought into being, and therefore, since there is no sacramental sign, the sacramental effects are not conferred. The distinction between these two scenarios is made in canonical language by the terms valid/invalid and licit/illicit.[12]

In brief: a sacramental celebration is understood to be "valid" if it is executed by the proper minister in such a way that the sacrament is truly brought into being. Invalidity happens when the celebration is executed by an unauthorized minister or when the matter and form are so defective that the sign is not brought about. An invalid celebration indicates, precisely, that a sacrament was never brought into being and thus, absent the sacrament, none of the sacramental effects are conferred.

A licit celebration is one that is performed according to the prescribed rite of the Church, while an illicit celebration is one that directly deviates in some way from the prescribed rite. An illicit sacramental celebration does not vitiate the validity and therefore reality of the sacrament; an invalid celebration, on the other hand, fails to bring about a sacrament at all and therefore cannot be cause of the effects intrinsic to the signification of the sign.

The Church, therefore, is not being restrictive, unspiritual, or excessively juridical by not allowing other elements to substitute for the water, wine, bread, oil, and other gestures or other verbal formulae to be introduced into the sacramental rites. The spirituality of the "mystery" — the very unfolding of the divine plan of salvation in Christ through the sacraments — is based on the conferral of the sanctifying effects through the established signs. Substituting the matter or altering the form thwarts the nature of the sign composed from the matter and form. If the sign is not brought into existence,

12. See the 1983 *Code of Canon Law*, §841.

its ability to confer effects by means of its signifying power is impeded.

This is so, returning to the principle of wisdom, because the primary meaning of the signs does not emanate solely from the culture or community in which the celebration takes place but rather is given by God, through his wisdom, for the sake of leading the faithful through the visible sign to invisible union with Christ in grace. As Christ is the primary agent in the sacramental celebration, the meaning of the signs depends upon his action and teaching. The meaning of the sacramental action is found, therefore, in the knowledge of faith and not in the natural or cultural significance (alone) of the matter and form used in the celebration.

FIVE

Sacramental Intention

A General Theory of Sacramental Intention

Proper matter and form are not the only requirements for the valid celebration of the sacraments. The Church teaches that, in addition to the proper matter and form, the proper intention is needed. The "sacraments are accomplished by three elements," the Council of Florence (1439) teaches, "namely, by things as the matter, by words as the form, and by the person of the minister who confers the sacrament with the intention of doing what the Church does. If any of these is absent, the sacrament is not accomplished."[1]

The doctrine of the requisite sacramental intention has an (overly) complicated interpretive history.[2] Yet it is important to comprehend this nuance, because it accentuates an underappreciated aspect of the nature of the sacraments, namely, that the sacraments are not

---

1. Heinrich Denzinger, *Enchiridion symbolorum*, 338 (§1312). The Council of Trent (Session 7, March 3, 1547) likewise declares in the "Canons on the Sacraments in General": "Can. 11. If anyone says that the intention at least of doing what the Church does is not required in the ministers when they are effecting and conferring the sacraments, let him be anathema." Ibid., 390 (§1611).

2. For a very historically thorough, but at times theologically ambiguous, treatment of sacramental intention, see Bernard Leeming, *Principles of Sacramental Theology*, 435–96. For a highly cogent but much less historical presentation, see Nicolas, *Synthèse dogmatique*, §727–28.

static, free-floating entities, like fruits on a tree, that are just there for the taking. On the contrary, although it is correct to speak of a sacrament as a *res* or reality, it is also true that the sacramental reality is brought about by the proper execution of the rite — the bringing together of the matter and the form.[3] Sacraments are celebrated through a prescribed liturgical action whose institution originates with Christ himself. It is through the valid sacramental celebration that the sacrament is operative, and the minister is the agent by whom the action is performed. "An animate instrument," Aquinas explains,

such as a minister, is not only moved, but in a sense moves itself, in so far as by his will he moves his bodily members to act. Consequently, his intention is required, whereby he subjects himself to the principal agent; that is, it is necessary that he intend to do that which Christ and the Church do.[4]

It follows from this that the valid conferral of a sacrament presupposes an authentic human action on the part of the minister.[5] This means, in the words of Nicolas, that "the act of conferring the sacrament is, on the part of the minister, a free personal act; it is also a moral or immoral act."[6] Sacraments, though, do not depend solely on the intentional agency of the minister, for they are ecclesial acts, and their force "depends exclusively on Christ's institution and on the norms of the Church."[7]

That the sacraments are human actions requiring the intention of the minister for validity *and* also are acts of the Church dependent upon Christ and ecclesial sanction is not a contradiction. "The human act of conferring the sacrament," Nicolas explains, "and the sacramental action are thus one and the same act, considered from two

---

3. For a helpful treatment of the sacraments as "reality" and as "action," see Nicolas, *Synthèse dogmatique*, §726.

4. *ST* III, q. 64, a. 8.

5. There is a corresponding doctrine of intention that applies to the recipient as well. Nicolas, *Synthèse dogmatique*, §728, describes this as "the intention to receive that which the Church intends to give: to receive the sacrament."

6. Ibid., §727.

7. Ibid.

different points of view, since to confer the sacrament is not different than to complete the sacramental action on the believer."[8]

The minister, therefore, confers what Christ has instituted and entrusted to the Church. To do this the minister must act with the intention to do what the Church understands herself to have received from Christ. This unifies the minister's action with Christ's, making the minister (presuming — normally — the sacrament of Holy Orders and ecclesial faculties) an instrument that Christ appropriates from heaven to continue his mission of sanctification. This means that normally the very performance of the action as prescribed by the Church is adequate to manifest the minimum requisite intention for validity.

The faithful need not be in a constant state of worry over whether the celebrant of a sacrament has the proper intention in mind. The minister, Aquinas explains, "acts in the person of the whole Church ... while in the words uttered by him, the intention of the Church is expressed; and ... this suffices for the validity of the sacrament, except the contrary be expressed on the part either of the minister or of the recipient of the sacrament."[9]

It is important to underscore, as Fr. Miralles notes, that sacramental *intention* is distinguishable from the notion of *attention*, which applies, not to the will and what is done, but to the intellect: "one can have the intention of doing something without paying attention."[10]

The summary phrase that the minister must have "the intention of doing what the Church does" clarifies several important points about the minister's role in the valid conferral of a sacrament. The fact that this threshold for validity is rather low should not be cause for alarm. In fact, to the contrary, it is, like the *ex opere operato* causality of the sacraments, a fundamentally consoling doctrine. It teaches that the human ministers, while essential and necessary, assume only the responsibility of performing the sacrament according

8. Ibid. 9. *ST* III, q. 64, a. 8, ad 2.
10. Miralles, *I Sacramenti Cristiani*, 356.

to the prescribed rite. In performing the prescribed rite the minister effects the sacramental sign, and by effecting the sacramental sign the minister effects the action ordained by Christ to confer the graces specific to the sacrament. There are, therefore, several points about sacramental validity that the doctrine of intention clarifies.

Intention and the Faith of the Minister

The valid celebration of a sacrament is not dependent on the faith of the minister. How can a minister "intend" to celebrate a sacrament without having correct (or even any) faith in the reality of the sacrament being celebrated? The intention of the agent, in the case of the sacraments, does not have as its object the content of the faith, but the performance of the action itself. What the minister is doing and whether or not he believes the theology supporting his action are two different questions.

For example, imagine that someone is given $1,000 by a friend and instructed to take the money to a stockbroker and invest it in "futures." The friend dutifully does as instructed. When later asked what he did on the errand, he responds, "I invested $1,000 in futures for my friend." He is then asked "What is a future?" — to which he replies that he has no idea. The point is this: lacking knowledge of futures, he was quite able to successfully perform the *action* of investing in them because the success of the action did not depend on the precision of the agent's knowledge.

Likewise with the sacraments: the intention to do what the Church does is met by actually doing what the Church prescribes *to be done*. The Church came to realize this when confronted with questions such as the validity of Baptism celebrated in heretical sects. To intend what the Church intends in regard to Baptism is to perform the rite of pouring or immersing in water with the Trinitarian formula. An extreme example of the fact that sacramental validity is not dependent upon the faith of the minister is the recognition by the Church that in cases of emergency even someone who is not baptized could validly perform the sacrament of Baptism:

The ordinary ministers of Baptism are the bishop and priest and, in the Latin Church, also the deacon. *In case of necessity, anyone, even a non-baptized person, with the required intention, can baptize, by using the Trinitarian baptismal formula. The intention required is to will to do what the Church does when she baptizes.* The Church finds the reason for this possibility in the universal saving will of God and the necessity of Baptism for salvation.[11]

Notice that the language used in this passage identifies the requisite intention as the "will to do what the Church does." This means that the minister must indeed intend something, but the object of the intention is the performance of the rite, not faith in or knowledge of its theological content.

Intention and Alterations to the Rites

The corollary to the first point is that by actually doing something *other* than what the Church does, the minister is not intending to do what the Church intends to be done and thereby negates validity.

Taking again the example given above of the person who invests $1000 in futures by following the instruction of his friend, What if he fails to perform the action according to the friend's instructions? What if, due to negligence, disingenuousness, or accident, he were to omit the word "futures" while handing over the money to the investment broker? He would thus fail to perform the investment action intended by his friend. By failing to perform the action intended by his friend, and indicating rather that the money be invested in Apple Inc., or not at all, instead of in futures, his omission would make his action into something other than what his friend intended. This failure makes his action an unsuitable instrument for effecting the specific reality envisioned by his friend.

Doing something other than what the Church intends to be done can admit of varying degrees of consequence and culpability. For example, Aquinas argues that, when it comes to adding or subtracting things from the performance of the sacramental action, if

11. *CCC* §1256 (emphasis added).

the minister "intends by such addition or suppression to perform a rite other from [sic] that which is recognized by the Church, it seems that the sacrament is invalid; because he seems not to intend to do what the Church does."[12]

Aquinas also considers the effect that changes to the words of the form, whether conscious or unconscious, can have on the meaning of the sign. By changing the meaning of the words, which are the formal part of the sign, the sign itself can be negated. However, sometimes mispronunciations, for example, do not change the meaning of the words. Aquinas argues that changes in the "essential sense of the words," including, obviously, the omission of an essential part of the form, renders the celebration invalid.[13] It is also the case, however, that some omissions do not change the essential meaning of the form. "In the form of the Eucharist," Aquinas observes, "*For this is my body*, the omission of the word *for* does not destroy the essential sense of the words, nor consequently cause the sacrament to be invalid; although perhaps he who makes the omission may sin from negligence or contempt."[14]

And, likewise, additions to the form can render similar results. "If one were to say" (when administering a Baptism), Aquinas explains,

I baptize thee in the name of the Father Who is greater, and of the Son who is less, with which form the Arians baptized: and consequently such an addition makes the sacrament invalid. But if the addition be such as not to destroy the essential sense, the sacrament is not rendered invalid.[15]

Taking a more contemporary example, baptisms done in the name of "the creator, redeemer, and sanctifier," fall into the same error as that of the Arians in Aquinas's example above. Creation, redemption, and sanctification are not names of the three Persons of the Trinity. As actions terminating outside of God, creation, redemption, and sanctification are common to all three persons and cannot serve as a formal invocation of the tri-personal reality of God.

---

12. *ST* III, q. 60, a. 8.
13. Ibid.
14. Ibid.
15. Ibid.

Intention and Unintended Sacramental Celebrations

Theologians have also considered situations in which a sacrament is celebrated with the proper matter and form in such contexts as wedding rehearsals, play of children, or acting. In the case of Baptism, for example, a child could pour water over the head of another child who is unbaptized with the Trinitarian formula without "accidentally" conferring a Baptism. The proper theological assessment of this scenario is that the sacrament is not valid, since the child's intention is to play, to imitate what adults do, and not to perform the rite intended by the Church. Age, too, limits the range of human action that can be intentionally pursued.

One can also imagine a scenario in which a priest playing a part in a play or drama acts out a sacramental rite, say Mass or Confession or witnessing marriage vows, using the proper matter and form. This does not effect a sacrament, because the priest's intention in this case is not to perform the action prescribed by the Church but to play the role of his character in the play.

Intention and the Awareness of the Minister

Finally, theologians have had to consider the relationship between a minister's actual conscious awareness during a sacramental celebration and sacramental intentionality. What if a minister is actually thinking of something else during the celebration of a sacrament? Thomas Aquinas addresses this problem by referring to the distinction between actual and habitual intention.[16] It is not uncommon for someone to be thinking about something else while engaged in some activity, say, for example, thinking about work while driving to the store to purchase milk. The habitual intention, Aquinas maintains, is sufficient to safeguard the validity of a sacrament.

Aquinas considers a case in which a priest goes to celebrate a Baptism with the intention to doing what the Church does: "During

---

16. *ST* III, q. 64, a. 8, ad 3.

the exercise of the act," however, "his mind be distracted by other matters." In such a case, Aquinas concludes that "the sacrament is valid in virtue of his original intention."[17]

The declaration of nullity in the case of matrimony is also related to this principle. The annulment process is, essentially, an inquiry into whether the celebration of Matrimony was carried out according to the proper sacramental form, with the correct matter, and the proper intention. Failing to intend what Christ and the Church intend, or lacking the form prescribed by the Church, as with all the other sacraments, prevents the sign from being effected. If the sign is not brought in to being, the bond effected by Matrimony cannot be conferred. An annulment, therefore, is merely a declaration that the effects caused by the sign (most importantly, the indissoluble bond) were never conferred on the spouses because some defect in the matter,[18] form, or intention nullified the sacrament from being brought about. This is why these procedures are called annulments — some defect *nullifies* the sacrament from being brought about.[19]

The requisite triad — matter, form, and intention — needed for a sacrament corresponds today to what is referred to in the *Catechism of the Catholic Church* as the "essential rite," which indicates the most basic and foundational principles necessary for a valid sacramental celebration. These considerations should not imply, however, that a sacramental minimalism vis-à-vis the matter, form and intention is adequate for a full spiritual engagement with the sacraments.

Just as the faithful commit sin — sometimes grave sin — in receiving sacraments unworthily, so too ministers can sin in failing

17. Ibid.

18. Nullity can be established as a result of material defect in cases of priestly or religious vows that have not been dispensed by ecclesiastical authority or in cases of physical and psychological conditions such as perpetual and antecedent inability to consummate the union (impotence). Impediments such as these, and others, prevent a sacramental union from taking place.

19. For a very helpful treatment of matrimonial nullity that offers a clear exposition of canonical principles and numerous examples and case studies, see Paolo Bianchi, *When Is Marriage Null? Guide to the Grounds of Nullity for Pastors, Counselors, and Lay Faithful*, trans. Michael Miller (San Francisco: Ignatius Press, 2015).

to be adequately attentive and reverent when celebrating the sacraments — even if the celebrations themselves are valid. Meeting the minimum requirements for validity is hardly an adequate criterion for a spirituality of priestly ministry and the universal call to holiness. Aquinas points out that, for example, when a sinful minister celebrates the sacraments, he commits "irreverence towards God and the contamination of holy things … although the holy things themselves cannot be contaminated."[20] The faithful and ministers need to retain a mindfulness of the gracious presence of the risen Christ in every sacramental celebration: "something greater than Solomon is here" (Mt 12:42, Lk 11:41).

Anglican Orders and John Calvin on the Sacrifice of the Mass: Two Test Cases

In light of the material covered in the last two chapters, two historical "test cases" will now be considered. These two cases bring to light the importance of a proper understanding of the sacraments as signs, as well as of the nature of sacramental matter, form, and intention.

Anglican Orders

Case 1 is the sacramental doctrine manifest in Pope Leo XIII's 1896 Apostolic Letter *Apostolica curae et caritatis*. In this letter Pope Leo

20. *ST* III, q. 64, a. 6. The faithful often struggle with the question of attending a parish that is well known for taking stances critical of the Church and her teachings. While this situation is understandably unsettling, the deeper question that many have is whether or not it is sinful to participate in the sacramental celebrations of a priest who is notorious for dissenting against the Church and even voices this dissent publicly during liturgical celebrations by word or action. Aquinas provides a very balanced answer to this question: "He who approaches a sacrament, receives it from a minister of the Church, *not because he is such and such a man, but because he is a minister of the Church*. Consequently, *as long as the latter is tolerated in the ministry, he that receives a sacrament from him, does not communicate in his sin, but communicates with the Church from whom he has his ministry*. But if the Church, by degrading, excommunicating, or suspending him, does not tolerate him in the ministry, he that receives a sacrament from him sins, because he communicates in his sin." *ST* III, q. 64, a. 6, ad 2 (emphasis added).

declared that ordinations in the Anglican Communion were sacramentally invalid. Pope Leo begins his letter by invoking the theology of sacramental matter and form: "In the rite of confecting and administering any sacrament, one rightly distinguishes between the ceremonial part and the essential part, usually called matter and form."[21]

Leo points out, however, that the matter of ordination, the laying of the bishop's hands on the ordinand, is specified by the words of the rite which refer to the power of the priesthood to consecrate and offer the Eucharistic sacrifice. The words referring to the power of the priestly office in relation to the Eucharist, however, had been removed from the Anglican *Ordinale* and replaced with "Receive the Holy Spirit."

Pope Leo teaches that the change in the words introduces a defect in form and the defect in form, in turn, indicates a defective intention. "With this inherent defect of form is joined the defect of intention, which is equally essential to the sacrament." Leo continues:

The Church does not judge about the mind or intention insofar as it is something by its nature internal; but insofar as it is manifested externally, she is bound to judge concerning it. When anyone had rightly and seriously made use of the due form and the matter requisite for effecting or conferring the sacrament, he is considered by the very fact to do what the Church does. On this principle rests the doctrine that a sacrament is truly conferred by the ministry of one who is a heretic or unbaptized, provided the Catholic rite be employed.

On the other hand, if the rite be changed, with the manifest intention of introducing another rite not approved by the Church and of rejecting what the Church does and what by the institution of Christ belongs to the nature of the sacrament, then it is clear that not only is the necessary intention wanting to the sacrament, but that the intention is adverse to and destructive of the sacrament.[22]

The position of the Catholic Church on Anglican orders, therefore, is not determined, as the common perception might indicate, by a

21. Heinrich Denzinger, *Enchiridion symbolorum*, 665–66 (§3315).
22. Ibid., 668 (§3318).

Roman prejudice against Anglicanism. Rather, the assessment of the Catholic Church is determined on the grounds of basic sacramental theology. Anglican orders are invalid because of a change in the form of the celebration, and the change in the form likewise indicated a defective intention.

Calvin and the Sacrificial Nature of the Mass

The second historical test case is from Book IV, Chapter XVIII, of John Calvin's *Institutes of the Christian Religion*. In this section of his *Institutes* Calvin develops a famous critique of the doctrine that the Mass is a true propitiatory sacramental sacrifice.[23] The Catholic understanding of the sacrifice of the Mass is put forward in the following decree from the Council of Trent:

In this divine sacrifice that is celebrated in the Mass, the same Christ who offered himself once in a bloody manner [*cf. Heb* 9:14, 27f] on the altar of the Cross is contained and is offered in an unbloody manner. Therefore, the holy council teaches that this sacrifice is truly propitiatory [*can.* 3] so that, if we draw near to God with an upright heart and true faith, with fear and reverence, with sorrow and repentance, through it "we may receive mercy and find grace to help in time of need" [*Heb* 4:15]. For the Lord, appeased by this oblation, grants grace and the gift of repentance, and he pardons wrongdoings and sins, even great ones. For, the victim is one and the same: the same now offers himself through the ministry of priests who then offered himself on the Cross: only the manner of offering is different.[24]

23. It is important to point out that the tension between the Lutheran, Reformed, and Catholic theology on the doctrine of the Eucharistic sacrifice is not, per se, about the notion of sacrifice generically. Generally, the negative reception of the Catholic doctrine pertains to the type of sacrifice that the Catholic Church identifies with the Eucharist. The Catholic Church does not maintain that the Mass is the sacrifice in the sense of a mere offering, as a tithe, vow, or fast. The Catholic Church teaches that in the Mass a true sacrificial victim — Jesus Christ, as he offered himself on the cross — is offered for sin, in an unbloody, sacramental way. It is the association of this specific type of sacrifice with the offering of the Eucharist that makes non-Catholics uncomfortable. See Romanus Cessario, "'Circa res ... aliquid fit' (*Summa theologiae* II-II, q. 85, a. 3, ad 3): Aquinas on New Law Sacrifice," *Nova et Vetera*, English Edition, 4, no. 2 (2006): 295–312.

24. Heinrich Denzinger, *Enchiridion symbolorum:* Session 22, September 17, 1562, Doctrine and Canons on the Sacrifice of the Mass, chap. 2, 418 (§1743). N.B.: Calvin wrote his *Institutes* prior to this decree from the Council of Trent. It is offered here merely to represent the Catholic position that Calvin rejects.

Calvin offers several formidable objections to the Catholic teaching on the Mass. Among them, the third engages directly the doctrine of sacrifice, which Calvin argues is to be rejected because "it obliterates the true and only death of Christ." Calvin's objection is (correctly) rooted in the biblical teaching that Christ's sacrificial death was a "once and for all offering" (Heb 9:28). The Mass obliterates Christ's death, Calvin argues, because the everlasting covenant was ratified in Christ's blood. Calvin thus contends that to view each Mass as a sacrifice of Christ's blood is to make each Mass "a new and altogether different testament."[25] "Therefore, let Christ come again," Calvin reasons, "and, by another death make this new testament; or rather, by innumerable deaths, ratify the innumerable testaments of the mass."[26]

The fundamental problem that Calvin identifies with the doctrine that the Mass is a true propitiatory sacrifice for sins is that such an offering, like Christ's sacrifice on the cross, requires his death. "It is necessary," Calvin observes, "that the victim which is offered be slain and immolated. If Christ is sacrificed at each mass, he must be cruelly slain every moment in a thousand places."[27] Calvin is aware that the Church speaks of the Mass as an unbloody sacrifice, but he views such language as mere semantics that fail to appreciate the true nature of sacrifice as established by God.[28]

The error in Calvin's assessment lies not in his instinct to protect the centrality and uniqueness of the cross, nor in his biblical understanding of propitiatory sacrifice as including the immolation of the victim. Rather, his error is sacramental in nature. The Catholic Church's understanding of the Mass as an "unbloody" sacrifice is not a semantic move to avoid contradicting biblical teaching about the "once and for all" nature of Christ's death. Rather, the Church understands the Eucharist, like all of the sacraments, from within the doctrine of signs, and this is what Calvin's articulation is lacking.

25. John Calvin, *Institutes of the Christian Religion*, vol. II, trans. Henry Beveridge (London: James Clarke, 1962), 610 (Book IV, chap. XVIII, #8).

26. Ibid.   27. Ibid., 611.

28. Ibid.

Calvin fails to consider that Christ connected the one-time event of his sacrifice on the cross with the sacramental institution of the Eucharist: the "my body" and "my blood" of the Last Supper and the Mass are "given" and "poured out." Calvin does not recognize in Christ's institution of the Eucharist a sacramental sacrifice. Why, for instance, does Christ institute a consecration over the bread *and* over the wine? What does the twofold consecration bring about? The twofold consecration brings about the presence of Christ precisely in his immolated form; namely, with his body and blood separated. Yet, the sacramental action of the Mass does not constitute another sacrificial event in which something must happen to Christ. The sacrifice takes place through the participatory signification of the sacramental forms. As a result of the twofold consecration, the priest intends to offer to God Christ's sacrifice with his body and blood separated (immolated) in and through the sacramental signs.

Contrary to Calvin's critique, the Church does not consider each Mass to be a sacrificial event, but the presentation of the sacrificial institution that Christ established at the Last Supper. "We do not choose," explains Charles Journet, "between the sacrifice of the Cross and that of the Last Supper, between the *sacrifice-event* and the *sacrifice-institution*; we preserve all of Scripture. The sacrifice-institution, in our eyes, does not multiply the sacrifice-event; *it multiplies the real presences of the sacrifice-event*."[29]

John Calvin's critique of the Catholic doctrine of the sacrifice of the Mass is rooted, in its foundation, in a sacramental error. Calvin neglects to distinguish adequately between the historical and proper reality of Christ's death on the cross and the reality of that presence in and through the sacramental signs. As signs the sacraments truly participate in and are derived from the realities that they signify, and yet as signs they also are distinguishable from those realities.

The presence of Christ's sacrifice in the Eucharist does not in any way require that Christ be sacrificed again, nor that the priest in-

29. Charles Cardinal Journet, *The Mass: The Presence of the Sacrifice of the Cross*, trans. Victor Szczurek, OPraem (South Bend, Ind.: St. Augustine's Press, 2008), 32.

tend to slay Christ; it requires only the presence of Christ's body and blood such that it can be offered sacramentally — in an unbloody mode — as a propitiation for sin.

The Anglican rite of ordination and Calvin's rejection of the sacrificial nature of the Mass both stem from sacramental errors. In the case of the former, a change in the form altered the nature of the sign, and thereby a lack of proper intention was made manifest; both the change of form and the lack of proper intention compromise validity. In the case of Calvin, he fails to recognize that the sacramental signs, precisely as signs, participate in the realities that they signify; in short, he conflates the historicity of the cross and the sacramentality of the Eucharist, leaving himself unable to embrace both.

SIX

The Necessity of the Sacraments

What is the end or purpose for which Christ instituted the seven sacraments of the Church? The answer to this question is related to the very essence and nature of Christ's own mission and the mission of the Church, which can be summarized in one word: holiness.[1] The "Universal Call to Holiness" is one of the central teachings of the Second Vatican Council's Dogmatic Constitution on the Church, *Lumen Gentium*:

Christ, the Son of God, who with the Father and the Spirit is praised as "uniquely holy," loved the Church as His bride, delivering Himself up for her. He did this that He might sanctify her. He united her to Himself as His own body and brought it to perfection by the gift of the Holy Spirit for God's glory. Therefore in the Church, everyone whether belonging to the hierarchy, or being cared for by it, is called to holiness, according to the saying of the Apostle: "For this is the will of God, your sanctification."[2]

The *Catechism of the Catholic Church* teaches the following in the context of the sacrament of Baptism:

---

1. For a helpful treatment of the divinizing power of the sacramental liturgy of the Church, see *Divinization: Becoming Icons of Christ through the Liturgy*, ed. Andrew Hofer, OP (Chicago/Mundelein: Hillenbrand Books, 2015).

2. *Lumen Gentium* §35.

The Lord himself affirms that Baptism is necessary for salvation. He also commands his disciples to proclaim the Gospel to all nations and to baptize them. Baptism is necessary for salvation for those to whom the Gospel has been proclaimed and who have had the possibility of asking for this sacrament. The Church does not know of any means other than Baptism that assures entry into eternal beatitude; this is why she takes care not to neglect the mission she has received from the Lord to see that all who can be baptized are "reborn of water and the Spirit." *God has bound salvation to the sacrament of Baptism, but he himself is not bound by his sacraments.*[3]

On this account the necessity of the sacraments seems obvious — following St. Thomas's definition, the sacraments are signs "of holy things so far as they make men holy" — the sacraments must be the necessary source of holiness in the life of the Church. Yet, the doctrine of the necessity of the sacraments is no longer so easy to affirm — at least for many.

Challenges to the Doctrine of the Necessity of the Sacraments

On the one hand, there is the fragmentation among Christians, which means that those outside of Catholicism (and Eastern Orthodoxy) lack some (or even all) of the seven sacraments.[4] On the other hand, there is the growing awareness of religious pluralism. If the sacraments are necessary, what is to be made of all those who do not have access to them? A few reflections can help bring some clarity to these issues.

First, it is unhealthy for theologians to put forward hypothetical theories of salvation that do not have some foundation in divine Revelation. This exercise ends up being more like gambling, in the sense that one makes a guess about a possible outcome, without any positive norm or data to guide it. The more Catholic and Christian approach to these questions is to ponder and develop what is

3. *CCC* §1257.
4. The Church teaches that certain sects, such as Mormonism, are not able to confer even Baptism validly.

revealed and to refrain from fostering ambiguity by hypothesizing about the realm of possibility. The teaching of the *Catechism* on the case of infant Baptism provides a sagacious example of this point:

As regards *children who have died without Baptism*, the Church can only entrust them to the mercy of God, as she does in her funeral rites for them. Indeed, the great mercy of God who desires that all men should be saved, and Jesus' tenderness toward children which caused him to say: "Let the children come to me, do not hinder them," allow us to hope that there is a way of salvation for children who have died without Baptism. All the more urgent is the Church's call not to prevent little children coming to Christ through the gift of holy Baptism.[5]

The Church declares her hope for unbaptized infants and her trust in God's mercy, but she also affirms the positive urgency of extending to infants the revealed truth that the baptized are, *de facto*, cleansed of original sin and made God's adopted children in the order of grace.

Second, the Church has never taught that God's power is bound solely to the sacramental actions of the Church. Aquinas, for example, addressing the case of someone desiring Baptism but lacking the actual reception of the sacrament, notes that "God, Whose power is not tied to visible sacraments" is able to "sanctif[y] [the] man inwardly."[6]

Third, God is not the author of many plans of salvation, as if the plan realized in Christ and passed on to the Church with the com-

---

5. *CCC* §1261.

6. *ST* III, q. 68, a. 2. It should be noted that Aquinas did not develop this principle abstractly. It applied only to those lacking sacramental Baptism but who also manifest a desire to receive the sacrament. More broadly, Aquinas does have a doctrine of implicit faith in Christ, but this implicit faith is manifest in assent to content that, in some way, is ordered to Christ. For example, Aquinas deemed fidelity to the Old Law to have been salvific because the rites and faith of Israel were ordered to fulfillment in Christ, and likewise natural knowledge of God is ordered implicitly to supernatural revelation. Thus, while Aquinas affirmed that God is not bound by the visible sacraments and that adherence to certain truths about God can be accredited as implicit faith, it is incorrect to present these doctrines as open theories of salvation that can be applied across the board. Aquinas consistently roots them in the Christian economy of salvation and connects them with specific requirements.

mission to "baptize all nations" was but one among many.[7] "[F]or some," the Congregation for the Doctrine of Faith's declaration *Dominus Iesus* explains, "Jesus would be one of the many faces which the Logos has assumed in the course of time to communicate with humanity in a salvific way."[8] This approach to the fact of religious pluralism fails to take into account Christ's unique standing as the one "mediator between God and man" (1 Tim 2:5). "The doctrine of faith regarding the unicity of the salvific economy willed by the One and Triune God must be *firmly believed*," *Dominus Iesus* explains,

at the source and centre of which is the mystery of the incarnation of the Word, mediator of divine grace on the level of creation and redemption (cf. Col 1:15–20), he who recapitulates all things (cf. Eph 1:10), he "whom God has made our wisdom, our righteousness, and sanctification and redemption" (1 Cor 1:30). In fact, the mystery of Christ has its own intrinsic unity, which extends from the eternal choice in God to the parousia: "he [the Father] chose us in Christ before the foundation of the world to be holy and blameless before him in love" (Eph 1:4); "In Christ we are heirs, having been destined according to the purpose of him who accomplishes all things according to his counsel and will" (Eph 1:11); "For those whom he foreknew he also predestined to be conformed to the image of his Son, in order that he might be the firstborn among many brothers; those whom he predestined he also called; and those whom he called he also justified; and those whom he justified he also glorified" (Rom 8:29–30).[9]

The presence and ongoing activity of the Holy Spirit in the world is not another — back door — means by which God bestows salvation on mankind. "The action of the Spirit is not outside or parallel to the action of Christ," *Dominus Iesus* teaches,

There is only one salvific economy of the One and Triune God, realized in the mystery of the incarnation, death, and resurrection of the Son of God, actualized with the cooperation of the Holy Spirit, and extended in its salvific value to all humanity and to the entire universe: "No one, therefore,

---

7. On this question, see Roger Nutt, "An Office in Search of Its Ontology: Mediation and Trinitarian Christology in Jacques Dupuis' Theology of Religious Pluralism," *Louvain Studies* 32 (2008): 383–407.

8. *Dominus Iesus* §9.1.

9. Ibid., §11.1.

can enter into communion with God except through Christ, by the working of the Holy Spirit."[10]

The affirmations that God's power is not bound to the visible sacraments and that there is but one divine plan of salvation realized through the unified missions of the Incarnate Word and the Holy Spirit are not contradictory. These two truths emerge from one unified, providential plan of salvation culminating in Christ and the outpouring of the Spirit upon the Church. The nature of the catholicity of the Church, in the words of *Lumen Gentium* 13, indicates that "all men are called to this catholic unity of the People of God."[11]

The Church likewise recognizes the peril, confusion, and vulnerability of life when lived without the aid and assistance of the Christian message, divine grace, and the guidance of the Church: "Very often, deceived by the Evil One, men have become vain in their reasonings, and have exchanged the truth of God for a lie, and served the creature rather than the Creator. Or else, living and dying in this world without God, they are exposed to ultimate despair."[12]

The necessity of the sacraments is not the result of some misguided Christian exclusivity. To the contrary, God's love for all people is the impetus of the Church's mission and the rich mercy that is available through the sacraments. "The Church's first purpose," the *Catechism* teaches, "is to be the sacrament of the *inner union of men with God*. Because men's communion with one another is rooted in that union with God, the Church is also the sacrament of the *unity of the human race*."[13] All are called to membership in the Church, and those who walk outside the Church are subject to deception and despair. In his mercy God has blessed the Church with sacraments that integrate people into the communion of the Church to which they are called and illumine them with the interior light of grace: "The seven sacraments are the signs and instruments," the *Catechism*

10. Ibid., §12.6, citing John Paul II's encyclical letter *Redemptoris Missio* §5.
11. Cited in *CCC* §836.
12. *Lumen Gentium* §15, cited in *CCC* §844.
13. *CCC* §775.

explains, "by which the Holy Spirit spreads the grace of Christ the head throughout the Church which is his body."[14]

Thomas Aquinas's Teaching on the Necessity of the Sacraments

Thomas Aquinas's teaching on the necessity of the sacraments offers some helpful resources for articulating this material in the contemporary context. In the Third Part of the *Summa*, Thomas first invokes necessity when asking whether or not the Incarnation was "necessary" for the "restoration of the human race."[15] In answering this question, Thomas distinguishes between two of the four senses of necessity put forward by Aristotle.[16] The first sense is "when the end cannot be without it; as food is necessary for the preservation of human life." The second sense is "when the end is attained better and more conveniently, as a horse is necessary for a journey." "In the first way," Aquinas explains, "it was not necessary that God should become incarnate for the restoration of human nature. For God with His omnipotent power could have restored human nature in many other ways. But in the second way it was necessary that God should become incarnate for the restoration of human nature."[17]

Aquinas therefore does not maintain that God could not have saved humanity in any other fashion, but he does maintain that the end of salvation is best obtained by the Incarnation. Building upon this foundation, in question 61 of the Third Part, Thomas then asks "Whether the sacraments are necessary for man's salvation?" Thomas answers this question in the affirmative, but given that he has already indicated that the Incarnation was necessary (according to the second sense of necessity) for the restoration of the human race, he needs to make several clarifications in affirming the necessity of the sacraments.

---

14. *CCC* §774.   15. See *ST* III, q. 1, a. 2.
16. See Aristotle, *Metaphysics*, book V, chap. 5, 1015a20–b15.
17. *ST* III, q. 1, a. 2.

Most importantly, it would seem that affirming the necessity of the sacraments would indicate a certain salvific insufficiency of the Incarnation and paschal mystery. Does not maintaining that both the Passion of the Christ *and* the sacraments are necessary imply the insufficiency of the first? Thomas's response to this question is:

> Christ's Passion is a sufficient cause of man's salvation. But it does not follow that the sacraments are not also necessary for that purpose: because they obtain their effect through the power of Christ's Passion; and Christ's Passion is, so to say, applied to man through the sacraments according to the Apostle (Romans 6:3): "All we who are baptized in Christ Jesus, are baptized in His death."[18]

The sacraments, therefore, are necessary because they are the means by which those who are separated temporally from Christ's life, death, and Resurrection can encounter him. The sacramental signs are not in competition with Christ's saving work; rather, through them the faithful are incorporated into Christ's saving mission.

The second sense of necessity invoked by Thomas in regard to the Incarnation also extends to the sacraments. Because God, in his wisdom, has saved humanity through the Incarnation, the sacraments are necessary in the bestowal of salvation in Christ. Thomas provides three reasons for this necessity. The first intersects with the importance of the visible aspect of the sacramental signs: since human beings are led to higher, spiritual realities through the senses, "Divine wisdom ... fittingly provides man with means of salvation, in the shape of corporeal and sensible signs that are called sacraments."[19]

The second is related to people's proclivity to be attached to corporeal things: the sacramental signs have a medicinal component: "if man were offered spiritual things without a veil, his mind being taken up with the material world would be unable to apply itself to them."[20]

---

18. *ST* III, q. 61, a. 1, ad 3.   19. Ibid., corpus.
20. Ibid.

The third reason is related to humanity's proclivity to the idolatry of material items, superstitions, and false worship: "lest, therefore, it should be too hard for man to be drawn away entirely from bodily actions, bodily exercise was offered to him in the sacraments."[21]

The sacraments are necessary in God's plan of salvation because, in Thomas's words, "Man, consistently with his nature, is instructed through sensible things; he is humbled, through confessing that he is subject to corporeal things, seeing that he receives assistance through them: and he is even preserved from bodily hurt, by the healthy exercise of the sacraments."[22] In short, in his love and wisdom, God bestows salvation on humanity through the sacraments in a way that corresponds perfectly to its fallen nature and deepest spiritual needs.

The doctrine of the necessity of the sacramental signs offers some insight, too, into the theological order and meaning of human history. Why did God come when he did, in the fashion that he did, teaching people the way that he did, and instituting visible sacraments for the Church to leave behind after his Ascension? Understanding history in relation to God's providential plan for salvation adds further clarification to what has already been considered. God does not bestow salvation abstractly. Original sin is a state of existence lacking the divine intimacy of grace, and every personal sin is an unjust offense against God with consequences that must be remedied for justice to be realized.

All of these factors come into play in Christ's foundation of the Church and the sacraments. "After sin," Aquinas explains, "no man can be made holy save through Christ."[23] The necessity of the sacraments stems from the fact that "they are sensible signs of invisible things whereby man is made holy."[24] The necessity of faith in Christ and the necessity of the sacraments are complementary doctrines: "The sacraments are signs," Aquinas explains, "in protestation of

21. Ibid.
22. Ibid.
23. *ST* III, q. 61, a. 3.
24. Ibid.

the faith whereby man is justified."[25] The faith without which it is "impossible to please God" (Heb 11:6) includes and points to the importance of the sacraments in accepting the gift of salvation that God has granted in Christ. Between Christ's first and second comings faith is necessary. Human history now stands in the position between the first beginnings of Christ's Kingdom and its full realization at the second coming. "The state of the New Law," Aquinas explains, "is between the state of the Old Law ... and the state of glory, in which all truth will be openly and perfectly revealed ... now, so long as we know *through a glass in a dark manner* (1 Cor 13:12), we need sensible signs in order to reach spiritual things: and this is the province of the sacraments."[26]

The meaning of the current age and the possibility of friendship with God at this point in human history is inextricably linked to his availability and presence to men and women in the sacraments of the Church.

25. Ibid., a. 4.
26. Ibid., ad 1.

PART III

Sacramental Causality, Grace, and Character

The effects of the sacraments (grace and character) and the nature of sacramental causality are so closely linked that it is best to pursue these topics in conjunction with each other. In fact, the necessity of the sacraments presupposes that the sacraments confer effects that make them necessary; further, if the sacraments confer necessary effects, their ability to do so is spiritually significant. As signs of holy realities that "make men holy," the sacraments produce in the soul the grace and character by which friendship with God takes place.

SEVEN

Sacramental Causality

Aquinas's doctrine of the causality of the sacraments stands out as a unique contribution to the question of the operative power of the sacraments. It merits close consideration and integration with the *ex opere operato* doctrine of the Church, especially in light of criticisms that it has received by contemporary theologians such as Louis-Marie Chauvet.[1]

Failing to appreciate the deeper theological, spiritual, and metaphysical sources underpinning sacramental causality, Chauvet reads Aquinas's doctrine as a post-Newtonian material, spatial, and external form of causality.[2] "Because of its distinctive metaphysical bent,"

1. Chauvet's most famous work is *Symbol and Sacrament: A Sacramental Reinterpretation of Christian Existence*, trans. Madigan and Beaumont (Collegeville, Minn.: Liturgical Press, 1995). For a critical engagement with Chauvet's thought from a Thomistic perspective, see E. Perrier, "Le Pain de Vie chez Louis-Marie Chauvet et saint Thomas d'Aquin. Représentation de l'inconnaissable ou terme de l'union spirituelle?" *Revue Thomiste* 113 (2013): 195–234; and T. Michelet, "Louis-Marie Chauvet et la sacramentalité de la parole entre analogie et paradigm," *Revue Thomiste* 113 (2013): 179–94. The essence of *Symbol and Sacrament* is presented by Chauvet in his much shorter book *The Sacraments: The Word of God at the Mercy of the Body*, trans. Madeleine Beaumont (Collegeville, Minn.: Liturgical Press, 2001). For a criticism of Chauvet's understanding and appropriation of the thought of Martin Heidegger within his sacramental doctrine, see Hal St John Broadbent, *The Call of the Holy: Heidegger — Chauvet — Benedict XVI* (London: T & T Clark, 2012).

2. Recall Newton's first law: "1. Every body continues in its state of rest, or of uniform motion in a right [i.e., straight] line, unless it is compelled to change that state by forces

Chauvet argues, "Western thought is unable to represent to itself the relations between subjects or of subjects with God in any way other than one according to a technical model of cause and effect."[3] This tendency, in Chauvet's view, ends up reducing personal relationships and even being itself "to the technico-productionist scheme oriented toward the finished product, the guaranteed outcome, the necessary first cause or the ultimate significance serving as the highest reason."[4]

However, Aquinas, having adopted Aristotle's fourfold understanding of causality, did not then rush to impose it on the Gospel. Rather, he appropriated a precise understanding of causality to explain how Christ influences the faithful in the sacraments because, as Revelation affirms, certain effects, like new birth, regeneration, illumination, and so on, are brought about by the sacraments. Liam Walsh insightfully corrects Chauvet on this point:

Much has been written in Scholastic theology about sacramental causality. The concentration has been on efficient causality in a way that often leaves aside the final and formal components of God's action. When Chauvet criticizes the reliance of a Scholastic theology of sacraments on the concept of causality, he seems to be envisaging causality as efficient, in isolation from final and formal causality. However, if one is to do justice to Aquinas' analysis of divine causality, one must recognize his position that when God acts he is simultaneously giving finality and form, as well as existence, to what he is doing.[5]

Causality: A Short Primer

Understanding realities in terms of causality and causal relations is far more contemplative and relational than what Chauvet is able

impressed upon it." See Newton's *Principia: The Mathematical Principles of Natural Philosophy*, trans. Andrew Motte (Whitefish, Mont.: Kessinger Publishing, 2008).

3. Chauvet, *Symbol and Sacrament*, 22.

4. Ibid., 26.

5. Liam Walsh, OP, "Sacraments," in *The Theology of Thomas Aquinas*, ed. Rik Van Nieuwenhove and Joseph Wawrykow (Notre Dame, Ind.: University of Notre Dame Press, 2005), 330.

to recognize from within his philosophical system.[6] Because of the Enlightenment's reduction of causality to extrinsic and mechanistic force, the original meaning of the Greek word for cause (*aitia*) needs some reintroduction.

Aristotle's approach to causality, as embodied in his famous "four causes," is really a contemplative quest to explain the existence of realities in the order of being. In his helpful edition of Aristotle's *Metaphysics*, Richard Hope renders "*aitia*" (cause) as "explanatory factor."[7] Aristotle's causes are not accurately understood as forms of force acting in a "technico-productionist" fashion on things. The causes are the explanations or explanatory factors of realities as they exist in their deepest being. The material and formal causes explain the internal principles constituting a reality, whereas the efficient and final causes explain the agency that brings about the reality and the end or purpose for which the agent acts.

Efficient causality,[8] which is the type of causality associated with the sacraments, is explained by Aristotle as "the agent whereby a change or state of rest is first produced."[9] And, again, "any agent generally is the factor whereby a change or state of being is initiated."[10] Each of these examples underscores that efficiency in the order of causality explains the cause of the motion (*aitia kinousa/causa agens*). Francis Meehan offers the following summary of Aristotle's position:

6. For a discussion of the metaphysical shortcomings of Chauvet's understanding of causality, especially as it pertains to the act of existence, see Jean-Philippe Revel, *Traité des sacrements: I.2, Baptême et sacramentalité. Don et réception de la grâce baptismale* (Paris: Les Éditions du Cerf, 2005): 43–45.

7. See *Aristotle's Metaphysics*, trans. Richard Hope, 26th ed. (Ann Arbor: University of Michigan Press, 2007), 88 (book V.2, 1013a20–1014a20). See also Hope's "Index of Technical Terms" in the same volume, where he offers "explanation" and "basic (explanatory) factor" as the two definitions of "*aitia*" (ibid., at 355).

8. For a helpful treatment of efficient causality in both Aristotle and Aquinas, see Francis Meehan, "Efficient Causality in Aristotle and St. Thomas" (Ph.D. Dissertation, The Catholic University of America, 1940).

9. *Aristotle's Metaphysics*, 88 (1013a30).

10. Ibid., 89 (1013b20).

Our study of Aristotle's concept of efficient cause has led us definitely to the conviction that what he had in mind was a cause that contributed to the being of another or influenced the existence of another by way of motion, in other words, a moving cause (*aitia kinousa*), a cause which is responsible for the initiation of change, becoming, and the like.[11]

The causality of the sacraments is presented in terms of efficient causality because the sacraments explain the action or "agency whereby" the state of sanctification through sacramental grace is brought about: the primary accent of efficient causation is the agency or action explaining a being. "Through its real, physical action," A. Challot explains, the efficient cause "produces a being that is distinct from itself."[12] This action or agency is not that of mechanistic force. It is intentional and purposeful and relational.

Causality and the Sacraments

When first introducing his theory of sacramental causality in the *Summa theologiae*, Aquinas affirms that "we must say in some way the sacraments of the New Law cause grace."[13] His reason for this is drawn not from excessive reliance on Aristotle but directly from divine Revelation: "for it is evident that through the sacraments of the New Law man is incorporated with Christ: thus the Apostle says of Baptism (Gal 3:27): *As many of you as have been baptized in Christ have put on Christ*. And man is made a member of Christ through grace alone."[14]

It is worth quoting John Gallagher's development of the biblical doctrine of sacramental causality at length. "The new testament," Gallagher explains, "sets before us a series of rites that are to be used in

---

11. Meehan, "Efficient Causality," 58.

12. A. Challot, "Cause," in *Dictionnaire de théologie catholique*, vol. 2, part 2, ed. A Vacant and E. Mangenot (Paris: Letouzey et Ané, 1905), column 2024 [III, 1].

13. *ST* III, q. 62, a. 1.

14. Ibid. For a helpful presentation of the biblical foundation of Thomas's doctrine of sacramental causality, see Bernhard Blankenhorn, OP, "The Place of Romans 6 in Aquinas' Doctrine of Sacramental Causality: A Balance of Scripture and Metaphysics," in *Ressourcement Thomism: Sacred Doctrine, The Sacraments, and the Moral Life*, 136–49.

the Church." "These rites," Gallagher continues, "are representative of something further: they are symbolic rites. And these rites somehow bring about the reality of which they are symbolic: they are efficacious rites."[15] In relation to the scriptural teaching on Baptism, for example, Gallagher identifies three interrelated points about causation:

1. We find described by the sacred authors a rite of initiation to the messianic kingdom to be used in the church.

This rite as such is not presented as an original invention of the messias. Rather the rite is used by the precursor, John the Baptist, who came preaching a baptism of repentance (Matt. 3:1–12; Mk. 1:1–8; Lk. 3:1–18; Acts 10:37; 13:24; 19:4).

The messias himself receives the rite, though known to be sinless, and thus not requiring it (Matt. 3:13–17; Mk. 1:9–11; Lk. 3:21; Jn. 1:32).

....

The rite to be inaugurated by the messias is spoken of as being superior to that of John, for it will be a baptism of fire and the Holy Spirit (Matt. 3:11; Mk. 1:7; Lk. 3:16; Jn. 1:19–33; Acts 1:5; 11:16)

The first step toward the realization of the new baptism is the use of a rite of baptism by the disciples of the messias, though He Himself did not baptize (Jn. 4:1). John 4:2   John 3:22

Having come to the end of His mission on earth, the messias sends His disciples to preach the gospel message to all the world, to make disciples of all men, baptizing those who believe with His new rite of baptism. He warns that those who believe and are baptized shall be saved, while the rest shall be lost (Matt. 28:19; Mk. 16:16).

....

2. This rite has a deeper signification: it is a symbolic rite.

There is first of all the obvious signification of cleansing; purification by a bath; the rite signifies the cleansing and purifying of the soul from sin, the death of the soul and its restoration to life in God (1 Cor. 6:11; Eph. 5:26; Tit. 3:5).

But there is a further signification. The descent into the baptismal waters suggests the descent of a body in burial; while the ascent from the waters suggests resurrection to new life. So Paul teaches that the baptized have been baptized in the death of Christ; they have been buried with Christ in baptism; and they are to rise with Christ to new life (Rom. 6:3–11;

15. John F. Gallagher, *Significando Causant: A Study of Sacramental Efficiency* (Fribourg: University Press, 1965), 5.

Col. 2:12). Thus the rite signifies the death and resurrection of Christ, and what that passion and resurrection means for the one baptized: death to sin; resurrection to new life. Christ Himself spoke of His passion as a baptism (Mk. 10:38; Lk. 12:50). And the baptismal rite is the communion in that passion and resurrection for the one baptized.

3. This rite of initiation brings about the effect of which it is symbolic and significative.

The effect signified, we have seen, is spiritual purification, restoration to life, resurrection to the new life through sharing in the passion of Christ. Now this effect, with its various aspects, is ascribed by the sacred authors to the baptismal rite, as used by God. God saves us; to do so, He uses as means the symbolic rite of baptism, which He makes somehow efficacious of the result it signifies, due to His use of it.

The new life signified by the rite is obtained by a rebirth accomplished by the baptismal rite (Tit. 3:5; Jn. 3:5). The rebirth corresponds to the resurrection to new life indicated in Rom. 6:4. It is a life in Christ that is to be eternal (Rom. 6:8; 6:22; Tit. 3:5–7). This life is salvation and justification, which are thus brought about by baptism, together with the elimination and remission of sin (Acts 2:38; 22:16; Rom. 6:6; Col. 2:12; 1 Cor. 6:11; Mk. 16:16; 1 Pet. 3:21). And this life brought about by baptism is life in Christ; it is to put on Christ, to be consecrated to Him (Gal. 3:27), and it is obtained by being joined to the body of Christ, the church (Acts 2:41; 1 Cor. 12:13, Eph. 4:4–6; Rom. 6:3). Baptism is thus the rite of incorporation: it makes us enter the body of Christ, which is the Church.

The baptismal rite, then, is an effective sign; it is a sign of the death and resurrection of Christ; and it realizes that death and resurrection in us, by making us dead to sin, and alive with the life of God, which is grace.[16]

The same could be said about each of the sacraments. For example, in John 6:54, 56, 57, 58, Jesus enumerates several effects of eating his body and drinking his blood: *"he who eats my flesh and drinks my blood* has eternal life, and I will raise him up at the last day . . . abides in me and I in him . . . will live because of me . . . will live forever."* In the Eucharist we finds the explanation of the "agency whereby" the grace of union with Christ is brought about.[17]

16. Ibid., 5–8.
17. For a treatment of sacramental causality in the Bible and the Fathers that dove-

Without needing to affirm that any of the biblical authors were familiar with Aristotle's four causes, it is clear that the Bible associates certain effects with the agency of (contact with) the sacraments. Or, to say it another way, the effects associated with the sacraments are, in fact, explained or caused by the operation of the sacraments.[18] Explaining the precise manner of the association between God, the sacraments, and the sacramental effects has a complex history, which came to a point of crisis at the time of the Reformation and remains, as Chauvet's work indicates, important in the present context. The weight of knowing that God has instituted the sacraments and works through them in such a way that he bestows the gift of grace, thereby deepening his intimacy and presence with the faithful, hardly needs to be underscored.

---

tails with Gallagher's presentation, see Jean-Philippe Revel, *Traité des sacrements: I. Baptême et sacramentalité, vol 2. Don et réception de la grâce baptismale*, 13–26.

18. Reformed theologian Peter J. Leithart, for example, forwards this standard caricature of the efficient causality of the sacraments without a single reference to the biblical foundations of Thomas's position: "Scholastic theology detached technical or mechanical questions of sacramental operation from patristic and early medieval typological mystagogy, so that, for example, Thomas construed sacramental 'causality' in the categories of Aristotle rather than according to biblical patterns of flood, Exodus, or the ablutions of Leviticus. Answers to scholastic questions (*quastiones*) were thus sought outside the typological reading of Scripture (*lectio*)." From P. Leithart, "Old Covenant and New in Sacrament Theology New and Old," *Pro Ecclesia* 14, no. 2 (2005): 177. Did not the typological mysteries cause by their agency effects within the created order? It is unclear how Leithart would characterize the causal-operative language that can be found in the sacramental theology of deeply typological Fathers such as Ambrose. Speaking of the power of the divine presence operating through the water of Baptism, Ambrose notes: "Believe, therefore, that the presence of Divinity is at hand there. Do you believe the operation (*operationem*)? Do you not believe the presence? Whence would the operation (*operatio*) follow, unless the presence went before?" Ambrose, *The Mysteries*, chap. 3.8, in Ambrose, *Theological and Dogmatic Works*, vol. 44 of The Fathers of the Church, trans. Roy J. Deferrari (Washington, D.C.: The Catholic University of America Press, 1963; reprint 2002), 8. It is simply not the case that the use of some philosophical categories to clarify or penetrate the revealed message is an imposition or foreign to the point that the inspired author sought to make. See also Gallagher's presentation of sacramental causality in the Fathers in *Significando Causant*, 15–37.

The Magisterium and the *Ex Opere Operato* Doctrine

The biblical and patristic affirmation of the objective efficacy of the sacraments is confirmed repeatedly by the Magisterium of the Church. This teaching developed first in conjunction with ascribing spiritual effects to specific sacraments, especially Baptism, such as grace, regeneration, washing away of sin, and incorporation into the Church.[19]

This teaching on the objective efficacy of the sacraments is gradually formalized as a general principle that applies to all seven sacraments. For example, in his 1341 *Libellus Cum dudum* to the Armenians, Benedict XII identifies the denial of a "gratia gratificans" as an error to be condemned.[20] And, furthermore, he condemns the position that holds that

> bishops and priests do nothing toward the remission of sins either principally or ministerially, but God alone remits sins; neither bishops nor priests are employed to perform the aforesaid remission of sins, except that they have received the power of speaking from God, and so when they absolve they say: "May God forgive you your sins" or, "I forgive you your sins on earth, and God forgives you in heaven."[21]

In the 1439 *Decree for the Armenians* issued by the Council of Florence, the use of causal language enters formally into the magisterial teaching to distinguish the objective efficacy of the seven sacraments from the rites of the Old Law:

> There are seven sacraments of the New Law ... which differ greatly from the sacraments of the Old Law. The latter, in fact, did not cause grace [non causabant gratiam], but they only prefigured the grace to be given through the Passion of Christ. These sacraments of ours, however, both contain grace and communicate it to those who worthily receive them.[22]

---

19. See Gallagher, *Significando Causant*, 37–38.

20. Ibid., 39.

21. Heinrich Denzinger, *Enchiridion symbolorum*, 304 (§1013). John Wyclif and Jan Hus both advocated similar positions, arguing that the sacraments celebrated by sinful ministers were not efficacious. These positions were condemned at the 8th and 15th sessions (May 4 and July 6, 1415) of the Council of Constance.

22. Ibid., 338 (§1310).

The teaching of the Council of Trent on sacramental causality is found in the 13 canons promulgated on March 3, 1547.[23] These canons affirm, in a converging fashion, that causation is intrinsic to the celebration of the sacramental signs, and not merely extrinsic and dependent on some other factor (such as the faith or devotion of the minister or recipient). Canon 6 affirms that the sacraments "contain" and "confer" the grace that they signify:

> If anyone says that the sacraments of the New Law do not contain the grace they signify or that they do not confer that grace on those who do not place an obstacle in their way, as if they were only external signs of grace or justice received through faith and marks of the Christian profession by which among men the faithful are distinguished from the unbelievers, let him be anathema.[24]

Commenting on this canon, Gallagher explains: "[H]ere the council opposes all the reformers, and especially Zwingli; it makes the sacraments efficacious signs; they confer the grace they signify."[25] This teaching is aimed especially at the 13th article of the Lutheran *Augsburg Confession*, which teaches that the purpose of the sacraments is to strengthen and arouse faith.[26] In light of this Lutheran position, Gallagher observes that Trent affirms that the sacraments

> do not merely arouse faith, or signify it, or pledge salvation, or protest faith. They do all these things and more: they contain and confer grace itself on those not placing an obstacle. In treating of the sacraments individually the same point is made; these rites effect or confer the grace they signify. The sacramental rites have a certain *vis* or power to confer that grace.[27]

---

23. Fr. Miralles points out that by the time of the Council of Trent the expression "*ex opere operato*" already had a very precise theological meaning that developed from the twelfth century onward in relation to the theology of merit. Two expressions, *opus operatum* and *opus operans*, were developed in this context to distinguish "the result of an action" (*opus operatum*) from an act as "voluntary and therefore morally qualifiable as good or bad, meritorious or punishable" (*opus operans*). See Miralles, *I Sacramenti Cristiani*, 302.

24. Heinrich Denzinger, *Enchiridion symbolorum*, Session 7, March 3, 1547, Decree on the Sacraments, 389 (§1606).

25. Gallagher, *Significando Causant*, 46.

26. For a Catholic response to the sacramental doctrine of Luther and Melanchthon as embodied in the Augsburg Confession, see Revel, *Traité des sacrements*: I.2, *Baptême et sacramentalité. Don et réception de la grâce baptismale*, 27–28.

27. Gallagher, *Significando Causant*, 46.

Against some false Protestant theories of predestination, such as Calvin's doctrine that the sacraments aid only those predestined, Canon 7 of Trent affirms that the sacraments give grace each time they are properly celebrated: *of the baptized*
We are the church

If anyone says that, as far as God's part is concerned, grace is not given through these sacraments always and to all, even if they receive them rightly, but only sometimes and to some, let him be anathema.[28]

Commenting on this canon Gallagher notes that "sanctification is objectively offered in the rite, and is actually received by all who *rite*, that is, properly disposed, come into contact with God in the sacrament."[29]

Canon 8 of Trent responds to the Protestant "faith alone" (*sola fide*) axiom, which maintains that faith alone suffices for one to receive grace. In response to this axiom, Trent teaches that grace is conferred in the sacraments by the very performance of the sacramental rite itself:

If anyone says that through the sacraments of the New Law grace is not conferred by the performance of the rite itself [*ex opere operato*] but that faith alone in the divine promise is sufficient to obtain grace, let him be anathema.[30]

This canon indicates that the sacramental celebration itself, that is, the valid celebration of the rite, exercises an agency in the conferral of grace. In its earliest instances in sacramental theology the phrase *ex opere operato* "was used to distinguish the sacrament itself, the *opus operatum*, from the act of giving the sacrament, the *opus operans*."[31]

Together these canons clarify, in the face of specific theses to the contrary held by the Protestants, that the conferral of grace in

28. Heinrich Denzinger, *Enchiridion symbolorum*, Session 7, March 3, 1547, Decree on the Sacraments, 389 (§1607).

29. Gallagher, *Significando Causant*, 49; "all who *rite*" is in the original. It seems that Gallagher means to say "receive."

30. Heinrich Denzinger, *Enchiridion symbolorum*, Session 7, March 3, 1547, Decree on the Sacraments, 389 (§1608).

31. Gallagher, *Significando Causant*, 49.

the sacraments is not dependent on external factors such as the faith of the recipient or minister, but rather stems from the sacramental operation itself.[32] "What the council teaches," Gallagher explains, "in Canons 6 and 8, is the infallible connection between the rite and the reception of grace, and the real dependence of that reception of grace on the rite itself."[33] As Revel demonstrates, Trent's teaching on the causality of the sacraments holds together the profound "*rapports*" between the sacraments and faith. The Protestants, Revel notes, could not accept sacramental efficiency in the face of Paul's teaching against works, whereas Catholics understood the sacraments — in faith — to be works of God in union with God's Word.[34]

The Magisterium of the Church has offered further clarification on the Tridentine doctrine of sacramental causality. Special emphasis is placed on the objective power of the sacraments through Christ's role and presence within the Church. For example, in his 1947 encyclical letter *Mediator Dei*, Pius XII teaches:

Sacraments and sacrifice do, then, possess that "objective" power to make us really and personally sharers in the divine life of Jesus Christ. Not from any ability of our own, but by the power of God, are they endowed with the capacity to unite the piety of members with that of the head, and to make this, in a sense, the action of the whole community.[35]

This passage affirms that the sacraments are actions of Christ and that they "possess" a power from Christ to communicate divine life to the faithful. Furthermore, in his 1965 encyclical on the Eucharist, *Mysterium Fidei*, Paul VI indicates the holiness of the sacraments as sources of grace for the soul when they are applied to the faithful: "the sacraments are the actions of Christ who administers them through men. And so the sacraments are holy in themselves

---

32. This does not mean, of course, that recipients cannot place obstacles in the way of the sacramental effects. It merely affirms that the effects themselves are not caused by the recipients' disposition, but by the sacramental operation itself.

33. Gallagher, *Significando Causant*, 52.

34. See Revel, *Traité des sacrements: I.2, Baptême et sacramentalité. Don et réception de la grâce baptismale*, 35.

35. *Mediator Dei* §29.

and they pour grace into the soul by the power of Christ, when they touch the body."[36]

The *ex opere operato* doctrine is hard to define in a single sentence because it affirms several things at one time, including: the agency of both God and the sacramental rite in the conferral of grace, and the fact that the faith or fervor of the minister or recipient are not internal causal factors in the efficient causation of the sacraments. The *Catechism of the Catholic Church* affirms these multiform factors in a compound definition that accentuates each aspect and founds the agency of the sacraments on the work of Christ:

> This is the meaning of the Church's affirmation that the sacraments act *ex opere operato* (literally: "by the very fact of the action's being performed"), i.e., by virtue of the saving work of Christ, accomplished once for all. It follows that "the sacrament *is not wrought* by the righteousness of either the celebrant or the recipient, *but by the power* of God."[50] From the moment that a *sacrament is celebrated in accordance with the intention of the Church, the power of Christ and his Spirit acts in and through it*, independently of the personal holiness of the minister. Nevertheless, the fruits of the sacraments also depend on the disposition of the one who receives them.[37]

The teaching of the Magisterium insists that the sacraments have an intrinsic causal power and that contact with the sacraments is operative in the outpouring of grace on the soul. This doctrine offers the greatest spiritual consolation to the faithful, for it clarifies that grace is conferred in the sacraments, as long as the rite is properly celebrated, through the very celebration itself. Human imperfections, therefore, such as a lack of perceptible devotion on the part of the minister, do not compromise the access to God that is available in the sacraments.

[handwritten left margin: it is intrinsic & it comes from God]

It is important to note that the patrimony of Trent indicates that the causation of the sacraments stems *ex opere* or "from the work" of the *operato* or operation of the rite that is being performed. Keeping this in mind, Reginald Lynch's development of Gallagher's distinc-

[handwritten: Sacrament]

36. *Mysterium Fidei* §38.
37. *CCC* §1128 (emphasis added).

[handwritten: God does 100% and the sacrament does its work]

[handwritten: as well]

[handwritten: w/o God establishing them as a sacrament, there wouldn't be anything]

tion between theories that posit the causality as intrinsic or as extrinsic to the operation of the sacramental rite is helpful when considering the merits of the various approaches:

While we are aware that historical metanarrative can have serious limitations, the distinction offered [here] between *intrinsic* and *extrinsic* approaches to sacramental causality is of great utility because it provides a workable framework for understanding the main lines of doctrinal development that shaped this issue through the centuries. This distinction between intrinsic and extrinsic approaches to sacramental causality is broadly congruent with the division between the physical and moral causality that emerged in the schools during the modern period.[38]

This does not mean, however, that there are no ambiguities to the doctrine, or that it is not in need of further elaboration. Does *"ex opere operato"* mean, for example, that the sacraments are merely occasions or disposing agents at the celebration of which, like an infallible promise, God gives grace? In this case the "operation" of the sacramental celebration would not be intrinsically involved in the causation. Birthdays, for example, occasion the bestowal of gifts, but the day itself exercises no intrinsic causal agency. Thomas Aquinas's theology of the instrumental efficient causality of the sacraments is an especially fruitful resource for pondering the objective and intrinsic efficacy of the sacraments.

Thomas Aquinas and Instrumental Efficient Causality

Aquinas points out an opinion on this that was held in his own day: "Some, however, say that [the sacraments] are the cause of grace not by their own operation [*non sunt causa gratiae aliquid operando*], but in so far as God causes grace in the soul when the sacraments are employed."[39] Thomas, however, rejects this opinion as being inconsistent with the revealed patrimony and the "authority of many

---

38. Reginald M. Lynch, OP, "The Sacraments as Causes of Sanctification," *Nova et Vetera*, English Edition, 12, no. 3 (2014): 791–836, at 803. See John F. Gallagher, *Significando Causant*, 80–81.

39. *ST* III, q. 62, a. 1.

saints," because "according to this opinion the sacraments of the New Law would be mere signs" and not causes of grace.[40] Thomas views the key flaw of this approach to sacramental causality to be the denial that grace is caused by the operation of the sacraments.

But how is it possible that the sacraments are truly and intrinsically causes of grace? Thomas's position on this point evolved, at least somewhat, over the course of his career.[41] In his earlier works, such as the *Commentary on the Sentences* (ca. 1256), Thomas devoted more attention to addressing how the instrumental causality of the sacraments was related to the immediate effect or the so-called "*res et sacramentum*," and how this, in turn, was related to the conferral of the sacramental grace or "*res tantum*."[42] By the time he wrote *De veritate*, question 27, article 4 (ca. 1259), Thomas's focus had shifted to addressing directly whether or not the sacraments cause grace.[43] In the body of this article he affirms that the sacraments, as instruments of God, do cause grace. He makes just two references to instrumental causality as dispositive (see ad 3 and ad 9) in this work.

By the time of the composition of the *Summa theologiae*, Miralles points out, Thomas does not "limit the instrumental action of the sacraments with respect to grace."[44] Furthermore, Ruggiero Biagi observes that, in using dispositive language, Thomas does not mean to indicate that the sacraments are some kind of temporal prerequi-

40. Ibid.

41. See Miralles, *I Sacramenti Cristiani*, 336–41. See also, for example, Bernhard Blankenhorn, OP, "The Instrumental Causality of the Sacraments: Thomas Aquinas and Louis-Marie Chauvet," *Nova et Vetera*, English Edition, 4, no. 2 (2006): 255–94. Blankenhorn provides a helpful description of the movement of Thomas's thinking on sacramental causality and also points out precisely where Chauvet's reading of Aquinas is incorrect. See also Leeming, *Principles of Sacramental Theology*, 324–32. See also Reginald Lynch, "Cajetan's Harp: Sacraments and the Life of Grace in Light of Perfective Instrumental Causality," *The Thomist* 78 (2014): 65–106.

42. See, for example, *In Sent.* IV, d. 1, q. 1, a. 4, s. 1, where Thomas speaks of the instrument causing the *res et sacramentum* (character or an *ornatus animae*), which disposes the subject to grace but does not cause the sacramental grace itself.

43. For a helpful discussion of Thomas's position in *De veritate* and the further trajectory of his thought, see Gallagher, *Significando Causant*, 102–9.

44. Miralles, *I Sacramenti Cristiani*, 341.

site to grace, which is unrelated to their instrumental action. Thus, even when Thomas does approach the question from the perspective of asking whether the *res et sacramentum* of the sacraments, especially character, is a disposition to grace, it is still one unified sacramental action that causes all of the sacramental effects.[45] It is not as if he maintains that one of the effects is caused by the sacrament, while the second is caused by God alone apart from (or only on the occasion of) the sacrament.

Thomas's use of instrumental causality enables him to articulate how the sacramental operation is employed by God in the causation of grace. "An efficient cause is twofold, principal and instrumental," Thomas explains. Aquinas's development of instrumental efficient causality has several sources. First, common experience indicates that agents frequently employ instruments (pens, pencils, knives, saws, axes, musical instruments, and so on) to bring about certain effects. These types of instruments contribute to the realization of the effect even though they must be employed by a primary (principal) agent. Second, Aristotle acknowledges instrumental causality in his doctrine of causality, although this concept is underdeveloped in his thought.[46] Third, the Fathers of the Church, especially those in the Greek tradition, such as Athanasius, Cyril of Alexandria, and John of Damascus, employed the notion of instrument (*organon*) very richly to explain the operational relation that exists between the divinity and humanity in Christ.

Christ's human nature, according to this line of thinking, works in the order of salvation as an instrument of the divinity. Aloys Grillmeier explains the importance that this concept has in Athanasius's thought accordingly:

In the word [*organon*, i.e., instrument] Athanasius sums up the whole significance of the Logos-sarx relationship. Here his deep insight into the

---

45. See Ruggero Biagi, *La Causalità dell' umanità di Cristo e dei Sacramenti nella "Summa Theologiae" di S. Tommaso d'Aquino* (Bologna: Edizioni Studio Domenicano, 1985), 11–25.

46. See, for example, *Metaphysics* 5.2 (1013b3).

Christ's human nature was an instrument to express His Divine Power - "laying of hands", "spitting to heal,"

conjunction of the divine Word with the flesh becomes particularly clear. . . . Athanasius wishes to make two points here: first the unity of subject in Christ, and secondly the difference between the instrument and the agent. The organon-concept allows him to stress the living power of the Logos in redemption and at the same time to emphasize his transcendence without relinquishing any of the closeness of the community of the Logos and sarx.[47]

Gilles Emery points out, in an insightful study on Aquinas and the Greek Fathers, that Thomas's theology of the hypostatic union and his use of the term "instrument" are "fundamentally" indebted to the Greek Fathers.[48] Emery further notes that Thomas's incorporation of these concepts and the teaching of the Second and Third Councils of Constantinople "designates Thomas as a pioneer" among the Latin Schoolmen.[49] Furthermore, as Bernhard Blankenhorn explains,

Thomas appropriates St. John Damascene's teaching that the operations of the Christ's flesh have a salvific efficacy through his divine power. Aquinas explains this teaching with the Aristotelian category of efficient causality. Behind Damascene stands none other than St. Cyril of Alexandria. Yet we are hardly witnessing the reduction of Greek Christology to the categories of Aristotle. Thomas's intention is to affirm the real emanation of divinizing power from the whole humanity of the suffering and resurrecting Christ, one that he can explain best with the Aristotelian concept of causal efficiency.[50]

Thomas's teaching on instrumentality is clarified by the twofold, divine and human, operation in Christ. "We must bear in mind that wherever there are several mutually ordained agents," Thomas explains, "the inferior is moved by the superior, as in man the body is moved by the soul and the lower powers by the reason."[51] This means that each (principal and instrumental cause) performs a caus-

47. Aloys Grillmeier, SJ, *Christ in the Christian Tradition: From the Apostolic Age to Chalcedon (451)*, trans. J. S. Bowden (New York: Sheed and Ward, 1965), 205–6.

48. Gilles Emery, "A Note on St. Thomas and the Eastern Fathers," in Emery, *Trinity, Church, and the Human Person: Thomistic Essays* (Ave Maria, Fla.: Sapientia Press, 2007), 193–207, at 202.

49. Ibid., 195.

50. Blankenhorn, "The Place of Romans 6 in Aquinas' Doctrine of Sacramental Causality," 139–40.

51. *ST* III, q. 19, a. 1.

ative role that can be distinguished, while it also shares in a common act of motion, namely, that of the principal cause. "The operation which belongs to the thing, as moved by another," Thomas explains,

is not distinct from the operation of the mover; thus to make a bench is not the work of the axe independently of the workman. Hence, wheresoever the mover and the moved have different forms or operative faculties, there must the operation of the mover and the proper operation of the moved be distinct; although the moved shares in the operation of the mover, and the mover makes use of the operation of the moved, and, consequently, each acts in communion with the other.[52]

The distinction between the instrument and the principal agent, and the fact that each is able to share, in a unified motion, in the operation of the other, enables Thomas to make this important conclusion about the real existence of divine and human actions in Christ:

Therefore, in Christ the human nature has its proper form and power whereby it acts; and so has the Divine. Hence the human nature has its proper operation distinct from the Divine, and conversely. Nevertheless, the Divine Nature makes use of the operation of the human nature, as of the operation of its instrument; and in the same way the human nature shares in the operation of the Divine Nature, as an instrument shares in the operation of the principal agent.[53]

It is important to keep in mind that the instrumentality of Christ's human nature is not static or inanimate. It is a living instrument, whose free acts of knowing and loving exercise agent causality meritoriously in the plan of salvation. "Grace was bestowed upon Christ, not only as an individual, but inasmuch as He is the Head of the Church," Aquinas observes,

so that it might overflow into His members; and therefore Christ's works are referred to Himself and to His members in the same way as the works of any other man in a state of grace are referred to himself. But it is evident that whosoever suffers for justice's sake, provided that he be in a state of grace, merits his salvation thereby, according to Matthew 5:10: "Blessed

52. Ibid.
53. Ibid.

are they that suffer persecution for justice's sake." Consequently Christ by His Passion merited salvation, not only for Himself, but likewise for all His members.[54]

Aquinas draws a special analogy between the instrumental causality of Christ's human nature in the order of merit and the instrumental efficient causality of the sacraments that helps to clarify the relation of the sacraments to Christ. "Now an instrument is twofold," Aquinas clarifies,

> the one, separate, as a stick, for instance; the other, united, as a hand. Moreover, the separate instrument is moved by means of the united instrument, as a stick by the hand. Now the principal efficient cause of grace is God Himself, in comparison with Whom Christ's humanity is as a united instrument, whereas the sacrament is as a separate instrument. Consequently, the saving power must needs be derived by the sacraments from Christ's Godhead through His humanity.[55]

From a spiritual standpoint, furthermore, the conjoined instrumentality of Christ's human nature enables him to influence the human soul interiorly through the sacraments. "Christ produces the inward sacramental effect, both as God and as man, but not in the same way,"[56] Thomas teaches. "As God, He works in the sacraments by authority: but, as man, His operation conduces to the inward sacramental effects meritoriously and efficiently, but instrumentally."[57] This principle extends from the salvific influence that Christ's human nature exercised in his Passion: "Christ's Passion which belongs to Him in respect of His human nature, is the cause of justification, both meritoriously and efficiently, not as the principal cause thereof, or by His own authority, but as an instrument, in so far as His humanity is the instrument of His Godhead."[58]

Speaking of Christ's human nature, Aquinas notes that "since it is an instrument united to the Godhead in unity of Person, it has

---

54. *ST* III, 48, a. 1. See also G. D. Lynn's "Christ's Redemptive Merit: The Nature of Its Causality According to St. Thomas" (S.T.D. dissertation, Pontifical Gregorian University, 1962).

55. *ST* III, q. 62, a. 5.   56. *ST* III, q. 64, a. 3.

57. Ibid.   58. Ibid.

a certain headship and efficiency in regard to the extrinsic instruments, which are the ministers of the Church and the sacraments themselves."[59]

This insight enables Aquinas to explain how the sacraments can truly work as efficient causes in the conferral of grace, as Revelation indicates, without in any way marginalizing or transgressing the primary and indispensable role that must be reserved for God (and Christ) in the bestowal of any divine gift.

In a motion of efficient causality in which the primary agent employs an instrument to help bring about or perfect a desired outcome, Aquinas explains that "the principal cause works by the power of its form, to which form the effect is likened."[60] This means that poetic words, for example, caused to be on paper by the instrumental causality of a pen, do not reflect the form of the pen, save as markings, but rather reflect the mind of the poet who employed the pen to mark them down.

In the order of principal efficient sacramental causality, therefore, as Aquinas explains, "none but God can cause grace: since grace is nothing else than a participated likeness of the Divine Nature, according to 2 Pet. 1:4: *He hath given us most great and precious promises; that we may be partakers of the Divine Nature.*"[61]

How, then, are the sacraments involved in the efficient causality of grace in any more than a dispositive or occasional fashion? "The instrumental cause," Thomas explains, "works not by the power of its form, but only by the motion whereby it is moved by the principal agent."[62] This point is extremely important for understanding Aquinas's insight into the revealed patrimony. The instrument acts according to its purpose as an instrument, as a true causal contributor in bringing about the effect. The instrument, however, does not cause the ultimate effect by way of its own motion alone; it causes, as an instrument, by being taken up by the principal agent.

The sacramental instrument, furthermore, is not an ontologi-

---

59. Ibid.
61. Ibid.

60. *ST* III, q. 62, a. 1.
62. Ibid.

cally static agent. Its existence is transient, working through the sacramental operation, and in a mode that is dependent on the principal cause. "The instrumental power," Aquinas explains, "has a being that passes from one thing into another, and is incomplete, just as motion is an imperfect act passing from agent to patient."[63]

The work of the instrument is, however, intrinsic to the completion of the action. "An instrument has a twofold action," Thomas explains:

one is instrumental, in respect of which it works not by its own power but by the power of the principal agent: the other is its proper action, which belongs to it in respect of its proper form.... In like manner the corporeal sacraments by their operation, which they exercise on the body that they touch, accomplish through the Divine institution an instrumental operation on the soul; for example, the water of baptism, in respect of its proper power, cleanses the body, and thereby, inasmuch as it is the instrument of the Divine power, cleanses the soul: since from soul and body one thing is made.[64]

The very purpose of the institution of the sacraments, by God, is that they "be employed for the purpose of conferring grace." So, following St. Paul's teaching on Baptism, Thomas concludes that each sacrament is instituted to be "an instrument by which someone works: wherefore it is written (Titus 3:5): *He saved us by the laver of regeneration.*"[65]

As a result, as Bernhard Blankenhorn observes, "What we find in Aquinas' manner of approaching sacramental causality does not involve the simple insertion of the sacraments into a pre-determined metaphysical model of causality, but rather a subtle, complex dialectic between metaphysics and history, between philosophy, Scripture, and the Fathers."[66] Any adequate treatment, therefore, of Aquinas's position must hold all of these together and resist the temptation to impose a strictly philosophical view that is not informed by the teaching of Scripture.

63. *ST* III, q. 62, a. 4.   64. Ibid., a. 1.
65. Ibid.
66. Blankenhorn, "The Place of Romans 6 in Aquinas' Doctrine of Sacramental Causality," 149.

Interpreting Thomas's Teaching: Dispositive and Perfective Physical Causality

There are two common interpretations that Thomas's followers have given to his doctrine of sacramental causality.[67] The division is between those who read his earlier sacramental teaching as dispositive *and* as obtaining throughout his career, and those who see the development in his teaching as bringing to fruition a more precise view, such as the one in the Third Part of the *Summa theologiae*. These two views are known, respectively, as "dispositive physical causality" and "perfective physical causality."[68] Each of these interpretations views the sacraments as instrumental causes. The following brief description by Reginald Lynch should provide an adequate sketch for the reader to appreciate the parameters of the debate:

> In the case of dispositive causality, the action of the instrument does not "touch" (*pertingere*) the finality of the completed act but awaits a completion that is accomplished by the principal agent beyond the scope of the individual instrument in question. In perfective instrumentality, on the other hand, the action of the instrument actually reaches or "touches" the completion of the action.[69]

Contemporary sacramental theologians tend to blanch at the language of physical causality. At its core, however, the language of "physical causality" is meant merely to point out the mode of contact by which the intended effect is brought about. "The word 'physical,'" Lynch explains, "indicates the motive potency of an instrumental ef-

---

67. For a presentation of the positions of Aquinas's principal commentators, see Revel, *Traité des sacrements: I.2 Baptême et sacramentalité. Don et réception de la grâce baptismale*, 90–121.

68. Aquinas himself identifies these two views in *In IV Sent.*, d. 1, q. 1, a. 4, sol. 1: "Ad cujus evidentiam sciendum est, quod causa efficiens dupliciter potest dividi. Uno modo ex parte effectus; scilicet *in disponentem, quae causat dispositionem ad formam ultimam; et perficientem, quae inducit ultimam perfectionem*" (emphasis added, cited in Lynch, "Cajetan's Harp," 71). For a brief summary of these views and their adherents, see Leeming, *Principles of Sacramental Theology*, 288–89 and 314–39. Leeming is obviously sympathetic to dispositive perfective causality. His treatment of both is detailed but lacks clarity on many points.

69. Lynch, "Cajetan's Harp," 71.

ficient cause in the Aristotelian sense, and eliminates those theories which rely on external forms of legal pact or moral coercion."[70] The term "physical" was adopted by theologians, not out of a commitment to a physicalist view of the sacraments, but to clarify that the causation of the sacraments is more than merely moral in nature. "That system which opposed 'moral' causality," Gallagher explains, "came to be called 'physical' causality. What the word means is that the sacraments are truly efficient causes, instrumental causes, of grace. The effect of grace flows from the sacraments as from true instrumental causes."[71]

In the case of the sacraments, therefore, to say that they work as "physical" instrumental causes indicates that the sacramental effects are bestowed by the very application of the sacrament to the recipient. This language does not mean that grace is physically forced into the soul. Rather, it means that, like other spiritual effects conferred through the operation of the healing touch of Christ's hand or cloak, the sacraments, when applied to the recipients, bestow the divine effects.

Thomas's commentators developed this language to help articulate the nature of instrumental efficient causality. In contrast to various late Medieval and Reformed theologians who rejected the idea that sacramental grace was an effect intrinsic to the sacramental operation, Thomas affirmed that the sacraments do, as instruments of Christ, cause grace through their operation. Physical causality merely affirms this basic point.

The theory of dispositive causality, spelled out in several variations, was held by many before St. Thomas (e.g., Alexander of Hales, William of Auxerre, and Albert the Great), and some of his interpreters maintain that "the sacrament causes a 'disposition' to grace.... [T]he sacraments, by placing the symbolic reality in the recipient of the sacraments, cause a real change or 'disposition' which,

---

70. Lynch, "The Sacraments as Causes of Sanctification," 813.
71. Gallagher, *Significando Causant*, 190.

in virtue of God's ordinary supernatural providence, carries grace with it, unless there be an impediment of ill-will."[72] One struggle that these authors sought to work through was the nature of grace itself as effected by the sacraments. Instrumental agents can bring about effects within the created order, but to what degree can they be said to "create" an effect – grace – by their agency?

Furthermore, authors point out cases such as valid Baptisms in which the sacramental grace is impeded from bearing fruit in the recipient – say in the case of the Donatist controversy, when people were seeking the sacraments from validly ordained ministers who had joined heretical or schismatic sects. Dispositive causality seeks, in a way, to deflect the causation of grace away from the sacramental operation, while affirming that the disposition to grace is truly perfected by the operation.[73] "*The main theological reason* for a 'dispositive' causality," Leeming argues, "is derived from the principle that the sacraments effect what they signify as present: The significance of the sacrament is not that grace is being here and now infallibly conferred, but that a state is conferred in which grace is requisite."[74] There are several aspects of this view that underscore important points of sacramental theology, but the view also includes some elements that are open to question.[75]

To argue that the sacraments effect a disposition to grace, but not grace itself, conflates the question of sacramental causality with the question of the relation of the various sacramental effects (*res et sacramentum* and *res tantum*) to each other. For example, when it comes to treating the three sacraments that confer character (Baptism, Confirmation, and Orders), articulating the relation between

---

72. Leeming, *Principles of Sacramental Theology*, 289.

73. For a helpful summary of dispositive sacramental causality in St. Thomas's followers and other schools, see Gallagher, *Significando Causant*, 135–48.

74. Leeming, *Principles of Sacramental Theology*, 330.

75. There is a variation of this theory that shifts the causal focus from disposition to the divine intention. According to this view, Leeming explains, "The sacraments express the divine intention to sanctify, and by expressing it produce the sanctity expressed." Leeming, *Principles of Sacramental Theology*, 290. See also Miralles, *I Sacramenti Cristiani*, 343.

the character and the grace is not the same as articulating how each is caused by the unified operation of the sacrament under the divine motion.

Furthermore, it is a component of sacramental spirituality that certain effects of the sacraments abide even after the celebration. The reception of communion, for example, bears spiritual fruits after the host is no longer present within the recipient. But the abiding sacramental fruit is as dependent on the sacrament itself as was the immediate reality of the consecrated host. That there be multiple effects of the sacraments that bear fruit after the transient celebration does not mean that these effects are not dependent on the operation of the sacrament.

To grasp fully the intelligibility of the causality of the sacraments, it may be helpful to think of other instruments besides the blunt force objects (axes) that Thomas frequently puts forward. Reginald Lynch points out that in his commentary on question 62, article 1 of the Third Part of the *Summa*, Cajetan invokes the image of the harp. The advantage of this type of example for instrumental causality is that it underscores the causative contribution of the principal agent *and the instrument* together: the music truly flows from the musician and the instrument. However, the music that is caused by the artist and instrument does not "produce two sounds," for example, a disposition (for hearing music) and a final effect (the actual music). The effect results from both the principal and the instrumental cause, with the latter's agency working under the motion of the primary agent.[76]

Many of the most profound interpreters of Thomas, including Cardinal Cajetan, Bañez, Gonet, Billurt, Robert Bellarmine, Suarez, and the Carmelites at Salamanca, held to perfective physical causality as the proper reading of St. Thomas (and Catholic sacramental theology). Bañez, for example, in his commentary on *ST* III, q. 62, a. 1, offers the following lapidary explanation of his (and Cajetan's)

76. See Lynch, "Cajetan's Harp," 89.

position: "The fourth opinion on this article is master Cajetan's, and it seems to be blessed Thomas's own in this article: that the sacraments efficiently coincide [*concurrunt*] and reach [*attingunt*] to the production of grace itself in the soul as instrumental causes, just as a paintbrush to a picture."[77]

St. Thomas's presentation of the instrumental efficient causality of the sacraments represents the mature fruit of a life of assiduous study and prayerful contemplation, but it was not the only attempt to offer a synthetic presentation of this aspect of the Christian faith. What are the other views of sacramental causality, besides that of Thomas and his interpreters on instrumental efficient causality, that theologians have invoked to explain the role of the sacraments in the conferral of grace?[78] Articulations of sacramental causality besides those offered by Thomas and his interpreters are too numerous to recount in full. What follows is a broad presentation of these theories according to their most representative articulations.

Other Theories of Sacramental Causality

Occasional Causality

Thomas's articulation of the efficacy of the sacraments in terms of the analogous forms of instrumental causality allowed him to affirm what he deemed to be the essential point of Revelation about

---

77. Domingo Bañez, OP, *De Sacramentis*, vol. 2 of *Comentarios Ineditos a la Tercera Parte de Santo Tomas*, ed. R. P. MTRO. Vicente Beltran de Heredia, OP (Madrid: Imprenta de Aldecoa-Burgos, 1953), on q. 62, a. 1, §3 (there are no page numbers in this volume). My translation.

78. Thomas, for the record, does not seem to think that there are innumerable logical possibilities on the question of sacramental causality. Either the sacraments themselves possess a productive power or the causation of grace is merely coincidental to them: "Those who hold that the sacraments do not cause grace save by a certain coincidence, deny the sacraments any power that is itself productive of the sacramental effect, and hold that the Divine power assists the sacraments and produces their effect. But if we hold that a sacrament is an instrumental cause of grace, we must needs allow that there is in the sacraments a certain instrumental power of bringing about the sacramental effects." *ST* III, q. 62, a. 5.

the sacraments, namely, in the words of Charles Morerod, "one and the same action can be accomplished entirely by God at his level, and by us at ours."[79] Not every thinker in the Catholic tradition, however, was able to provide such a coherent systemization. The most common approach to sacramental causality that was developed outside of Thomism, and to some degree in criticism of it, is that of "occasional causality."[80]

Leeming provides the following general definition for this position: "In this view, God says: 'Whenever the sacraments are duly conferred, I will give grace.' There is no power or force in the sacrament itself which causes grace, but God makes the sacrament an infallible condition of his own immediate action on the soul."[81]

This theory of sacramental causality often uses the word "condition" (*sine qua non*) to explain the causal mode in which the sacraments work. The sacrament, as such, is the occasion or condition for the conferral of grace. The problem with this approach is that the causal relation between the occasion or condition and the effect to which it is related is extrinsic. "A good road," Leeming explains, "is a necessary condition for the movement of motor cars but it is not in the strict sense a cause of their movement."[82] The consequence of this is that "there is nothing in the sacrament itself which causes the grace, unless the word 'cause' be used in a very wide sense."[83]

John Duns Scotus

This position exercised significant influence in the theology of the later Middle Ages. For example, Richard Cross explains Scotus's theory of sacramental causality in the following terms: "the reception of a sacrament is no more than an occasion for a merely divine

---

79. Charles Morerod, OP, *Ecumenism and Philosophy: Philosophical Questions for a Renewal of Dialogue* (Ave Maria, Fla.: Sapientia Press, 2006), 67.

80. In *Principles of Sacramental Theology*, 287, Leeming identifies, inter alia, Henry of Ghent, Ockham, Gabriel Biel, and with some qualification, Bonaventure and Scotus as adherents of this view.

81. Ibid.   82. Ibid., 291.

83. Ibid., 290.

action. On this view, the reception of a sacrament has no *causal* role in the divine gift of grace."[84] The reason for this is that "on Scotus's account, no natural agent could have a supernatural causal power."[85] "The reception of the sacraments," Scotus argues,

is a disposition which necessarily leads to the effect signified by the sacrament, not as by an intrinsic form, however, through which this disposition would attain to its goal or give rise to a preceding disposition, but solely through God's assistance: it is God who calls this effect into being, and not with absolute necessity but only with a necessity that follows from the divine ordinance. This means that God has generally ordered things (and informed His Church of his design) in such a way that He Himself wills to communicate to the recipient of such a sacrament the effect signified [in the sacramental sign].[86]

For obvious reasons, this principle makes Scotus suspicious of Aquinas's version of instrumental causality.[87]

---

84. Richard Cross, *Duns Scotus* (Oxford: Oxford University Press, 1999), 136.

85. Ibid., 137. For a number of thoroughly developed responses to this objection, which refers specifically to the sacraments and other instrumental actions conducive of supernatural effects such as the inspiration of Scripture and miracles, see Edouard Hugon, *La causalité instrumentale: dans l'ordre surnaturel* (Paris: Pierre Téqui, 1924).

86. *Opus Oxoniense* IV, d. I, q. 5, cited in Johann Auer, *A General Doctrine of the Sacraments and the Mystery of the Eucharist*, trans. Erasmo Leiva-Merikakis (Washington, D.C.: The Catholic University of America Press, 1995), 79–80.

87. Aquinas was familiar with the basic position that Scotus came to adopt, and he responded as follows: "A spiritual power cannot be in a corporeal subject, after the manner of a permanent and complete power, as the argument proves. But there is nothing to hinder an instrumental spiritual power from being in a body; in so far as a body can be moved by a particular spiritual substance so as to produce a particular spiritual effect; thus in the very voice which is perceived by the senses there is a certain spiritual power, inasmuch as it proceeds from a mental concept, of arousing the mind of the hearer. It is in this way that a spiritual power is in the sacraments, inasmuch as they are ordained by God unto the production of a spiritual effect." *ST* III, q. 64, a. 4, ad 1. It should be noted, too, that while it is true, in the words of Gallagher, that with Scotus "the extrinsic causality school reaches its highest point" (149), Scotus did not view his own position as occasionalism. "[Scotus's doctrine] is true causality but not what we call physical. It is moral causality, not as used later, but in the sense that the sacraments cause grace for God intends them to do so, and He has so ordered them by His divine will." Gallagher, *Significando Causant*, 150. From this perspective, while Scotus does not subscribe to Aquinas's view of instrumental efficient causality or perfective physical causality, his intention is to affirm the causality of the sacraments, even if his extrinsic theory of causation raises questions about the association of the sacraments with their effects.

The problem with Scotus's rejection of a position maintaining the intrinsic causality of the sacraments themselves is that he fails to recognize how Aquinas, at least, claims that instruments act properly as instruments such that their causal agency acts in dependence on the motion of the primary agent. So, although a twofold causation can be identified in composite actions, there is but one unified motion, namely, that of the primary agent (God) taking up the instrument for the sake of perfecting the soul with grace by applying the instrument to the recipient. The instrument, therefore, works properly as an instrument, but the (supernatural) motion by which it works is that of God as the primary agent.

Cross points out, interestingly, that Scotus develops his theory of sacramental causality "on philosophical premises."[88] It is important to recall that Aquinas's doctrine of the instrumental efficient causality of the sacraments, having a remote and underdeveloped foundation in Aristotle, is also the positive fruit of his reading of sacred Scripture and the Greek Fathers of the Church. Therefore, while Scotus's philosophical critiques of instrumental causality fail to appreciate Aquinas's claims, they also fail to measure up adequately to the theological patrimony, which received Revelation as affirming a causal dependency of certain spiritual effects on the operation of the sacraments.[89]

Theories that sever the intrinsic connection between the sacramental operation and the sacramental effects are not unrelated to the positions on the sacraments that were developed at the time of the Reformation. This is not to say that Scotus would have endorsed those positions. However, the negation of the causality of the sacramental operation (*opus operatum*) opened the way for a greater emphasis on God's agency independent of the sacraments and, par-

88. Richard Cross, *Duns Scotus*, 137.
89. In *Principles of Sacramental Theology*, 293, Leeming notes: "Scotus, although there is some difference of opinion [about this] among his interpreters, seems clearly to reject any power in the sacrament itself and to affirm that it is 'the assistance' of God which causes the effect."

adoxically, on the salvific significance of the faith of the recipient (*opus operantis*).

Martin Luther and Late Medieval Theories of Sacramental Causality

It is interesting to note that Martin Luther expressed reservations about the implications of Scotus's doctrine of univocity of being (which he erroneously imputed to medieval authors generally, not only to Scotus), fearing that it compromised the doctrine of divine transcendence.[90]

What is this doctrine of univocity and how is it related to the causality of the sacraments? Scotus took issue with Thomas's doctrine of analogy because, in the words of Charles Morerod, "[He] perceives analogous concepts as being too different (corresponding more to what Thomas called equivocal concepts). From this he deduces that if discourse about God is to be possible, we should be able to engage in it using our own concepts in their unique and thus comprehensible sense."[91]

Scotus claims, against Aquinas's doctrine of analogy, that God can be known and affirmed "quidditatively." But for this to be possible, a closer comparative relation than an analogous one is needed. "I say," Scotus explains, "that God is not conceived only in a concept analogous to the concept of the creature, namely in a concept which might be altogether different from that which is spoken of the creature, but in a concept which is univocal to him [God] and to the creature."[92]

A great deal of historical work has been done to unearth possible links between Luther's rejection of Aquinas and the similarities

---

90. For a detailed presentation of theories of sacramental causality that were rejected by the Church, including Reformed creeds and Luther's writings, see the entry "Sacrements, Causalité, Négations Hérétiques," in *Dictionnaire de théologie catholique*, vol. 14, part 1, ed. A. Vacant, E. Mangenot, and É. Amann (Paris: Letouzey et Ané, 1939), columns 593–99.

91. Morerod, *Ecumenism and Philosophy*, 65.

92. Duns Scotus, *Ordinatio* I, dist. III, pars I, q. 1, in *Opera Omnia*, vol. 3, 16–18, cited in Morerod, *Ecumenism and Philosophy*, 65–66.

between Luther's thought and late Medieval intellectual trends. It is helpful, in this regard, to take account of Luther's familiarity with (and dependence on) the work of Gabriel Biel, who was an influential thinker in Luther's lifetime. "Luther," Morerod explains, "had come to know Scholasticism primarily through reading Gabriel Biel (1408–95), whose writings guided his studies and whom, Melanchthon asserts, he could still quote by heart at the end of his life."[93]

The problem with Luther's knowledge of Scholasticism through Biel is that "Biel was an 'open' nominalist and often quoted Thomas Aquinas favorably; consequently," Morerod observes, "Luther assumed that he had had access to Thomas's thought [through Biel], whereas he did not actually know Thomas directly (it should be noted that some Thomists were not very faithful to St. Thomas on topics such as merit)."[94]

Thus, to bring this point full circle, the sacramental theology that Luther learned from Biel's writings denied the intrinsic causality of the sacraments in the sense that Thomas had outlined, while presenting itself in a Thomistic mode. In short, Luther learned a nominalist version of Aquinas from Biel. For example, Biel argued that "it should not be said that there is in the sacraments of the new law some supernatural virtue through which they would possess the status of cause, in relation to the sacramental effect."[95] In Luther's German milieu, this type of discourse sounded not unlike semi-Pelagianism, which seemed to cast human freedom into a competitive relationship with divine agency. Luther, therefore, conflated Aquinas's position with a position that was a very poor representation of his actual teaching. It is difficult to assess the degree to which Luther was turned against certain articulations by a preference for nominalist theology itself. Or possibly whether his unconscious

---

93. Morerod, *Ecumenism and Philosophy*, 53.

94. Ibid., 54. For a summary presentation of the sacramental doctrine of the nominalist school, see *Dictionnaire de théologie catholique*, vol. 14, part 1, columns 590–593.

95. Biel, *Collectorium circa IV libros sententiarum*, IV/I, d. 1, q. 1, a. 2, conclusion 4, p. 23, cited in Morerod, *Ecumenism and Philosophy*, 76.

absorption of some principles nominalist theology determined his own sacramental doctrine in a more implicit fashion.

For example, Luther critiques Aquinas's teaching that Baptism possesses a spiritual power, something that Luther extends only to God's Word, and not to the sacraments or elements used in the sacramental celebration. In the Smalcald Articles, which Luther composed as a summary of his doctrine in 1537, he declares: "we do not hold with Thomas and the monastic preachers [or Dominicans] who forget the Word (God's institution) and say that God has imparted to the water a spiritual power, which through the water washes away sin."[96] Similarly, in his earlier work, *The Pagan Servitude of the Church* [*Babylonian Captivity of the Church*], Luther teaches: "Unless faith is present, or comes to life in baptism, the ceremony is of no avail; indeed it is a stumbling-block not only at the moment we receive baptism but for all our life thereafter."[97]

Luther is, of course, quite right to affirm the close union that exists between faith and Baptism, as well as the necessity of faith for salvation. But his assertion that the actual rite "is of no avail" does not follow. This places the soteriological efficacy of Baptism in the fervor of the recipient's faith and not in the divine power acting through the rite. One can see here a tinge of the late Medieval philosophical influence that denies that any instrumental cause could confer a divine effect.

A helpful analogy can be drawn between the position on free will that Luther developed against the semi-Pelagian tendencies of his day and his sacramental doctrine. The humanists of Luther's day, Reinhard Hütter explains, maintained that human freedom could merit grace by its own unaided power: "freedom [according to the

96. Smalcald Articles, Part III, Article V. Luther also disagrees with Scotus in this section, but his disagreement with Scotus is not for placing causality in Baptism itself, but for placing the causation in God's will and not in his Word. See Denis Janz, *Luther on Thomas Aquinas: The Angelic Doctor in the Thought of the Reformer* (Stuttgart: Franz Steiner Verlag Wiesbaden GMB, 1989), 66.

97. Martin Luther, "Pagan Servitude of the Church," in *Martin Luther: Selections from His Writings*, ed. John Dillenberger (New York: Anchor Books, 1961), 293.

humanists] must be understood as just this power, a power essentially unaffected by original sin."[98] "This, in a nutshell," Hütter explains, is the position of the dominant theological school in Germany in the fifteenth and early sixteenth centuries — a position with which also many humanists, not least Erasmus, sympathized. Martin Luther received his philosophical and theological training in this school. However, under the influence of his intense study of the Apostle Paul and of the late Augustine, he began to reject, branch and root, his school's *theological* account of grace and free will, rightly understanding its position to be incompatible with the teaching of St. Paul. But never rejecting the *philosophical* tenets of nominalism, Luther's corrective move veered to the opposite extreme: God is not merely the first but the sole agent of the act of conversion, with the human in a state of utter passivity.[99]

The long and short of this examination is that Luther's position, when read in the context of late Medieval disputes played out in the schools of Germany, appears to be touched by the philosophical doctrines that he assimilated from the "open nominalism" imbedded in Biel's work and other trends of his day. In particular, these tenets place divine and human agency in an irrevocably competitive relationship. Whether or not he was an open advocate or critic of the sacramental doctrine of occasionalism is somewhat beside the point, inasmuch as his position seems effectively to deny that there is any operative or causal power intrinsic to the operation of the sacramental rite itself.

Moral Causality

Moral causality is another theory of sacramental theology. It is historically associated with Melchior Cano (†1560) and John of Lugo (†1669), but it has a wide and popular appeal, and some indirect resonance in Reformed theology.[100] In this view the sacraments

98. Hütter, "'Thomas the Augustinian' — Recovering a Surpassing Synthesis of Grace and Free Will," in Reinhard Hütter, *Dust Bound for Heaven: Explorations in the Theology of Thomas Aquinas* (Grand Rapids, Mich.: William B. Eerdmans, 2012), 253.

99. Ibid., 253–54.

100. See Gallagher, *Significando Causant*, 154–61.

cause by "having in themselves a moral worth or value which moves God to give grace to their recipients."[101] Lugo, for example, relates the causation of the sacraments to their effects in terms of prayer: they stand as Christ's "visible manifestations" to the Father of his prayer for those receiving the sacraments.[102] As Leeming explains, "a moral cause always acts by presenting motives why another should act."[103] Often advocates of this theory view Christ's intercession as the operative moral agency moving God to act in the sacraments.

Some moral causes do indeed work in the order of efficiency, but it is difficult to see how this theory applies in regard to the operation of the sacraments, when the operative moral efficiency would stem from Christ's petitioning of the Father and not from the celebration of the rite itself. When applied to the sacraments, it is God, not the sacraments as instruments, who causes grace, whereas the moral cause works by way of "command, counsel, merit, or prayer."[104]

This is why, in his assessment of approaches to moral causality, Gallagher asks, "If the sacraments are our acts that move God, why are they efficacious *ex opere operato*, and in such a special way, when our other acts, prayer, and so forth, are not so?"[105] This question raises difficulties for the theory of moral causality in two opposing directions. On the one hand it "seems to make the sacraments signs for God.... But certainly God needs no sign to remind Him of the passion," Gallagher argues. On the other hand,

[t]he Sacraments, then, must be signs for men, but in that case how are they causes of grace, which is caused by God alone; for the sacraments signify and cause, and thus should be signs and causes used by God. They cannot

---

101. Leeming, *Principles of Sacramental Theology*, 287.

102. See Mirallles, *I Sacramenti Cristiani*, 342.

103. Leeming, *Principles of Sacramental Theology*, 300.

104. Miralles, *I Sacramenti Cristiani*, 341. Related to moral causality is the theory of intentional causality, which maintains that the sacramental signs have an instrumental power as manifestations of Christ's will in instituting them to bestow grace. The signs thus serve, not as direct causes of grace, but as visible manifestations of Christ's promise or intention to bestow grace. See ibid., 343. For a presentation of the theory of intentional causality as developed by Cardinal Billot, see Gallagher, *Significando Causant*, 161–88.

105. Gallagher, *Significando Causant*, 160.

be at once causes used by men to move God, and signs used by God to signify that He is giving grace.[106]

What makes a moral cause differ from an occasional cause is that a moral cause provides a motivating factor that explains the causal action — for example, Christ's merit or intercession — whereas the motive of an occasional cause is the occasion itself and not some motive or moral trait that incites the action.

The Mystery-Presence Theory of Dom Odo Casel

An important variation of moral theory of sacramental causality is the influential "mystery-presence" (*mysteriengegenwart*) theory of twentieth-century Benedictine Dom Odo Casel. Casel was a monk of the famed Monastery of Maria Laach, which was an influential center of the liturgical movement.[107] His most original contribution is his presentation of the Church's liturgy and sacraments in light of his careful study of the ancient notion of "mystery" in biblical, patristic, and pagan sources. "The mystery," according to Casel, "is a sacred ritual action in which a saving deed is made present through the rite; the congregation, by performing the rite, take part in the saving act, and thereby win salvation."[108] The name "mystery-presence" is derived from Casel's unification of the rite or "ritual action" with the presence of the "saving deed" in the mystery.

Casel's work contains many insights, but his theory of the efficacious presence of Christ's saving deeds in the sacraments creates, perhaps, even more ambiguities about the nature of the sacraments and their mode of causation than the insights that it contains. In particular, Casel never clarifies how a completed historical event, a

---

106. Ibid.

107. The treatment of Casel's theory as a variation of moral causality is not iron-clad; it could easily be viewed from another perspective. The rationale is simply that the conflation of the rites with the saving events gives them an efficacy that is derived from the operative power of Christ's merit in the events, and not from the operational efficacy of the rites themselves.

108. Odo Casel, OSB, *The Mystery of Christian Worship and Other Writings*, trans. I. T. Hale (Westminster, Md.: Newman Press, 1962), 54.

saving action, is made present to a recipient who is separated from the event in time and space. For Casel, it is not the power of Christ's saving acts, or a mediation or participation in them through the signification of the signs, but the presence of the events themselves that constitutes the mystery of the sacraments.[109]

Furthermore, as Edward Schillebeeckx points out, Casel's view of Christ's saving deeds in history fails to account for their "perennial character." Given that "time itself is irreversible," Schillebeeckx observes, "a contradiction is inherent" in Casel's thesis.[110] "As the realization in human form of the redeeming Trinity," Schillebeeckx argues against Casel, "the historical mysteries of Christ's life, which were the personal acts of the God-man, are a permanent, enduring reality in the mode of the Lord's existence in glory. The mystery of saving worship, or Christ's act of redemption is, in the mode of glory, an eternally actual reality, as the Epistle to the Hebrews repeatedly stresses."[111]

Leeming points out that Casel's presentation constitutes, fundamentally, a redefinition of mystery as an event. "What is present is not some mysterious efficacy in the symbols, nor the life of God, nor the person of Christ, nor the effect produced," Leeming notes, "but there is present the saving act itself as it existed in Christ's human life and it is present to produce conformity to the 'mystery' of Christ in us." This means, Leeming continues, that "it is not *Christus passus* who is present, but *ipsa passio*, as advocates of the opinion so often assert and insist. The presence is said to transcend space and time, and sometimes the 'saving acts' are said to be present *per modum substantiae* …"[112]

---

109. For a critique of Casel from a liturgical perspective, see Louis Bouyer, *Liturgical Piety* (Notre Dame, Ind.: University of Notre Dame Press, 1955), 15–22.

110. Edward Schillebeeckx, *Christ the Sacrament of the Encounter with God* (Franklin, Wis.: Sheed and Ward, 1963), 55–56.

111. Ibid., 58–59. Leeming points out, furthermore, that a basic problem with Casel's thesis is that it conflates sacramental effects with the sacramental mode of causation: "To insist that a conformity [to Christ] is produced [by the sacraments], and that the mysteries are present, does not explain how the mysteries produce the conformity." Leeming, *Principles of Sacramental Theology*, 312.

112. Bernard Leeming, "Recent Trends in Sacramental Theology," *Irish Theological Quarterly* 23 (1956): 195–217, at 207.

Furthermore, the subject of Casel's mystery-presence theory is the experience that the worshipping community has of the salvific deed. "Some scholars," Reginald Lynch explains, "see the emphasis on mystery that appears during the modern period as an extension of the nominalist emphasis on the radical omnipotence and freedom of God and its accompanying reticence regarding causal connections."[113] As a result of this trend, "the rhetoric of mystery can appear as a supplement for metaphysical explanation."[114] Lynch observes that under the influence of Casel's "methodological choices," therefore, "there was a decided shift [in the twentieth century] toward liturgy-as-event using the category of symbol or sign."[115]

It is the sacraments, precisely as causes in the order of instrumental efficiency, which make the power of Christ's saving action and his risen life present throughout time by their signification. There is no need to conflate sacrament and historical event — or to insinuate that the sacrament becomes the historical event in mystery. Christ instituted the signs precisely for the sake of actively using their signification as the causal (instrumental) means of applying the power of his Passion and risen life.

Trent, the Protestants, and Various Theories of Sacramental Causality

Where do all of these different theories of sacramental causality stand in light of the *ex opere operato* doctrine of Trent? In an important and influential study, Daniel Iturrioz has argued that the teaching of Trent on the *ex opere operato* causality of the sacraments (especially canon 8) was not meant by the Council Fathers to stand as an exclusive affirmation of Thomas's position, nor was it meant as a condemnation of the other positions of the schoolmen.[116] Tri-

---

113. Lynch, "The Sacraments as Causes of Sanctification," 827.
114. Ibid.
115. Ibid., 828.
116. Iturrioz's work was published in article form as "La definición del Concilio de

dentine historian Hubert Jedin, and many others, have consistently invoked Iturrioz's work, underscoring that the primary aim of Trent was to condemn specific errors (codified as theses at Trent) of the Protestants without taking sides on the intramural debates within the Catholic Church between the schools. This went so far, according to Jedin, as avoiding "as much as possible the use of the apparatus of scholastic concepts" in the formulation of Trent's decrees.[117]

This historical assessment, though accurate regarding the diverse schools represented at Trent, has led subsequent authors in sacramental theology to an extension of the historical point that lacks logical and theological coherence. Kenan Osborne, for example, makes the following assertion when commenting on Trent's intention to condemn only the position of the Protestants and not any of the positions held by the schoolmen: "Each theory [on sacramental causality advocated before and at the time of Trent] remains acceptable teaching within the Catholic Church."[118]

The problem with the logic of this reasoning is that it falsely assumes that although no specific Scholastic theory of sacramental causality was explicitly condemned by Trent (as a result of the Council's wish to focus on the Protestants), each pre-Tridentine theory is equally able to account for the *ex opere operato* doctrine promulgated by the Council. Even if one follows Gallagher's conclusion that "objective efficacy ... but no decision for or against any of the opinions taught by Catholic theologians, is the council's teaching," it is not clear just how many of these theories of sacramental causality affirm an objective efficacy.[119]

Trento sobre la causalidad de los sacramentos," *Estudios eclesiásticos* 24 (1950): 291–340. The work was also published in book form under the same title (Madrid: Estudios Oniensis, 1951).

117. Hubert Jedin, *The First Sessions at Trent 1545–47*, vol. 2 of *A History of the Council of Trent*, trans. Dom Ernest Graf, OSB (London: Thomas Nelson and Sons, 1961), 372–76, at 374.

118. Kenan Osborne, *Sacramental Theology: A General Introduction* (New York: Paulist Press, 1988), 57.

119. Gallagher, *Significando Causant*, 52.

Refraining from explicitly condemning an extant position does not by default mean that the position is judged to be commensurate with a promulgated teaching going forward. This would be tantamount to saying that any theory about Christ's relation to the Father prior to Nicaea stood as "acceptable teaching" after Nicaea, as long as it was not explicitly included in the Arian condemnation.

There were many prudential reasons why the Fathers at Trent focused on the positions of the Protestants and shied away from debates between the various schools within the Catholic Church. But after the condemnation of the Protestants and the positive articulation of the *ex opere operato* doctrine, Catholic theologians of any school or theological sympathy alike have stood under and accountable to the teaching put forward by Trent, which affirms an objective efficacy of the operation of the sacramental rites themselves. The decrees of Trent and subsequent magisterial interventions, after all, are not mere negations of Protestant theses. They contain positive theological content about the operative power of the sacramental rites. It is not enough for Catholic theologians to rest in historical positions that, for whatever reasons, were not mentioned in Tridentine condemnations. Theologians ought, to the best of their ability, to refine and develop theories in light of magisterial teaching. "Trent clearly ruled out," Fr. Lynch notes,

among other things, theories which reduced the sacraments to mere external signs. Aquinas' original objection to the extrincisist approach was that it reduced the causality operative in the sacraments of the new law to the accidental status of sign, no different from the sacraments of the old law. To this extent, Trent's determination to avoid sacramental models which reduce the sacraments to mere outward signs broadly reflects Aquinas' original concerns.[120]

Furthermore, in the Decree on Justification, Trent teaches that "the instrumental cause is the sacrament of baptism, which is the 'sacrament of faith', without which [faith] no one has ever been jus-

---

120. Lynch, "The Sacraments as Causes of Sanctification," 821–22.

tified."[121] The common reading of the Council of Trent points out that none of the canons were directed against Catholic authors or schools, yet it is the case, as Miralles explains, that with the sacraments "every theological solution must be coherent with this dogma [*ex opere operato*]" of Trent.[122] St. Thomas's doctrine of the instrumental efficient causality of the sacraments is especially helpful in manifesting the objective and intrinsic efficacy of the sacraments.

Sacramental causality is an indispensable doctrine of the Christian faith. It indicates the consoling revelation that the grace merited by Christ is continually available in the sacraments of the Church in such a fashion that their efficacy (to be distinguished from their fruition) is safeguarded by the infallible agency of Christ himself. As such, the sacraments are the surest, most direct path to the bestowal and increase in the participation in the divine life that is made possible by the gift of grace.

---

121. Heinrich Denzinger, *Enchiridion symbolorum*, Session 6, Janurary 13, 1547, Decree on Justification, 377 (§1529). Miralles points out that "this genre of causality is not exclusive to baptism, but common to all the other sacraments." Miralles, *I Sacramenti Cristiani*, 332.

122. Miralles, *I Sacramenti Cristiani*, 332.

EIGHT

Sacramental Grace

The Christian theology of grace begins with the doctrine of the triune God. This does not mean, of course, that God, who is uncreated and infinite, somehow gives himself additional perfections through grace. Rather, the doctrine of grace explains what it is that God gives to humanity, in addition to the created order, through the visible and invisible missions of the persons of the Son and Holy Spirit, to heal the wounds of sins and to reorient humanity to God in the justice of Christ. There is a very real sense in which the whole message of the gospel is contained in seed form, at least, in the fact that, in addition to the eternal generation of the Son and the eternal spiration of the Spirit in God, the Son and Spirit have missions in creation. As the oft-quoted Bible passage John 3:16 indicates: "God so loved the world that he *gave* his only Son."

The Trinitarian and Christological Foundation of Sacramental Grace

How are followers of Christ to understand the Father's giving of the Son? The giving of the Son by the Father signifies, Aquinas explains, his "becoming man, according to His visible mission, or likewise by dwelling in man according to His invisible mission."[1] What do the missions of the Son and the Holy Spirit have to do with the question of grace, let alone sacramental grace? The temporal missions of the Son and the Holy Spirit, Thomas explains, following St. Augustine, are for no other purpose than "the creature's sanctification." "Since then," Thomas continues, "the creature's sanctification is by sanctifying grace, it follows that the mission of the divine person is only by sanctifying grace."[2] The implications of this doctrine are profound — even mystical.

Is it not true, however, that God is omnipresent to creation? How could God come to people through grace, if God is already present to every part of his creation? Is he not already present everywhere? Or, from a religious perspective if someone were to know that he has been touched by God (i.e., "saved," as the evangelicals like to put it), how can the Son or Holy Spirit be sent (again) to where they already are? The answer to such questions accentuates the profundity of the gift of grace and the seminal importance of each of the seven sacraments in the unfolding of the Christian life. "God is in all things," Thomas acknowledges, affirming the divine omnipresence, "by his essence, power and presence, according to His one common mode, as the cause existing in the effects which participate in his goodness."[3] Intimacy with God, however, is not exhausted by this "common mode."

"Above and beyond this common mode," Thomas teaches,

there is one special mode belonging to the rational nature wherein God is said to be present as the object known is in the knower, and the beloved in the lover. And since the rational creature by its operation of knowledge and love attains to God Himself, according to this special mode God is said not only to exist in the rational creature but also to dwell therein as in His own temple. So no other effect can be put down as the reason why the divine person is in the rational creature in a new mode, except sanctifying grace.[4]

1. *ST* I, q. 43, a. 2.   2. Ibid., a. 3, sed contra.

3. Ibid., a. 3.   4. Ibid.

The visible mission of the Son and the invisible missions of the Son and Holy Spirit through the outpouring of sanctifying grace do not imply that God comes to be where he was not already present prior to the sending, for he was already there (and everywhere) according to the common mode. Rather — and here is the profundity of this doctrine — the mission accomplished in grace means that God "begins to exist where he was before, but in a new way, in which sense mission is ascribed to the divine persons. Thus, mission as regards the one to whom it is sent implies two things, the indwelling of grace, and a certain renewal by grace."[5]

As a result, Catholic theology does not deny the general presence of God in creation; rather, it affirms that through the additional gift of grace God comes to be in a newer and fuller way in the hearts of the faithful. In his unfathomable generosity and love, God makes the growth, augmentation, and renewal of this indwelling possible through the causality of grace by the sacraments.

This does not mean, Thomas clarifies, that the sacraments themselves are the objects of the divine mission. Rather, God ordains that the mission of the divine Persons be fulfilled in the faithful by their receiving the gift of grace through the sacraments: "the mission of the divine person is not sent to the sacraments, but to those who receive grace through the sacraments."[6] This reception is where the triune God, grace, and the sacramental life of the Church connect. Through the invisible mission of grace, mediated by the instrumental causality of the sacraments, God comes to the faithful in a new and fuller way — each time a sacrament is fruitfully received. Thus the affirmation that grace is caused by the sacraments does not lead to a denial of God's presence within the created order. Moreover, sacramental causality of grace does not, as Chauvet alleges, reduce the sacraments to a technical means of production. Rather, the doctrine of sacramental causality is a positive affirmation that God's

5. Ibid., a. 6.
6. Ibid., ad 4.

presence is augmented and deepened in the faithful through the operative power of the sacraments.

Catholic theology needs a new integration of the doctrine of grace, in all of its moral and spiritual implications for the Church, with the doctrine of sacramental causality. Aquinas is a tremendous resource for this task. In his teaching on grace, Thomas displays a full awareness of the connections that exist between the economy of salvation, Christ, and the sacraments:

> As in the person of Christ the humanity causes our salvation by grace, the Divine power being the principal agent, so likewise in the sacraments of the New Law, which are derived from Christ, grace is instrumentally caused by the sacraments, and principally by the power of the Holy Ghost working in the sacraments, according to John 3:5: "Unless a man be born again of water and the Holy Ghost he cannot enter into the kingdom of God."[7]

It is a significant theological mistake, therefore, to divorce the general doctrine of grace, the Christian moral life, which depends on grace, and the universal call to holiness from the sacraments, especially since they are instrumental causes of the grace on which they depend.

Sacramental Grace

The question of sacramental grace brings into focus the transformation and ongoing sanctification that takes place in the justification of the sinner. In the second article of the question 62 of the Third Part of the *Summa theologiae*, Thomas asks "whether sacramental grace confers anything in addition to the Grace of the Virtues and Gifts?" This question gets at two issues relating to the sevenfold sacramental life of the Church.

First, if one has been baptized or been converted to Christ, is there any benefit in receiving the other sacraments on a regular basis? That is: do the various sacraments accomplish anything more in

---

7. *ST* I-II, q. 112, a. 1.

the soul than the general grace of justification? In popular evangelical language, is there any further grace needed than the grace of "being saved"? Second, why are there so many sacraments, rather than just one, absolutely necessary sacrament (i.e., Baptism)?

The answer to the first question (is there any grace specific to the sacraments beyond the general state) requires some understanding of the nature of grace. In his discussions of grace, Thomas consistently refers to 2 Peter 1:4, which declares that the faithful are made "partakers of the divine nature." This does not mean that God destroys the persons in whom he dwells according to grace by assimilating them to himself. Rather, the divine life is in men and women through grace "inasmuch as a habitual gift is infused by God into the soul."[8]

This gift therefore elevates the graced individual's existence, because by it he participates in a new mode of communion with God. "Inasmuch as [grace] is the expression or participation of the Divine goodness," Thomas explains, "it is nobler than the nature of the soul" in which it dwells; thus the soul's union with God is elevated by the gift of grace beyond the natural mode of participation to the supernatural.[9] Grace, understood in this sense, does not correspond to just one aspect or faculty of human existence (such as a specific gift, like healing, which is understood as another type of grace); rather it perfects and elevates human existence at its core. This "core elevation" of the soul corresponds to the inner healing that is needed as a result of sin. Certain serious sins, Christ teaches, such as "evil thoughts, fornication, theft, murder, adultery, coveting, wickedness, deceit, licentiousness, envy, slander, pride, foolishness," proceed "from within, out of the heart of man.... All these evil things come from within, and they defile a man" (Mk 7:21–23).

Thomas brings this basic understanding of grace and humanity's need for inner healing and rectitude into the theology of sacramental grace. Grace, Thomas explains,

8. *ST* I-II, q. 110, a. 2.
9. Ibid., ad 2.

perfects the essence of the soul, in so far as it is a certain participated likeness of the Divine Nature. And just as the soul's powers flow from its essence, so from grace there flow certain perfections into the powers of the soul, which are called virtues and gifts, whereby the powers are perfected in reference to their actions.[10]

This catechesis on grace enables Thomas to offer a clear teaching about the grace that is specific to the sacraments and thus distinguishable from the broad category of grace and virtue understood generically. Thomas identifies the grace specific to the sacraments by reasoning from the purpose which the divine wisdom ordained each sacrament to fulfill in the Christian life to the grace which makes this fulfillment possible. "The sacraments are ordained unto certain special effects," Thomas reasons,

which are necessary in the Christian life: thus Baptism is ordained unto a certain spiritual regeneration, by which man dies to vice and becomes a member of Christ: which effect is something special in addition to the actions of the soul's powers: and the same holds true of the other sacraments.[11]

The conclusion to this line of reasoning is as follows:

Consequently just as the virtues and gifts confer, in addition to grace commonly so called, a certain special perfection ordained to the powers' proper actions, so does sacramental grace confer, over and above grace commonly so called, and in addition to the virtues and gifts, a certain Divine assistance in obtaining the end of the sacrament. It is thus that sacramental grace confers something in addition to the grace of the virtues and gifts.[12]

In direct answer to the first question put forward above, then, it must be affirmed that there is much benefit to receiving sacraments frequently. Even if one could have absolute knowledge of being among the elect, which the Church denies,[13] in the frequent recep-

---

10. *ST* III, q. 62, a. 2.

11. Ibid.

12. Ibid.

13. In the Decrees on Justification, Can. 15, Trent teaches: "If anyone says that he has absolute and infallible certitude that he will surely have the great gift of perseverance to the end, ... unless he has learned this by special revelation, let him be anathema." Heinrich Denzinger, *Enchiridion symbolorum*, 386 (§1566).

tion of the sacraments one avails himself of the ongoing divine assistance that God offers to help him reach the intended purpose of the sacraments — ultimately eternal life.

Furthermore, the reality of sacramental grace corresponds perfectly to the spiritual truth about grace that Thomas developed in his theology of the Trinitarian missions: namely, God can always come to someone in a newer and fuller way — even if he is already present to them. "The fruit of the sacraments," Gilles Emery explains, "is not only of the moral order, but rather it concerns first and foremost the *being* of believers. By the coming of the Son of God and the gift of the Holy Spirit, believers are renewed and transformed in their very being."[14] Sacramental grace is not only a beginning point, with Baptism, of the supernatural life of the soul. It is the normative means by which God has established that his presence within the very being of the faithful grow and increase unto eternal life.

The reality of sacramental grace leads to the answer, which is now rather obvious, to the second question, namely, why is there a sevenfold sacramental system. These celebrations are not redundant; they are not just seven different ways of obtaining grace, as if grace were just a generic reality. Rather, in each of the seven sacraments, God provides graces that are ordered to the full flowering and perfection of the purpose that each sacrament is ordered to have within the Christian life. This is why having seven sacraments is not repetitive: each offers grace, healing, and assistance that enable the recipient to grow and deepen in that area of the Christian life that each sacrament perfects. "Thus grace, in passing through the sacraments," Charles Journet explains, "is enriched with various modalities and hues, like light passing through a window of seven different colors."[15]

14. Gilles Emery, *The Trinity: An Introduction to the Catholic Doctrine of the Triune God*, trans. Matthew Levering (Washington, D.C.: The Catholic University of America Press, 2011), 3.

15. Charles Journet, *The Meaning of Grace*, trans. A. V. Littledale (Princeton, N.J.: Scepter Publishers, 1996), 120.

the invisible mission of the Son & the Holy Spirit and the visible mission of the Son & the Holy Spirit

Catholic theologians and interpreters of St. Thomas have debated the proper category (sanctifying or actual) of grace within which to situate sacramental grace. The position associated with the interpretation of John of St. Thomas and the Carmelites of Salamanca, that sacramental grace is a modality of sanctifying grace, seems nearest to Thomas's own position, which Leeming defines thus: "Sacramental grace is sanctifying grace with a special modification, which one can call a special energy or strength or 'virtuality' with regard to the activities demanded by reception of the sacrament."[16]

When Thomas articulates the specific effects of individual sacraments he speaks his mind more openly. For example, when treating the effect of the sacrament of Confirmation, Thomas asks pointedly, "whether sanctifying grace [gratia gratum faciens] is bestowed in this sacrament?" In his answer to this question, he connects the theology of grace that he developed in question 43 of the First Part in conjunction with the Trinitarian missions to the effect of Confirmation:

In this sacrament ... the Holy Ghost is given to the baptized for strength: just as He was given to the apostles on the day of Pentecost, as we read in Acts 2; and just as He was given to the baptized by the imposition of the apostles' hands, as related in Acts 8:17. Now it has been proved in I, 43, 3 that the Holy Ghost is not sent or given except with sanctifying grace. Consequently it is evident that sanctifying grace is bestowed in this sacrament.[17]

This means, in the words of John of St. Thomas (†1644), that Thomas intends by "sacramental grace" not grace "as commonly meant but as sacramental, that is, as in a special way medicinal of sin and healing by the aid of God and by participation in the redemption of Christ in the Christian life."[18] As Revel explains by means of the analogy of the musical instrument, playing the same piece of music with different instruments realizes the sound of the composition in different ways, according to the specific musical modality of each

16. Leeming, *Principles of Sacramental Theology*, 100.

17. *ST* III, q. 72, a. 7.

18. John of St. Thomas, *Introduction to the Summa Theologiae of Thomas Aquinas*, trans. Ralph McInerny (South Bend, Ind.: St. Augustine's Press, 2004), 169.

particular instrument. The same is true with the gift of grace as bestowed by God on the faithful by the unique instrumental agency of each of the seven sacraments.[19]

This point is accentuated by the fact that the guilt of a past sinful action remains with the sinner after the sinful action has been completed. Hence, Thomas teaches that "in regard to past sins, the acts of which are transitory whereas their guilt remains, man is provided with a special remedy in the sacraments."[20] There is medicinal benefit in receiving the sacraments in relation to past sins, as well as in regard to growth in holiness. Both aspects, cleansing and growth in sanctity, are associated with sanctifying grace, which Thomas, again in relation to Confirmation, affirms: in Confirmation "sanctifying grace is given not only for the remission of sin, but also for growth and stability in righteousness. And thus it is bestowed in this sacrament."[21]

This positive conferral of growth and stabilization in grace by the sacraments accentuates why the sevenfold sacramental system is not redundant, and why each sacramental grace is important in the development of the Christian's spiritual and moral life. "The sacramental grace adds to the sanctifying grace taken in its wide sense," Thomas teaches,

something that produces a special effect, and to which the sacrament is ordained. If, then, we consider, in its wide sense, the grace bestowed in this sacrament [Confirmation], it does not differ from that bestowed in Baptism, but increases what was already there. On the other hand, if we consider it as to that which is added over and above, then one differs in species from the other.[22]

Thomas's presentation of sacramental grace outlines positive and negative aspects, both of which are important for the full un-

---

19. See Revel, *Traité des sacrements: I.2, Baptême et sacramentalité. Don et réception de la grâce baptismale*, 165–67, at 166.
20. *ST* III, q. 62, a. 2, ad 2.
21. *ST* III, q. 72, a. 7, ad 1.
22. Ibid., ad 3. Thomas articulates a similar position in *De veritate*, q. 27, a. 5, ad 12.

folding of the Christian life. Negatively, sacramental grace has a remedial and healing power in relation to sin and the inner disorder resulting from sin. Positively, the sacraments provide specific graces that assist the faithful in reaching the full end or purpose that corresponds to each sacrament. These graces provide healing, forgiveness, restoration and/or growth, and increase in the divine life and intimacy that is present in the soul as a result of the divine indwelling through grace. This doctrine brings the sacraments full circle with St. Paul's teaching that "the charity of God is poured forth in our hearts, by the Holy Spirit, who is given to us" (Rom 5:5).[23]

Grace, Causality, and the Distinction between the Old Law and the New

The two interrelated topics of sacramental grace and causality lie at the core of an important Catholic teaching on a real distinction that exists between modes of causal efficacy operative in the Old Law and in the New.[24] Central to the teaching of St. Paul is that the New Law of grace in Christ accomplishes a spiritual renewal and justification of the sinner that the Old Law was unable to realize through the power of its prescribed rites and observances.

This does not mean that according to Christian theology the practice of the Old Law was not efficacious. But it does mean that there is a distinction between the way in which those who lived under the Old Law prior to Christ were saved and how those who live under the New Law are incorporated into Christ through the sacraments. Thomas taught, for example, that the saints of the Old Law prior to Christ were saved through their practice of the Old Law.

---

23. The Fathers of the Church referred to the progressive transformation of the sinner by grace into the image of Christ as "divinization" or "deification." For a discussion of the Fathers' teaching on role of the sacraments in deification, especially Baptism and the Eucharist, see Daniel A. Keating, *Deification and Grace* (Ave Maria, Fla: Sapientia Press, 2007), 41–61.

24. For an extremely helpful treatment of the relationship between the Old and the New Covenant, with special emphasis on Christ, grace, and the sacramental life of the Church, see Levering, *Christ's Fulfillment of Torah and Temple*.

However, he clarifies that the rites or sacraments of the Old Law did not bestow salvific grace in the same way that the sacraments of the New Law do.[25] Rather, by adherence to the Old Law, Aquinas reasons, those who lived under it manifested a faith in the coming Messiah that had a saving value. Thomas explains the principle as follows: "Whatsoever is set down in the New Testament explicitly and openly as a point of faith, is contained in the Old Testament as a matter of belief, but implicitly, under a figure."[26]

Aquinas integrates this with his understanding of the instrumental efficient causality of the seven sacraments by affirming that "the Fathers of old were justified by faith in Christ's Passion, just as we are." However, he also distinguishes the sacraments of the New Law from those of the Old precisely on the grounds of their internal power to cause grace:

the sacraments of the Old Law were a kind of protestation of that faith, inasmuch as they signified Christ's Passion and its effects. It is therefore manifest that the sacraments of the Old Law were not endowed with any power by which they conduced to the bestowal of justifying grace: and they merely signified faith by which men were justified.[27]

The inability of the sacraments of the Old Law to cause grace, intrinsically, through their own operation, is the fault-line that distinguishes them from the seven sacraments of the New Law.

In its *Decree for the Armenians*, the Council of Florence (1439) takes up this distinction, declaring that the seven sacraments "differ greatly from the sacraments of the Old Law. The latter, in fact, did not cause grace, but they only prefigured the grace to be given through the Passion of Christ."[28]

As a result of their denial of the *ex opere operato* causality of the sacraments, the Protestants generally rejected the idea that the sacraments of the Old Law differed in any way from those of the New

---

25. See ibid., 15–30.
26. *ST* I-II, q. 107, a. 3, ad 1.
27. *ST* III, q. 62, a. 5.
28. Heinrich Denzinger, *Enchiridion symbolorum*, 338 (§1310).

Law with respect to their operational efficacy. Luther, for example, placing the primary agency of justification on the faith of the recipient, argues: "for it is wrong to hold that the sacraments of the New Law differ from those of the Old Law in point of their effective significance." His reason for this assertion is that one and the same God operates through each covenant: "For the God who now saves by baptism and the Supper saved Abel by his sacrifice, Noah by the rainbow, Abraham by circumcision, and the others by their own signs." Luther further argues that "with regard to the meaning of the sacraments, there is no difference between those of the Old Covenant and those of the New, except that you may describe as belonging to the Old Law everything which God did among the patriarchs and their fathers at the time of the Law."[29]

This position fails to appreciate Christ's intention in founding the sacramental system of the Church to aid the faithful in their growth in holiness and divine intimacy through the bestowal of sacramental grace. Denial of any causal distinction between the sacraments of the Old Law and those of the New Law greatly compromises the spiritual importance of each of the sacraments, with the graces and effects specific to them.

As a result of these implications, the Council of Trent issued the following canon: "If anyone says that these same sacraments of the New Law do not differ from the sacraments of the Old Law, except that the ceremonies and external rites are different, let him be anathema."[30]

The doctrine of sacramental grace underscores the immensity of the gift that Christ has given to the Church in the sacraments. As *ex opere operato* causes of grace, the sacraments provide a sure wellspring for the faithful to renew and deepen the presence of the divine life within them. Furthermore, the effects specific to each

29. Martin Luther, "Pagan Servitude of the Church," in *Martin Luther: Selections from His Writings*, 299.

30. Heinrich Denzinger, "Decree on the Sacraments," in *Enchiridion symbolorum*, 389 (§1602, Canon 2).

sacrament indicate both the tremendous aid that each sacrament is ordered to provide within the whole panorama of the Christian life, from life to death, as well as the divine intention to be present to the faithful, concretely, during each major stage and vocation of the Christian life.[31]

---

31. For a helpful treatment of the distinction between the Old and the New Law sacraments that is developed explicitly in terms of causality, see Aquinas's disputed question *De veritate*, q. 27, a. 4.

NINE

Sacramental Character

Sacramental grace is not the only effect of the sacraments.[1] The Church has consistently taught, and continues to do so, that

> [t]he three sacraments of Baptism, Confirmation, and Holy Orders confer, in addition to grace, a sacramental character or "seal" by which the Christian shares in Christ's priesthood and is made a member of the Church according to different states and functions. This configuration to Christ and to the Church, brought about by the Spirit, is indelible; it remains for ever in the Christian as a positive disposition for grace, a promise and guarantee of divine protection, and as a vocation to divine worship and to the service of the Church. Therefore these sacraments can never be repeated.[2]

priest
prophet
king

see picture of chalk board

The reality of character noted in this passage is an effect of the sacraments distinct from sacramental grace. As the passage from the *Catechism* just quoted indicates, character gives Christians a share in Christ's priesthood, configuring them to Christ in such a way that by it they are ordered to the life of worship and various forms of service in the Church. As a result, sacramental character provides an important theological foundation for understanding the point of contact between the acts of worship of the members of the Church

---

1. See Leeming, *Principles of Sacramental Theology*, 129–279; Nicolas, *Synthèse dogmatique*, §756–62.

2. *CCC* §1121.

and Christ's action and presence in the Church through the liturgy. It is the configuration of the soul to Christ by sacramental character that joins his priestly activity from heaven to the worship and ministry that takes place in the Church.

For example, how can it be that a baptized child who has reached the age of First Communion can go to Confession, receive Communion, be confirmed, and even receive (if it is needed) Anointing of the Sick, while an unbaptized adult who has a very advanced understanding of the Christian faith and manifests a desire for Holy Communion, cannot receive any of the sacraments of the Church until the reception of Baptism? Or, why it is that a devout adult who is Baptized and Confirmed cannot hear confessions or celebrate Mass, but a priest who has lost his faith can do both validly? The answer to these scenarios lies in the reality of sacramental character. The child (by Baptism) and the priest (by Orders) are joined to Christ's priesthood by character, while an unbaptized adult with advanced faith lacks the configuration to Christ that is needed to share in his priestly acts.

Biblical Foundation

The basis for the Church's teaching on character is rooted in the Old Testament affirmation of God's irrevocable fidelity to his people and in two aspects of St. Paul's teaching. The first of these Pauline aspects is the affirmation that Christ carries the very stamp of God. The second is his affirmation that the followers of Christ have likewise been sealed (stamped) or marked by God.[3]

The word "character" is used in the Letter to the Hebrews to affirm the co-equality and consubstantiality of the Son and the Father: "He reflects the glory of God and bears the very stamp (*character*) of his nature, upholding the universe by his word and power" (Heb 1:3). St. Paul also used variations of the word *sphragis/signacu-*

3. For a helpful presentation of the biblical foundation of the doctrine of character, see Miralles, *I Sacramenti Cristiani*, 263–67.

lum (seal) to indicate that Christians have been marked or signed by God. For example, Paul teaches that God "has put his seal upon us and given us his Spirit in our hearts as a guarantee" (2 Cor 1:22).[4]

The Contribution of St. Augustine

The basis of the distinction between sacramental grace and the permanent seal was brought into focus in the early Church, especially in North Africa, as a result of the persistence of schismatic groups such as the Donatists.[5] Since from the time of the apostles onward the Church never accepted re-baptism as an authentic apostolic practice, clarification and judgment were needed in cases involving the celebration of the sacraments by schismatics.[6] In cases such as the celebration of Baptism (with the proper matter and form) by schismatics or when a priest ordained within the Church joined a schismatic group for a period of time and then returned to the Church, the real distinction between sacramental grace and the seal of character helped the Church understand why the apostles never re-baptized or re-ordained those who had fallen away.

St. Augustine is an important Father of the Church to turn to on this question.[7] The schismatic group known as the Donatists, which strongly advocated re-baptism and the invalidity of sacraments cel-

4. See also Ephesians 1:13 and 4:30. For a summary of the use of *sphragis* in the Fathers of the Church, see J. Daniélou, *The Bible and the Liturgy* (South Bend, Ind.: University of Notre Dame Press, 1956), 54ff.

5. For an historic and systematic examination of the doctrine of character in Scripture, the Apostolic Fathers, the Greek Fathers, Augustine and the Latin patristic tradition, the schoolmen, and the teachings of the Magisterium, see Revel, *Traité des sacrements: I.2, Baptême et sacramentalité. Don et réception de la grâce baptismale*, 651–87.

6. There is no instance in the New Testament of the conferral of rebaptism on anyone who had previously received Baptism validly. During the pontificate of Pope Stephen I (ca. 254–57) the practice of re-baptism was officially condemned as contrary to the faith of the apostles. See Revel, *Traité des sacrements: I.2, Baptême et sacramentalité. Don et réception de la grâce baptismale*, 616–17.

7. For Augustine's contribution to the development of the doctrine of character, see Leeming, *Principles of Sacramental Theology*, 145–61. For a treatment that includes the doctrine of character in Augustine and many other Fathers, including Basil, Gregory Nazianzen, and John Chrysostom, see Miralles, *I Sacramenti Cristiani*, 267–72.

ebrated in the Catholic Church, was very prominent in his day. At the most basic level, Augustine argues that the error of advocates of re-baptism (or re-ordination) stems from their inability "to distinguish between the sacrament and the efficacy or working out of a sacrament."[8] Not every valid sacramental celebration is fruitful. Those who receive sacraments in a state of sin place an obstacle in the way of the fruition of the sacrament. The problem, however, in these cases does not lie in the sacrament that was validly received. The recipient's sins do not invalidate the sacramental reality, which is a work of Christ, but they do prevent the grace that is available in the sacrament from flowering in their lives.

Augustine teaches "that a man can be baptized with the true baptism of Christ, and that yet his heart, persisting in malice or sacrilege, may not allow remission of sins to be given." This same man, however, because he was baptized "is purged by faithful discipline and truthful confession, which he could not be without baptism, so that what was given before becomes then powerful to work his salvation."[9]

As can been seen, Augustine does not reduce the sacramental reality merely to the transient celebration of the external sign.[10] Rather, something of the sacrament remains or abides after the celebration, even if the sacramental grace is lost or impeded by sin.

8. Augustine, *On Baptism, Against the Donatists*, 6.1, cited in Colman O'Neill, *Sacramental Realism: A General Theory of the Sacraments* (Chicago: Midwest Theological Forum, 1998), 131.

9. Augustine, "On Baptism, Against the Donatists," in *Augustine: The Writings against the Manicheans, and Against the Donatists*, vol. 4 of Nicene and Post-Nicene Fathers, ed. Philip Schaff (Peabody: Hendrickson, 1994), 419 (book 1, chap. 12.18).

10. Nicholas Haring argues with ample evidence that Augustine's primary intention with his use of the word "character" was to affirm the permanence and lasting nature of a validly celebrated sacrament because of the primacy of Christ's agency in the efficacy of the sacraments. "Since it is *He who baptizes*," Haring explains, summarizing Augustine's usage of character, "Baptism both as a transitory action and lasting effect is final and above human interference. Its form or *character* is inviolable and cannot be destroyed or changed. Its effect cannot be undone by man because the consecration and *sanctitas* which Christ produces in the recipient is a lasting *sacramentum*. Any attempt to repeat it is ultimately an insult and injustice to Christ who baptized and to the form prescribed by Him." See Nicholas M. Haring, SAC, "St. Augustine's Use of the Word *Character*," *Mediaeval Studies* 14 (1952): 79–97, at 96.

When the impediment of sin is removed by reconciliation with the Church, Augustine explains, "the sacrament now begins in unity to be of avail for the remission of his sins, which could not so avail him as received in schism."[11] To express the permanence of a validly celebrated sacrament Augustine draws on the word character, using phrases such as *"character sacramenti," "character dominicus," "character Imperatoris (Christi)," and "character regius."*[12]

Theological insights of these sorts helped the Church to gain a deeper appreciation for the distinction between sacramental grace, which can be lost or impeded by sin, and the abiding reality of the sacrament. There is more to character, however, than simply its indelibility.

St. Thomas on Character and Christ's Priesthood

St. Thomas utilizes the reality of the Christian's deputation to worship as an example for better understanding sacramental character.[13] When someone is deputed for a specific role, such as a police officer or soldier, that person is commissioned by way of the deputation, which normally comes with a visible marking such as a badge, uniform, or, in the ancient world, a tattoo to perform a task that those lacking the deputation are unable validly to perform (e.g., non-police officers have no authority to issue traffic tickets).

In deputing Christians to the life of sacramental worship, God marks or seals their souls with sacramental character. "Since," Thomas teaches, "by the sacraments men are deputed to a spiritual service pertaining to the worship of God, it follows that by their means the faithful receive a certain spiritual character."[14]

---

11. Augustine, "On Baptism, Against the Donatists," 419 (book 1, chap. 12.18).

12. See Augustine's *Sermo ad Caesar.* Plebem. 2 and Sermo 71, 19, 32 [PL vol. 38, p. 462]; all cited in Leeming, *Principles of Sacramental Theology*, 154.

13. See *ST* III, q. 63, a. 1.

14. Ibid. Nicolas notes that "from this point of view, character is a consecration of the believer, analogous to the consecration of an object, reserved for God." *Synthèse dogmatique*, §758.

Distinguishing Grace and Character: Character as a Spiritual Power

Just what is this spiritual character and how does it differ from grace? The faithful, Thomas explains, "are deputed to a two-fold end. First and principally to the enjoyment of glory. And for this purpose they are marked with the seal of grace." The second end to which the faithful are deputed is "to receive, or to bestow on others, things pertaining to the worship of God. And this, properly speaking, is the purpose of the sacramental character."[15] To receive divine gifts or bestow them on others, Thomas recognizes, "[S]ome power is needed; for to bestow something on others, active power is necessary; and in order to receive, we need a passive power."[16]

This teaching is very important for understanding the nature of character, its role in the Church and Christian life, and how it is distinct from grace. Recall that grace is not in the soul as a power or faculty, but rather it perfects the very essence of the soul, such that all acts and faculties flowing from the essence of the soul take on a sanctified quality when the soul is in grace. Character, however, is not ordered to the end of the "enjoyment of glory" but for the receiving or giving of divine things.

What is needed for this is not a gift seated in the essence of the soul, like grace, but "a certain spiritual power ordained unto things pertaining to the Divine worship."[17] In searching for the most scientific articulation of the reality of character within the soul, Thomas relates it to the second species of Aristotle's accident of quality.[18] This insight is very helpful in identifying character's standing within the soul. As contrasted with a disposition, which may be fleeting, or even a firmer habit, Aristotle defines the second species of quality as "an inborn capacity to accomplish something with ease."[19]

As a power or capacity in the soul to give and receive those things

---

15. *ST* III, q. 63, a. 3.   16. Ibid., a. 2.
17. Ibid.   18. Ibid.
19. See Aristotle's *Categories* 9.20.

pertaining to divine worship, character is what capacitates the faithful to share and participate in Christ's priestly activity, which is the foundation of the sacramental liturgy. "The whole rite of the Christian religion," Aquinas teaches, "is derived from Christ's priesthood." As a result of the fact that Christ's priestly worship is the source and foundation of Christianity, "it is clear that the sacramental character is specially the character of Christ, to Whose priesthood the faithful are likened by reason of the sacramental characters, which are nothing else than certain participations of Christ's Priesthood, flowing from Christ Himself."[20] The capacity or power that is infused into the soul as a sacramental character is a share or participation in Christ's own priesthood.

Since Christ is the Incarnate Word, his priestly actions are unique in the order of worship. By nature and even more so as a result of the Fall, humanity has no natural share or participation in these privileged actions. What Aquinas clarifies is that sacramental character is the means by which fallen humanity is capacitated to participate in Christ's ongoing priestly mediation from heaven, which is realized on earth in the sacraments.[21]

What makes the sacramental liturgy of the Church uniquely efficacious is not the mere horizontal gathering of the faithful, but the fact that the liturgical synaxis is joined in a special way to Christ's heavenly and eternal priesthood by sacramental characters.[22] Be-

---

20. ST III, q. 63, a. 3.

21. See Nicolas, Synthèse dogmatique, §759.

22. While this is true of all the faithful who have received Baptism (and Confirmation), the teaching of Vatican II on the uniqueness of the sacerdotal characters caused by Holy Orders is important to keep in mind: "Though they differ from one another in essence and not only in degree, the common priesthood of the faithful and the ministerial or hierarchical priesthood are nonetheless interrelated: each of them in its own special way is a participation in the one priesthood of Christ. The ministerial priest, by the sacred power he enjoys, teaches and rules the priestly people; acting in the person of Christ, he makes present the Eucharistic sacrifice, and offers it to God in the name of all the people. But the faithful, in virtue of their royal priesthood, join in the offering of the Eucharist." Lumen Gentium §10.2, emphasis added. For a discussion of Vatican II's doctrine of sacerdotal character, see Guy Mansini, "Sacerdotal Character at the Second Vatican Council," The Thomist 66 (2002): 369–94; Roger W. Nutt, "Sacerdotal Character and the Munera Christi: Reflections on the

What character do the faithful who are Baptized or Confirmed receive?,

cause character is a share in Christ's own priesthood, sacramental actions are participatory in Christ's own ongoing ministry as eternal high priest from heaven.[23]

Because of its nature as participating in Christ's own priesthood, character is indelible. From that participatory nature also flows the non-repeatability of the three sacraments — Baptism, Confirmation, and Orders — that confer it. Whereas the power corresponding to a badge or some other sign indicating a deputation is only coextensive with the office or term-limit of the commission by which it is bestowed, sacramental character gives the soul a participation in an eternal reality, namely, Christ's priesthood. The Letter to the Hebrews, following Psalm 110:4, indicates the eternity of Christ's priesthood: "thou art a priest forever according to the order of Melchisedek." The character, therefore, that is seated in the soul of the Christian faithful is rooted in the eternity of Christ's priesthood. This is why the character, and therefore the ability to return to the Church through Penance, remains even if grace is lost.

Sacramental Character in the Life of the Christian and the Church

The answers to the questions raised at the beginning of this chapter are now evident. The reason why a baptized child is able to receive Holy Communion and other sacraments but an unbaptized adult who has well-formed faith cannot receive Holy Communion or participate in the sacramental life of the Church can be given in one word — character. By Baptism the child has been consecrated or deputed to join in the sacramental worship of the Church. To ac-

---

Theology of Charles Cardinal Journet in Relation to the Second Vatican Council," *Gregorianum* 90, no. 2 (2009): 237–53; Larry Welch, "The Decree on the Ministry and Life of Priests, *Presbyterorum Ordinis*," in *Vatican II: Renewal within Tradition*, ed. Matthew Lamb and Matthew Levering (Oxford: Oxford University Press, 2008), 205–27.

23. For a treatment of the theology of Christ's priestly activity, see Matthew Levering, "Christ the Priest: An Exploration of *Summa Theologiae*, III, Question 22," *The Thomist* 71 (2007): 379–417.

complish this deputation to participate in these supernatural realities, Baptism (and Confirmation) causes a spiritual power in the soul that gives it a participation in Christ's own priesthood. The unbaptized adult, by contrast, while perhaps enjoying a very mature faith, lacks the capacity to join in the sacramental liturgy because his soul has not been elevated spiritually by the character of Baptism to share in Christ's priestly activity.

This doctrine also reminds us that although Baptism, from the perspective of absolute necessity, is considered by the Church to be the most necessary of the sacraments, it is not intended to be the sole or stand-alone source of supernatural life and divine assistance in the Christian life. Baptismal grace gives the Christian supernatural birth unto new life, and baptismal character gives the Christian spiritual power to participate in the sacramental life of the Church, but birth is not to be equated with full Christian maturity. The new life of Baptism stands, in relation to the other sacraments of initiation, in need of further perfection and elevation.[24]

On the character of Confirmation, for example, the *Catechism*, following St. Thomas, teaches: "This 'character' perfects the common priesthood of the faithful, received in Baptism, and 'the confirmed person receives the power to profess faith in Christ publicly and as it were officially (*quasi ex officio*).'"[25]

---

24. For example, in §17 of his Post-Synodal Apostolic Exhortation *Sacramentum Caritatis*, Benedict XVI teaches: "If the Eucharist is truly the source and summit of the Church's life and mission, it follows that the process of Christian initiation must constantly be directed to the reception of this sacrament. As the Synod Fathers said, we need to ask ourselves whether in our Christian communities the close link between Baptism, Confirmation and Eucharist is sufficiently recognized. It must never be forgotten that our reception of Baptism and Confirmation is ordered to the Eucharist. Accordingly, our pastoral practice should reflect a more unitary understanding of the process of Christian initiation. The sacrament of Baptism, by which we were conformed to Christ, incorporated in the Church and made children of God, is the portal to all the sacraments. It makes us part of the one Body of Christ (cf. 1 Cor 12:13), a priestly people. Still, it is our participation in the Eucharistic sacrifice which perfects within us the gifts given to us at Baptism. The gifts of the Spirit are given for the building up of Christ's Body (1 Cor 12) and for ever greater witness to the Gospel in the world. The Holy Eucharist, then, brings Christian initiation to completion and represents the centre and goal of all sacramental life."

25. *CCC* §1305.

Furthermore, even though the baptized and confirmed receive spiritual power through their participation in Christ's priesthood given by the characters, these sacraments do not conform their souls to Christ in such a manner that they are able to act in the very person of Christ by consecrating the Eucharist, confirming the baptized, forgiving sins, ministering to the sick, and ordaining other ministers. By these powers the character of each of the Orders adds a type of perfection in the life of the Church that serves the spiritual needs of the faithful by making Christ's ministerial powers present in an especially unique, personal, and necessary manner.[26]

Moreover, the connection between the character conferred by the sacrament of Holy Orders and the Church's mark of apostolicity is underappreciated. The apostolicity of the Church is not only the result of a historical genealogy of the Church traceable back to the first century, or even the possession of the Bible and creeds, although both of these are extremely important. The primary mark of apostolicity is the possession and continuation of the sacerdotal ministries (such as the forgiveness of sins and the celebration of the Last Supper) that Christ himself exercised and passed on to the apostles and their successors. This is why the *Catechism*, following *Lumen Gentium*, includes "apostolic succession through the sacrament of Holy Orders" in its articulation of the bonds necessary for the unity of the Church.[27] It is precisely through the unique powers that are conferred by the characters of orders, which conform the souls of priests and bishops to Christ's own priestly ministry, which he continues in the Church today through his ministers.[28]

Failing to appreciate the distinction between grace and charac-

26. For a helpful presentation of the unique ministerial power transmitted by Christ to the apostles (and not to the entire apostolic community), especially according to 1 Corinthians and the Gospel of Matthew, see Matthew Levering, *Christ and the Catholic Priesthood: Ecclesial Hierarchy and the Pattern of the Trinity* (Chicago: Hillenbrand Books, 2010), 135–55.

27. *CCC* §815.

28. On this point the *CCC* teaches: "The ordained minister is the sacramental bond that ties the liturgical action to what the apostles said and did and, through them, to the words and actions of Christ, the source and foundation of the sacraments" (§1120).

ter, especially the participatory nature of character in Christ's own priesthood, has immensely negative effects in the life of the Church. Specifically, when the participation that exists between Christ and the faithful and the unique way that Christ perpetuates his priestly ministry in the Church through character are not adequately appreciated, the Church and her worship tend to become horizontal and anthropological in emphasis.

Luther, for example, denied the permanence of orders and that any essential difference exists in the Church between the laity and the ordained: "As far as we are taught from Scripture, since what we call the priesthood is a ministry, I do not see at all for what reason a man who has once been made a priest cannot become a layman again, since he differs in no wise from a layman, except by his ministerial office."[29] The problem with this is that it does not account for the distinction between grace and character, which is the basis for the Church's rejection of the heretical practice of re-baptism and re-ordination. The ministerial office requires powers to perform Christ's ministries. If the permanent characters of Baptism, Confirmation, and Orders are denied, Augustine's important distinction between the reality of the sacrament and its working out in grace crumbles. Tradition has discerned that character is the foundation of the theology of the non-repeatability of Baptism, Confirmation, and Orders.

Furthermore, such a position on ministry fails to take into account the fact that Christ deputed the apostles to many of his own ministries (e.g., the forgiveness of sin [Jn 20:21], binding and loosing [Mt 18:18], and the ministry of the keys [Mt 16:18]), which he did not share with the wider apostolic community.[30] Ministry is not merely an appointment received from one's peers or elders; it is a vocation to share in Christ's own priesthood: "'Peace be with you. As the Fa-

---

29. From Luther's *Babylonian Captivity* [*Pagan Servitude of the Church*] cited in Leeming, *Principles of Sacramental Theology*, 137. Leeming also points out that all of the major Protestant confessions (Augsburg, Westminster, and the Thirty-Nine Articles) are silent on sacramental character.

30. On this point, again, Levering's *Christ and the Catholic Priesthood*, 135ff., is extremely helpful.

ther has sent me, even so I send you.' And when he had said this, he breathed on them, and said to them, 'Receive the Holy Spirit. If you forgive the sins of any, they are forgiven; if you retain the sins of any, they are retained'" (Jn 20:21–23). This collaboration with Christ is made possible by the special conformity of the soul to Christ by the power of character.

Because of the major gap in Lutheran and Reformed theology on the doctrine of character, the Council of Trent affirmed the following: "If anyone says that in three sacraments, namely, baptism, confirmation, and orders, a character is not imprinted on the soul, that is, a kind of indelible spiritual sign by reason of which these sacraments cannot be repeated, let him be anathema."[31]

The Lack of Understanding of Character in Contemporary Theology

Unfortunately, a lack of appreciation for the spiritual and ecclesial significance of sacramental character in the period after Vatican II has hindered Catholic theology from fully harvesting the important ecclesial and sacramental teachings of the Council. For example, writing shortly after the Council, Karl Rahner argues that Aquinas's treatment of the general principles of sacramental theology in questions 60–65 of the Third Part of the *Summa theologiae* "turns out to be problematical."[32] One of the elements that Rahner finds inadequate is that Aquinas's treatment of the sacraments follows his treatment of Christ, and thus the treatise on the sacraments "does not include any developed ecclesiology."[33]

---

31. See Heinrich Denzinger, *Enchiridion symbolorum*, 390 (§1609). The Council of Florence had already taught: "Among these sacraments, there are three, namely; baptism, confirmation, and orders, that imprint an indelible character on the soul, which is a type of spiritual sign that is distinct from the rest. As a consequence, they may not be repeated in the same person. The other four, however, do not imprint a character and allow for repetition." Ibid., 338 (§1313).

32. Karl Rahner, "Introductory Observations on Thomas Aquinas' Theology of the Sacraments in General," in *Ecclesiology, Questions in the Church, The Church in the World*, vol. 14 of *Theological Investigations*, trans. David Bourke (New York: Seabury Press, 1976), 150.

33. Ibid., 151.

In Rahner's view this negates any proper (and needed) ecclesial reference for Aquinas's sacramental theology, leaving it without the "connecting member" of intelligibility.[34] Despite the fact that in the whole of the *Summa theologiae* Thomas devotes just one question, comprising but six articles, to sacramental character, Rahner states that the treatment of character "seems disproportionate."[35]

Rahner's assessment of Aquinas's teaching on character concludes as follows:

Thomas interprets sacramental character as deputing the subject concerned to the Christian cult, and at which, as a result, there is a suggestion of an ecclesiological view of the sacraments, the Church is still not clearly included as a vital factor. For as Aquinas presents it this Christian cult is precisely viewed too much as a task of the individual functionary officially appointed in each case.[36]

The horizontal implications of Rahner's position are made more explicit by Sr. Judith Kubicki, CSSF, who, writing after Rahner, argues: "For Rahner, this presence of Christ in the Church necessarily precedes the possibility of Christ in the Eucharistic species."[37] Closely following Rahner's critique of Aquinas, Kubicki maintains that "although Thomas Aquinas does identify the *res sacramenti* as the unity of the Church, his treatment of the Eucharist fails to situate his sacramental theology within ecclesiology."[38] As a result, Kubicki asserts, the importance of the Church community gathered for worship "has no apparent role in Aquinas' theological system. For Aquinas, it is the ordained minister who is the complete subject of the liturgical action."[39]

Sr. Kubicki's Rahnerian critique of Aquinas betrays a lack of appreciation for the spiritual insight and theological nuance of Aquinas's

34. Ibid., 152. 35. Ibid., 150, f. 3.
36. Ibid., 152.

37. Kubicki, "Recognizing the Presence of Christ in the Liturgical Assembly," *Theological Studies* 65 (2007): 817–37, at 821. Kubicki has also authored a book on the same topic: *The Presence of Christ in the Gathered Assembly* (New York: Continuum International, 2006).

38. Kubicki, "Recognizing the Presence of Christ in the Liturgical Assembly," 824.

39. Ibid., 824–25.

position. One is hard-pressed to read Aquinas's treatment of character and find anything indicating the ordained minister as the "complete subject" of the liturgical action. Aquinas views the characters conferred in Baptism, Confirmation, and Holy Orders as instrumental powers whose principal agency is rooted in Christ. He also clearly teaches that all Christians are "deputed" to worship by Baptism.

"But an instrumental power follows rather the condition of the principal agent," Aquinas teaches, "and consequently a character exists in the soul in an indelible manner, not from any perfection of its own, but from the perfection of Christ's Priesthood, from which the character flows like an instrumental power."[40] The Church is Christ's body. Although certain parts of a body, for instance, the head, do have a certain priority, the body exists together in a unified fashion; the body does not temporally precede the head.

In Aquinas's theology of sacramental character, the whole Church, head and members, are joined together in Christ's priestly activity. Character gives the Church a participatory share in Christ's priestly activity, thus joining organically the worship of the body with the priestly ministry of the head. It is true that some members of the body, through the characters of Orders, perform ministries that the nonordained cannot, but this unique role stems from the clergy's conformity to Christ as his special instruments.

As a result, even though Aquinas's theology of the sacraments is not developed within a modern treatise on the Church,[41] his theology of sacramental character is the linchpin that joins together the worship of the body with that of Christ as priest and head. Aquinas's understanding of the Church is heavily influenced by the participatory metaphysics of Dionysius's *Ecclesiastical Hierarchy*.[42] "Jesus who

40. *ST* III, q. 65, a. 5, ad 3.
41. It should be noted that, even though a fully developed treatise on the Church is lacking in Aquinas's work, he clearly understands Christ to stand as head of the Church, joining the members to himself and to each other invisibly through the spiritual effects of the sacraments. See, for example, Aquinas's treatment of Christ's headship in *ST* III, q. 8.
42. Aquinas explicitly refers to Dionysius's *Ecclesiastical Hierarchy* three times in *ST* III, q. 63, in articles 2 and 6.

is transcendent mind," Dionysius teaches, "who is the source of the being underlying all hierarchy ... who is the ultimate divine power. He assimilates them ... to his own light. ... He makes our life, disposition, and activity something one and divine, and he bestows on us the power appropriate to a sacred priesthood."[43]

The perennial insight that Kubicki and Rahner fail to appreciate in Aquinas's doctrine of sacramental character is that the foundation of the worshipping Church is Christ's high priesthood. What would the Church's worship be without an ontological participation in Christ's priesthood? The seal of Christ's character gives to Christ's members a real participation in this hierarchical and heavenly reality. The assessment of John M. Donahue, writing just after the Council, seems unfortunately still unrealized: "My own conviction is that a more vigorous presentation of the Thomistic doctrine on sacramental character ... would contribute to a broad understanding of the Church and her members as a sacramental community of faith and worship."[44]

Character is therefore the foundation upon which the Church shares and participates in Christ's ongoing priestly activity. Also, the permanence of character works in the soul as "a positive disposition for grace."[45] This explains how someone who has lost sacramental grace through sin is able to return to the life of grace through the sacrament of Penance. The graces lost through sin are brought back to life or "revivified" by the reconciliation with God and the Church that takes place through sacramental absolution. Character, therefore, is a fundamental reality for the life of the Church and a largely unexplored resource for developing the rich ecclesial teaching of the Second Vatican Council.

43. Pseudo-Dionysius, *The Complete Works*, trans. Colm Luibheid (New York: Paulist Press, 1987), 195–96 [1.1, 372a–372b].

44. John M. Donahue, "Sacramental Character: The State of the Question," *The Thomist* 31 (1967): 464.

45. *CCC* §1121.

TEN

Sacramentum Tantum, Res et Sacramentum, Res Tantum

Understanding the Formula

The distinction between sacramental grace and sacramental character, as well as the distinction between a valid sacramental celebration and a fruitful one, reveals the many-layered (or symbolic) nature of the sacraments. As an external rite or celebration, a sacrament is a brief, transient reality. However, as the doctrines of grace and character reveal, there is more to each sacrament than merely the external rite. To explain the relationship between the external celebration and the diverse aspects and effects of the sacraments, theologians in the Catholic tradition have had recourse to the tripartite formula: *sacramentum tantum* (sacrament only), *res et sacramentum* (reality and sacrament), and *res tantum* (reality only).[1] Theologians have understood the *sacramentum tantum* to be the sacramental sign or the external rite; the *res et sacramentum* corresponds to the immediate effect of the sacramental sign, such as sacramental

---

1. See Leeming, *Principles of Sacramental Theology*, 251–66; Miralles, *I Sacramenti Cristiani*, 197–212; Nicolas, *Synthèse dogmatique*, §730; Ronald F. King, CM, "The Origin and Evolution of a Sacramental Formula: *SACRAMENTUM TANTUM, RES ET SACRAMENTUM, RES TANTUM*," *The Thomist* 31 (1967): 21–82.

character, the indissoluble marriage bond, or the reality of the body and blood of Christ in the Eucharist; *res tantum* refers to the deepest or ultimate interior effect and full fruition of the sacrament.

An immediate mistake that students of sacramental theology often make when first confronted with the formula is to think of these three points as somehow distinct from the sacrament itself. The sacrament is a multi-layered reality that can include in its causal motion more than one effect. The effects are distinguishable from one another, but they are all contained in and caused by the sacramental reality itself.

Why did the theologians adopt this tripartite formula, which comes off rather clumsily in English, to present the rich and multi-layered reality of the sacraments? In many ways the formula is implicit in Augustine's distinction between a valid sacrament and a fruitful sacrament: the valid sacrament is not devoid or empty of any sacramental reality just because the recipient has placed some obstacle in the way of the fruitfulness of the grace.

The controversy over Berengar's denial of the real presence of Christ in the Eucharist gave the Church a special occasion to reflect more deeply on the nature of the sacraments as signs. "Berengar," Leeming explains, "insisted that the bread and wine upon the altar are a sacrament, and, as such, a sign; but a sign, he argued, cannot be the thing it signifies, and hence the bread and wine are not the body and blood of Christ."[2] As a result of this position, "Berengar limited the concept of a sacrament to a visible, corporeal, mutable element. Therefore, the Body of Christ, which is invisible, eternal and immutable, could not possibly be the sacrament of the Eucharist."[3]

To use the language of the tripartite formula, Berengar reduced the sacramental reality to the *sacramentum tantum*, and denied the existence of any further or deeper realities (*res et sacramentum* and *res tantum*) within the sign itself. Berengar, in Leeming's words, adopt-

2. Leeming, *Principles of Sacramental Theology*, 252.
3. King, "The Origin and Evolution of a Sacramental Formula," 22.

ed a sacramental "either-or," whereas his opponents rightly affirmed that "the Eucharist is indeed a sacrament, but this does not deny that it is also the reality of the body and blood."[4]

St. Thomas provides an interesting and helpful example of this formula in his treatment of Baptism in the *Summa theologiae* III, question 66, article 1. The question that Thomas poses in this article is somewhat counterintuitive. He asks whether Baptism is a "mere washing," that is, whether Baptism is reducible to the washing itself (*ipsa ablutio*), or, in other words, is Baptism reducible to the external rite (*sacramentum tantum*). Given that Thomas was not a follower of Berengar, it seems obvious that his answer would deny that Baptism is a mere washing, especially since it confers character and grace. However, Thomas answers this question in the affirmative — sort of. His reason for this is that he understands that the external sign, or the "mere washing," contains and confers interior realities through its signification and operation. Therefore, while Baptism is a "mere washing" in that it is a transient rite involving the application of water to the recipient, the mere washing effects interior realities.

"In the sacrament of Baptism," Thomas explains,

three things may be considered: namely, that which is "sacrament only" [*sacramentum tantum*]; that which is "reality and sacrament" [*res et sacramentum*]; and that which is "reality only" [*res tantum*]. That which is sacrament only, is something visible and outward; the sign, namely, of the inward effect: for such is the very nature of a sacrament. And this outward something that can be perceived by the sense is both the water itself and its use, which is the washing.[5]

Thomas's teaching, unlike that of Berengar, does not reduce the sacramental reality to the external element, the water or the "mere washing." This position is not true, Thomas argues, because "since the sacraments of the New Law effect a certain sanctification, [there] the sacrament is completed where the sanctification is completed."[6]

4. Leeming, *Principles of Sacramental Theology*, 253.
5. *ST* III, q. 66, a. 1.
6. Ibid.

Thus, returning to the question of the article, the sanctification is not completed merely in the water or the "mere washing." The external sign, however, possesses "a certain sanctifying instrumental virtue, not permanent but transient, [that] passes from the water, in which it is, into man who is the subject of true sanctification."[7] While the performance or external rite of Baptism is made up of the application of water to the recipient, the perfection or completion of the action terminates not in the external action but in the interior effects caused by the exterior rite.

The *sacramentum tantum*, therefore, is brought to perfection in the recipient by the conferral of the *res et sacramentum* and the *res tantum*. Thomas explains the character and grace conferred by Baptism accordingly:

The baptismal character is both reality and sacrament [*res et sacramentum*]: because it is something real signified by the outward washing; and a sacramental sign of the inward justification: and this last is the reality only [*res tantum*], in this sacrament — namely, the reality signified and not signifying.[8]

Another way of thinking about the distinction between the *sacamentum tantum, res et sacramentum*, and the *res tantum*, is to trace the movement of the sacramental celebration to its ultimate perfection: exterior (rite) to interior (character or the immediate sacramental reality) to superior reality (the ultimate grace or purpose of the sacrament).[9]

The Formula and the Seven Sacraments

The application of the tripartite formula to each of the sacraments is, in certain cases, a subject of considerable debate. The following is a basic sketch of how to apply the schema to each of the sacraments: with the three sacraments that cause character (Baptism, Confirmation, and Orders), the character is associated with the *res et*

---

7. Ibid.
8. Ibid.
9. See Nicolas, *Synthèse dogmatique*, §730.

sacramentum. In the Eucharist, the actual body and blood of Christ received in the sacrament is considered the *res et sacramentum,* and the unity of the Church vis-à-vis the charity that is brought about by fruitful communion with Christ is held to be the *res tantum.*[10] With Matrimony the indissoluble bond effected by the sacrament is identified as the *res et sacramentum,* and the graces leading to the perfection of the sacrament constitute the *res tantum.*[11] In the sacrament of Penance, two distinguishable effects are closely related: reconciliation with the Church (exterior penance) and reconciliation with God (interior penance). Indeed, can one be friends with God without being friends with God's friends (the Church), and vice versa?[12] Finally, the anointing with oil in the Sacrament of the Sick is viewed as bestowing a special consecration of the sick person to

10. On this point the teaching of *CCC* §1396 is helpful: "The unity of the Mystical Body: the Eucharist makes the Church. Those who receive the Eucharist are united more closely to Christ. Through it Christ unites them to all the faithful in one body — the Church. Communion renews, strengthens, and deepens this incorporation into the Church, already achieved by Baptism. In Baptism we have been called to form but one body. The Eucharist fulfills this call: "The cup of blessing which we bless, is it not a participation in the blood of Christ? The bread which we break, is it not a participation in the body of Christ? Because there is one bread, we who are many are one body, for we all partake of the one bread" (1 Cor 10:16–17). See also Gilles Emery, "The Ecclesial Fruit of the Eucharist," trans. Therese C. Scarpelli, in Emery, *Trinity, Church, and the Human Person,* 155–72.

11. John Paul II, in his Apostolic Exhortation *Familiaris Consortio* §13, explains: "Like each of the seven sacraments, so also marriage is a real symbol of the event of salvation, but in its own way. 'The spouses participate in it as spouses, together, as a couple, so that the first and immediate effect of marriage (*res et sacramentum*) is not supernatural grace itself, but the Christian conjugal bond, a typically Christian communion of two persons because it represents the mystery of Christ's incarnation and the mystery of his covenant.'" [He is quoting himself from an address earlier in his pontificate.]

12. For example, a person conscious of two mortal sins who confesses only one of them while consciously withholding the other leaves the confessional in the state of mortal sin. So it is, putatively at least, impossible to obtain the one effect (reconciliation with God) without the other (reconciliation with the Church): God does not unite himself to those who do not seek communion with the Church, and those who withhold their sins from God are not granted communion with the Church. The two effects go together. See Gilles Emery, "Reconciliation with the Church and Interior Penance: The Contribution of Thomas Aquinas on the Question of the *Res et Sacramentum* of Penance," *Nova et Vetera,* English Edition, 1 (2003): 283–301. (Reprinted in Emery, *Trinity, Church, and the Human Person.*)

Christ's Passion (*res et sacramentum*), and the graces of strengthening and perseverance in suffering correspond to the *res tantum*.[13]

Pastoral Implications

What is the value of retaining this formula in Catholic sacramental theology today? Even though it may not be immediately evident, these clumsy Latin phrases have significant pastoral application in the Church. For example, what happens when someone in the state of mortal sin receives a validly celebrated sacrament (other than Penance)? The tripartite distinction helps to understand that in receiving the *sacramentum tantum* unworthily, the recipient places an obstacle in the way of the fruition of the gracious effects.[14]

Receiving the body and blood of Christ, therefore, in an unworthy state not only offends against the sanctity of the sacrament and the divine gratuity but also thwarts the flowering in the recipient of the spiritual effects to which the sacrament is ordered. The same is true regarding the sacraments that bestow character: if these sacraments are celebrated validly, the character is impressed on the soul, but the recipients do not enjoy the grace of the sacrament unless and until they turn to Christ in Penance. This explains why these sacraments do not need to be repeated. What needs to be brought to life or renewed is the grace that was impeded by sin, which is removed by sacramental penance.

The Church faces many pastoral challenges today concerning people who are in a persistent state of mortal sin. Many of these challenges, such as the situation of the divorced and remarried and those in same-sex relationships, are especially exploited against the

---

13. See *CCC* §1521. "Union with the passion of Christ. By the grace of this sacrament the sick person receives the strength and the gift of uniting himself more closely to Christ's Passion: in a certain way he is consecrated to bear fruit by configuration to the Savior's redemptive Passion. Suffering, a consequence of original sin, acquires a new meaning; it becomes a participation in the saving work of Jesus."

14. St. Thomas teaches that the unworthy reception of the Eucharist, for example, constitutes the sin of sacrilege.

Church by the mass media.[15] Regarding such cases, it should be recalled that simply receiving the body of Christ does not guarantee that the *res tantum* or interior graces of the sacrament are automatically brought to fruition.

Validly celebrated sacraments are not fruitful if the faithful impede their fruition by receiving them in an unworthy state. This means that, not only is it sacrilegious for the faithful to knowingly receive the sacraments unworthily, but also it is pastorally misleading to encourage those in the state of mortal sin to receive Holy Communion. Therefore, in addition to sinning against the sanctity of the sacrament, the faithful could also be induced to presume that their external reception of the sacrament is fruitfully communicating its interior effects when, in fact, those effects would be impeded by the obstacle of mortal sin.

In point of fact, the very word "communion" implies union between the recipient and God that is incompatible with being in the state of mortal sin. St. Thomas presents this truth very beautifully by distinguishing between eating the Eucharist spiritually *and* sacramentally, or merely sacramentally. "There are two things to be considered in the receiving of this sacrament," Thomas explains:

the sacrament itself, and its fruits.... The perfect way, then, of receiving this sacrament is when one takes it so as to partake of its effect.... [I]t sometimes happens that a man is hindered from receiving the effect of this sacrament; and such receiving of this sacrament is an imperfect one. Therefore, as the perfect is divided against the imperfect, so sacramental eating, whereby the sacrament only is received without its effect, is divided against spiritual eating, by which one receives the effect of this sacrament, whereby a man is spiritually united with Christ through faith and charity.[16]

This clarifies why the sacraments do not work as "vending machines" of grace, despite the fact that their causality works *ex opere operato*.

15. For an extremely helpful and theologically astute treatment of the delicate issue of the reception of the Eucharist by the divorced and remarriage, see John Corbett, OP, et al., "Recent Proposals for the Pastoral Care of the Divorced and Remarried: A Theological Assessment," *Nova et Vetera*, English Edition, 12, no. 3 (2014): 601–30.

16. *ST* III, q. 80, a. 1.

ng validly celebrated sacraments is not the same as re-
spiritually and fruitfully.

oral situations are indeed difficult. But more spiritual
e had when the faithful persevere with hearts open
nce in the midst of a difficulty, than when they re-
Eucharist unfruitfully. As Charles Cardinal Journet
ne discussion of the presentation of matrimonial indissolubility in *Gaudium et Spes* at the Second Vatican Council, "the
Church, which cannot not obey Christ's command, looks respect-
fully, with the measureless mercy of God, on those unfortunate situations which summon towards the heroic life and which, from that
circumstance, to human eyes alone — not however before God — remain without a solution."[17] Unfruitful reception of the sacraments,
especially Holy Communion, is by no means a proper solution to
these difficult situations.[18]

One final implication of this doctrine is worthy of consideration.
Namely, since the sacraments are ordered, ultimately, to eternal life,
and since the sacraments produce multiple spiritual effects in the
soul and not merely grace generically conceived, there is an especial
advantage to seeking intimacy with God through the sacraments.
To illumine this question, Thomas Aquinas considers the hypothetical situation of someone who is known to be sanctified apart from
Baptism (e.g., John the Baptist in the womb of his mother). Would
someone like John the Baptist benefit in any way from the sacraments, given that he has already received grace abundantly? Such
persons, Aquinas argues "receive indeed grace which cleanses them
from original sin, but they do not therefore receive the character, by
which they are conformed to Christ. Consequently, if any were to
be sanctified in the womb now, they would need to be baptized, in

---

17. See Roger W. Nutt, "*Gaudium et Spes* and the Indissolubility of the Sacrament
of Matrimony: The Contribution of Cardinal Journet," *Nova et Vetera*, English Edition,
11, no. 3 (2013): 619–26, at 625.

18. See Paul Jerome Keller, OP, "Is Spiritual Communion for Everyone?" *Nova et
Vetera*, English Edition, 12, no. 3 (2014): 631–55.

order to be conformed to Christ's other members by receiving the character."[19]

Hence there is an "ecclesial" advantage to seeking and receiving grace through the sacramental system of the Church. The sacraments are rich, multi-layered realities. It is wrong to reduce them to the visible, external rite. Indeed, the rite, when applied and received worthily, is the causal source of rich spiritual realities ordered to honoring God with proper worship and, ultimately, to eternal life.

19. *ST* III, q. 68, a. 1, ad 3.

ELEVEN

The Institution and Authority of the Sacraments

Consideration of the theology of the nature of the sacraments, their causality, and their effects brings our narrative back to some of the book's initial questions. Indeed, if the sacraments were merely a kind of emanation of Christian sentimentality or experience, something like linguistic expressions or symbols of what the faithful hold dear, they would not be able to cause grace and participation in Christ's priesthood. Sacraments are not superstitious attempts to somehow gain control of God, like a rain dance seeking to bend divine favor in a certain direction. Sacraments are truly actions of the Church, but they are causal, efficacious, and fruitful because they have God, not humanity, as their author and primary agent.

Sacramental theology is not philosophy of religion. The sacraments do correspond to fallen humanity's deepest anthropological needs, but this is not because they are merely religious expressions of people's search for God. Rather, they embody God's loving and all-wise initiative to save man in Christ.[1] As a result, it is important

---

1. It is important to underscore this point, because many philosophers of religion and anthropological approaches to religion seek to equate early Christian forms of worship, especially the Eucharist, with mystery rites of the pagan cults. Their approach views

to come to an understanding of the relationship between the divine and the human contributions to the sacraments.

The Institution of the Sacraments: Theological Parameters

Agency, with respect to the sacraments, Aquinas teaches is "twofold; namely, he who institutes the sacraments, and he who makes use of the sacrament instituted, by applying it for the production of the effect."[2] People's role in the sacraments is not as author but as recipient or minister of what has been given. The power that produces the spiritual effects that are available in the sacraments is, therefore, dependent on "God alone"; from this it follows that "God alone can institute the sacraments."[3] In Thomas's teaching, this point extends to the authority of the apostles as well:

The apostles and their successors are God's vicars in governing the Church which is built on faith and the sacraments of faith. Wherefore, just as they may not institute another Church, so neither may they deliver another faith, nor institute other sacraments: on the contrary, the Church is said to be built up with the sacraments "which flowed from the side of Christ while hanging on the Cross."[4]

As part of the fabric of the Church that Christ founded and the patrimony of faith, therefore, the sevenfold sacramental system of the Church constitutes part of the fullness of faith or catholicity that is an essential mark of the Church. The sacraments are not the private property of the local community. They are the means by which the one, holy, catholic, and apostolic Church is made present in and through the local community. When a newborn is baptized (in a Catholic Church), he becomes a member of the one, holy, catholic, and apostolic Church. The membership in the community that Bap-

---

the Christian rites as but one cultic expression among many in the ancient world. See Leeming, *Principles of Christianity*, 385–93.

2. *ST* III, q. 64, a. 1.   3. Ibid.

4. Ibid., ad 3.

tism confers is not circumscribed by the local parish in which it takes place. The faithful belong to the Universal Church, which is present to them through the jurisdictional structure of the local diocese by means of the fullness of the sacramental ministry of the bishop.

This same principle, with due respect for prescribed variations and legitimate traditions such as the feast days of local saints, is applicable for all of the sacraments. This is why Vatican II in *Sacrosanctum Concilium* (§22.3) teaches: "Therefore no other person, even if he be a priest, may add, remove, or change anything in the liturgy on his own authority." In simple terms, the faithful have a right to the celebration of the sacraments as prescribed by the Church to which they belong, which is the Catholic Church, and ministers are deputed by the Church to carry out her rites, not their own variations thereof.

This does not mean that the Church has not introduced elements into the sacramental rites or that the rites have not undergone genuine development.[5] It means only that the sacramental system and the essential rite of each of the sacraments is not a human creation. The magnificence of the Easter Vigil, for example, is surely a manifestation of the centrality of Christ's Resurrection and its relation to the new life bestowed in the sacraments of initiation. Aquinas understands the broader rites that have grown up around the essential aspects of the sacraments in terms of the reverence and devotion that is proper to them.

"Human institutions observed in the sacraments," Aquinas explains, "are not essential to the sacrament; but belong to the solemnity which is added to the sacraments in order to arouse devotion and reverence in the recipients."[6] The Church seeks to assist the

5. For a helpful discussion of the principles of liturgical development, see Alcuin Reid, *The Organic Development of the Liturgy: The Principles of Liturgical Reform and Their Relation to the Twentieth-Century Liturgical Movement Prior to the Second Vatican Council* (San Francisco: Ignatius Press, 2005).

6. *ST* III, q. 64, a. 2, ad 1. See also Sr. Thomas Augustine Becker, OP, "The Role of *Solemnitas* in the Liturgy According to Saint Thomas Aquinas," in *Rediscovering Aquinas and the Sacraments*, ed. Michael Dauphinais and Matthew Levering (Chicago: Hillenbrand Books, 2009), 114–35.

faithful, through the broader aspects of the rites, to share more fully and prayerfully in the sacramental celebration.

What is to be made, then, of those sacramental rites and verbal formulae that do not have an explicit institutional narrative in the Gospels, as well as the material aspects of the essential rites of those sacraments, such as the chrism oil of Confirmation, which are not explicitly mentioned in the Gospels? These are legitimate questions that the Church has been aware of from the beginning.

The first point to recall is that Catholics do not reduce the totality of divine Revelation to the written word of God. The lack of explicit mention of something in the Bible is not equivalent to the conclusion that it was therefore not revealed. The theological conviction that every Christian doctrine and practice must be reducible to an explicit passage in the Bible is inaccurate. "It is not from Sacred Scripture alone," *Dei Verbum* (§9) teaches, "that the Church draws her certainty about everything which has been revealed. Therefore both sacred tradition and Sacred Scripture are to be accepted and venerated with the same sense of loyalty and reverence."[7]

In addressing these questions, *Dei Verbum* teaches very much in continuity with Aquinas's understanding of tradition. "Those things that are essential to the sacrament," Aquinas notes, "are instituted by Christ Himself, Who is God and man. And though they are not all handed down by the Scriptures, yet the Church holds them from the intimate tradition of the apostles, according to the saying of the Apostle (1 Corinthians 11:34): 'The rest I will set in order when I come.'"[8]

Regarding the specific question of Christ's institution of Confirmation and the use of chrism oil as its matter, Aquinas makes an interesting deductive argument from Christ's words about the Holy Spirit in the Gospel of John:

---

7. For a treatment of tradition as a source of Revelation in the Fathers, especially in St. Basil the Great, see Yves Congar, *Tradition and Traditions: The Biblical, Historical, and Theological Evidence for Catholic Teaching on Tradition*, 47.

8. *ST* III, q. 64, a. 2, ad 1. For a treatment of the liturgy as a "monument or witness" of Revelation, see Congar, *Tradition and Traditions*, 427–35.

we must say that Christ instituted this sacrament not by bestowing, but by promising it, according to John 16:7: "If I go not, the Paraclete will not come to you, but if I go, I will send Him to you." And this was because in this sacrament the fullness of the Holy Ghost is bestowed, which was not to be given before Christ's Resurrection and Ascension; according to John 7:39: "As yet the Spirit was not given, because Jesus was not yet glorified."[9]

It is important to understand that, for the sake of deepening the unity of the Church around his headship and authority, Christ exercised a certain sapiential and prudential reservation in his establishment of the sacraments. Aquinas concedes that Christ, in fact, could have communicated a certain power to the apostles such that "they themselves might institute sacraments, and by their mere will confer the sacramental effect without observing the sacramental rite."[10] However, Thomas then clarifies that "it was in order to avoid the incongruity of many heads in the Church, that Christ was unwilling to communicate to ministers His power of excellence" by which he instituted the sacraments.[11]

In reference to the sacraments that they retained, the Protestants all held (with the Catholic Church) that they were instituted by Christ. However, they came to deny that each of the seven held by the Catholic Church was a legitimate sacrament owing their origin to Christ.[12] Luther, for example, sees in the Gospels no evidence of Christ's institution of Anointing of the Sick. With regard to the affirmation of the sacrament of the sick in James 5:14ff., Luther contends "that this epistle was not written by the apostle James, and is not worthy of the spirit of an apostle."[13] Likewise, Luther concludes

9. *ST* III, q. 72, a. 1, ad 1.　　　　10. *ST* III, q. 64, a. 4.
11. Ibid., ad 3.

12. Article XXV of the "39 Articles of Religion" of the Anglican communion states: "There are two Sacraments ordained of Christ our Lord in the Gospel, that is to say, Baptism, and the Supper of the Lord. Those five commonly called Sacraments, that is to say, Confirmation, Penance, Orders, Matrimony, and Extreme Unction, are not to be counted for Sacraments of the Gospel, being such as have grown partly of the corrupt following of the Apostles, partly are states of life allowed in the Scriptures, but yet have not like nature of Sacraments with Baptism, and the Lord's Supper, for that they have not any visible sign or ceremony ordained of God."

13. See Martin Luther, "Pagan Servitude of the Church," in *Martin Luther: Selections*

that "there is no Scriptural warrant whatsoever for regarding marriage as a sacrament."[14]

In the face of these errors about the number and institution of the sacraments, the Council of Trent affirmed the following:

> If anyone says that the sacraments of the New Law were not all instituted by Jesus Christ our Lord; or that there are more or fewer than seven, that is: baptism, confirmation, the Eucharist, penance, extreme unction, orders, and matrimony; or that any one of these seven is not truly and properly a sacrament, let him be anathema.[15]

The specificity of the Council's use of the phrase "instituted by Jesus Christ our Lord" has been the subject of sustained debate.

The Meaning of Trent's Teaching on Christ's Institution of the Sacraments

The teaching of Trent indicates that the origin of the sacraments is not God understood abstractly, but "Jesus Christ our Lord." This language implies, Miralles argues, that the sacraments all originated prior to Christ's Ascension into heaven.[16]

The debate hinges on what this teaching requires regarding Christ's manner of institution; namely, whether Christ instituted all seven sacraments by explicitly fixing their specific matter and form (immediate institution) or if the institution of the seven was more vague and left some of the details to the apostles and/or the authority of the Church (general institution). *for example, Baptism Conform*

---

from His Writings, 351. In fairness to Luther's position, his rejection of Anointing of the Sick is not based solely on his ambivalence toward the epistle associated with the apostle James. His primary point is that the sacrament, in his view, was not instituted by Christ, and so the reference in James, regardless of its authorship, must be incorrect.

14. Ibid., 326. The denial of Christ's institution of all seven of the sacraments is not exclusive to Martin Luther among the Protestants. However, his positions are an especially important point of reference in relation to the object of the decrees of Trent. In regard to Christ's institution of Matrimony, Trent appeals directly to Christ's elevation of matrimony to a sacrament in Matthew 19:4. For a helpful catalog of patristic and scriptural texts indicating Christ's institution of the sacraments, see Leeming, *Principles of Sacramental Theology*, 398–400.

15. Session 7, "Canons on the Sacraments in General," Canon 1. See Heinrich Denzinger, *Enchiridion symbolorum*, 389 (§1601).

16. See Miralles, *I Sacramenti Cristiani*, 149–53.

At the level of the concrete, however, it is more difficult to explain in every detail the full manner of Christ's institution of each sacrament, given the diversity of celebration that exists among the rites of the Catholic Church and the different external forms that the celebration of some of the sacraments has taken over the course of the centuries. With Baptism and the Eucharist, the sacramental matter and form indicated by Christ are easily detectable in the written component of the deposit of faith. It is not so easy for all of the other sacraments.

When speaking about the Church's role in the administration of the sacraments, the Council of Trent adds the following clarification about the manner of Christ's institution:

In the administration of the sacraments — provided their substance is preserved — there had always been in the Church that power to determine or modify what she judged more expedient for the benefit of those receiving the sacraments or for the reverence due to the sacraments themselves — according to the diversity of circumstances, time, and places.[17]

Theologians point to the distinction made in this teaching between the "substance" of the sacraments and the rite, or form of celebration, that each sacrament assumes under the prudential administrative guidance of the Church. There is something of what Christ instituted, the "substance" of the sacraments, which cannot be altered, even by the authority of the Church. Substance indicates, at least vaguely, the notions of both matter and form. Subsistent substances can vary according to their particular accidents, but individuals of a common genus have an underlying principle of unity that locates them in the same category. This distinction helps clarify the historical diversity and nuance that can be found in the celebration of some of the sacraments.[18]

---

17. Session 21, chap. 2. See Heinrich Denzinger, *Enchiridion symbolorum*, 415 (§1728).

18. *In Lamentabili*, §40, Pius X identifies the following position as erroneous: "the Sacraments have their origin in the fact that the Apostles and their successors, swayed and moved by circumstances and events, interpreted some idea and intention of Christ." The modernist position that the sacraments were instituted "mediately" by Christ, as if the Church and sacraments were later outgrowths of a more basic divine "seed," is also condemned by Pius X in the encyclical *Pascendi*. See Leeming, *Principles of Sacramental Theology*, 395.

Furthermore, if the substance of the sacraments was not instituted by Christ, the supernatural efficiency and fruit of each sacrament, which depend immediately on Christ's authority, could not be affirmed. The conferral of these effects is, furthermore, intrinsic to the sacramental sign. As a result, there must be some connection between Christ's authority in relation to the effects, the substance of the sacraments, and the nature of the signs through which the effects are conferred.[19] Just as some fluctuation in accidental properties does not change the nature of a substance, so too some diversity in celebration does not compromise the integral substance of each sacrament. It does mean, however, that there are important boundaries. Accidents are ordered to the being of the substances in which they inhere. Likewise, the Church's practices are related to the substance established by Christ in his institution of each sacrament.

As a result, some historical diversity in the celebration of the sacraments does not negate that Christ instituted them according to their substance. For example, it is well documented that the external form of the sacrament of Penance evolved over the course of the first six or seven centuries of the Church from a public to a private ceremony.[20] However, each of the external forms of celebration that the Church has used in the administration of penance manifests a unified understanding of the substance of the sacrament: namely, that in transmitting the power of "binding and loosing" to the apostles, Christ intended the Church to be intrinsically involved in the penitential life of the faithful. Beneath the various external forms the sacrament has assumed is the fact that Christ instituted an ecclesial form of penance, the substance of which is retained across diverse forms of celebrating of the sacrament.

While there have been many historical attempts to articulate the

---

19. Nicolas affirms, "It is clear that Christ, being the one savior and sanctifier of man, that he alone could have given to a rite this saving significance." Nicolas, *Synthèse dogmatique*, §731.

20. For a very helpful historical and doctrinal treatment of Penance (and Anointing of the Sick), see Bernhard Poschmann, *Penance and the Anointing of the Sick,* trans. by F. Courtney, SJ (New York: Herder and Herder, 1964).

teaching of Trent in more explicit ways and attempts to generalize Trent's teaching on Christ's institution, there is, as Miralles points out, "a boundary that cannot be crossed," and this boundary is the substance of the sacraments established by Christ.[21] In his Apostolic Constitution *Sacramentum Ordinis* (November 30, 1947), Pius XII develops the teaching of Trent on Christ's institution of the sacraments:

In the course of the ages, the Church has not and could not substitute other sacraments for these sacraments instituted by Christ the Lord, since, as the Council of Trent teaches, the seven sacraments of the New Law have all been instituted by Jesus Christ, our Lord, and the Church has no power over the "substance of the sacraments", that is, over those things that, with the sources of divine revelation as witnesses, Christ the Lord himself decreed to be preserved in a sacramental sign.[22]

It is clear, then, that the spiritual effects that the sacraments cause in the Christian life are derived from the authority and ministry of Christ himself, who, as author and principal agent of the sacraments, continues his office of "mediator between God and man."[23] The Church is the custodian of the sevenfold sacramental system, but the power of the sacraments is the result of Christ's instituting authority. As such, the sacraments are not static institutions; they are dynamic encounters with the risen Christ.

21. Miralles, *I Sacramenti Cristiani*, 164.

22. *Sacramentum ordinis*, §1. See Heinrich Denzinger, *Enchiridion symbolorum*, 791 (§3857).

23. In his work *The Church and the Sacraments*, Karl Rahner states: "The institution of a sacrament can (it is not necessarily implied that it must always) follow simply from the fact that Christ founded the Church with its sacramental nature." (This work was printed as a stand-alone volume and also within a series. Cited here from Rahner's *Inquiries: Questiones Disputatae 9* [New York: Herder and Herder, 1964], 223.) While this theory retains the instituting authority of Christ in a virtual fashion, it lacks accountability to the full parameters mapped out by Trent's teaching. The Church certainly gained clarity about each of the seven sacraments over the centuries, but none of the seven can be viewed as merely an emanation of the arch-sacramentality of the Church.

Conclusion

Principles of a Sacramental Spirituality

The profundity of the sacramental patrimony of the Church is in need of reintegration with the everyday spirituality of the faithful. "Therefore in the Church," the Second Vatican Council teaches, "everyone whether belonging to the hierarchy, or being cared for by it, is called to holiness, according to the saying of the Apostle: 'For this is the will of God, your sanctification'" (1 Thes 4:3).[1] The pursuit of holiness in the Church is inextricably linked to the sacraments. As *ex opere operato* causes of grace, the sacraments communicate the supernatural life of the risen Christ to the faithful, drawing them closer and closer to the full union with God that is consummated in heaven. "In that Body," which is the Church, "the life of Christ is poured into the believers who, through the sacraments, are united in a hidden and real way to Christ who suffered and was glorified."[2]

In this closing chapter a few points of reflection will be offered toward the end of reintegrating the sacraments with the broader project of renewing the spiritual life of the Church.

The Liturgy and the Life of Prayer

A first point of reflection, which is foundational and somewhat obvious, but which has been underemphasized, is that the sac-

---

1. *Lumen Gentium* §39.
2. Ibid., §7.2.

ramental liturgy of the Church *is* prayer; indeed, it is the highest prayer that can be offered to God. God intends for the sacraments, as causes of grace (and character), to be the foundational source of supernatural life and divine intimacy within the soul, which private prayer and devotions seek to nourish and deepen. The teaching of the Second Vatican Council should serve as an important source of renewal on this point: "every liturgical celebration, because it is an action of Christ the priest and of His Body which is the Church, is a sacred action surpassing all others; no other action of the Church can equal its efficacy by the same title and to the same degree."[3]

This does not mean that private prayer and devotion are not essential to the Christian life and the pursuit of holiness, but it does mean that the faithful should maintain a healthy, complementary, and well-ordered relationship between liturgical and non-liturgical forms of prayer. It is best, following the guidance of the Second Vatican Council, to practice private prayer and devotion with a liturgical awareness: "Devotions should be so drawn up that they harmonize with the liturgical seasons," Vatican II teaches, "accord with the sacred liturgy, are in some fashion derived from it, and lead the people to it, since, in fact, the liturgy by its very nature far surpasses any of them."[4]

Participating in the liturgy fruitfully is, therefore, the fundamental and highest way that Christians can seek and find intimacy with God. Not only is the sacramental celebration itself, because of its connection to Christ, the highest form of prayer that the Church can offer, but certain privileged moments within the liturgy, such as just after receiving communion or absolution, are especially fertile times of mental prayer.[5]

The richness and profundity of liturgical prayer saves the faithful from the burden and stress of having to be creative and technical within the spiritual life. God has provided privileged means of prayer

3. *Sacrosanctum Concilium* §7.4.
4. Ibid., §13.3.
5. For a helpful treatment of the relation of liturgical piety to the contemplative life, see Jacques and Raïssa Maritain, *Liturgy and Contemplation*, trans. Joseph W. Evans (New York: P. J. Kenedy and Sons, 1960).

and encounter with him in the sacraments and the liturgy of the hours, as well as in sacred Scripture. The faithful do not have to master any techniques to encounter God, because, in his love and mercy, he has already made himself available in the liturgy and the Bible, Word and Sacrament. Of course, good habits and discipline can make prayer, liturgical or private, more fruitful. But the spiritual benefits of the sacraments are not produced by a technique or method; they are generously given by God, and the faithful need to cultivate the appropriate virtues so that these benefits may be abundantly received.

This means that a well-ordered Christian life looks to and relies on the sacraments as the key to the pursuit of holiness and the cultivation of a rich life of prayer.

The Sacraments Make Christ Present in Every Phase of Life

People from every continent, age group, and economic status are in search of God. Especially in the face of so much suffering, violence, and disenchantment, the question of God's presence to humanity cannot be escaped. The Church is sent by Christ to all people of every nation. Her ministry is not primarily that of external works and social initiatives, though these efforts are important. The world is fundamentally in need of redemption from sin. As Charles Journet points out, "The very *raison d'être* of the Church is to bring to men the blood of Christ, not the benefits of civilization."[6] The sevenfold system of the sacraments integrates the gift of redemption — the fullness of God's love for people — with each major phase and point of development in life, from birth to death.

Thomas Aquinas viewed the spiritual life bestowed in the sevenfold system of the sacraments as corresponding, in an especially profound way, to the manner in which natural, bodily life unfolds. This correspondence between the natural and the spiritual life dem-

6. Charles Journet, *Theology of the Church*, trans. Victor Szczurek, OPraem (San Francisco: Ignatius Press, 2004), 36.

onstrates the way in which God is present to humanity and provides for it according to its deepest spiritual needs. Human life at the natural level, Aquinas argues, is perfected in a twofold manner: "first, in regard to his own person; second, in regard to the whole community of the society in which he lives, for man is by nature a social animal."[7]

At the individual level, humanity needs the basic gift of life and the basic means of sustaining life if it is to reach its perfection. Without adequate care and sustenance, life, even at the biological level, would degenerate. With the supernatural life of grace, therefore, Thomas teaches that life comes first by

Baptism, which is a spiritual regeneration, according to Titus 3:5: "By the laver of regeneration." Second, by growth whereby a man is brought to perfect size and strength: and corresponding to this in the spiritual life there is Confirmation, in which the Holy Ghost is given to strengthen us. Wherefore the disciples who were already baptized were bidden thus: "Stay you in the city till you be endued with power from on high" (Luke 24:49). Third, by nourishment, whereby life and strength are preserved to man; and corresponding to this in the spiritual life there is the Eucharist. Wherefore it is said (John 6:54): "Except you eat of the flesh of the Son of Man, and drink His blood, you shall not have life in you."[8]

Human life, moreover, needs more than generation and sustenance to flourish. For example, when someone breaks an arm, the mere healing of the fissure in the bone does not fully remedy the injury. The arm is left in a weakened and vulnerable state and needs rehabilitation to return to its former strength. Sin has a similar effect in the spiritual life. Being forgiven may not rectify the weakness and vulnerability that sin can leave behind. "Corresponding to this in the spiritual life," Thomas teaches, "there is Penance, according to Psalm 40:5: "Heal my soul, for I have sinned against Thee."[9] What about any residual effects of sin? "The other [form of healing] is the restoration of former vigor by means of suitable diet and exercise: and corresponding to this in the spiritual life there is Extreme Unction, which removes the remainder of sin, and prepares man for final

7. *ST* III, q. 65, a. 1.   8. Ibid.
9. Ibid.

glory. Wherefore it is written (James 5:15): 'And if he be in sins they shall be forgiven him.'"[10]

Besides generating, sustaining, nourishing and healing the life of the individual, the perfection of human life also requires communal goods:

First, by receiving power to rule the community and to exercise public acts and corresponding to this in the spiritual life there is the sacrament of order, according to the saying of Hebrews 7:27, that priests offer sacrifices not for themselves only, but also for the people. Secondly in regard to natural propagation. This is accomplished by Matrimony both in the corporal and in the spiritual life: since it is not only a sacrament but also a function of nature.[11]

Thomas also sees the sacraments as medicinal remedies to the multiform effects of sin:

For Baptism is intended as a remedy against the absence of spiritual life; Confirmation, against the infirmity of soul found in those of recent birth; the Eucharist, against the soul's proneness to sin; Penance, against actual sin committed after baptism; Extreme Unction, against the remainders of sins — of those sins, namely, which are not sufficiently removed by Penance, whether through negligence or through ignorance; order, against divisions in the community; Matrimony, as a remedy against concupiscence in the individual, and against the decrease in numbers that results from death.[12]

This teaching offers several important avenues for the renewal of Church life and spiritual and pastoral theology. First, and most importantly, the integration of seven sacraments with the major phases of growth and areas of need in the spiritual life reveals the wide-ranging access that people have to God through the sacramental life of the Church. From birth to death, in remedy to sin, and in service to the community, God makes himself present to the faithful in the sacraments.

This aspect of sacramental spirituality is underappreciated. In the case of the Anointing of the Sick, to provide one example, God is present to those in danger of death who often, because of serious ail-

---

10. Ibid.   11. Ibid.

12. Ibid. Aquinas closes this article by connecting each of the seven sacraments with the cardinal and theological virtues and the sinful vices that each opposes.

ment or old age, are most vulnerable to doubt, loneliness, and even despair. In the sacrament of the sick, Christ, who suffered, unites himself to the sick and pours out special graces on them. God is not far away from those who suffer, and their suffering is not pointless; in the sacrament of the sick, God is intimately present to them, helping them to persevere and make of their suffering an offering to God. "By the grace of this sacrament," the *Catechism* explains,

the sick person receives the strength and the gift of uniting himself more closely to Christ's Passion: in a certain way he is consecrated to bear fruit by configuration to the Savior's redemptive Passion. Suffering, a consequence of original sin, acquires a new meaning; it becomes a participation in the saving work of Jesus.[13]

In short, through the sacraments God helps and assists the faithful and journeys with them at those important and difficult moments and situations when the gift of his grace is most needed. The Church's daily celebration of the Eucharist especially manifests God's openness and desire for deep intimacy with humanity.

The Spiritual Life of the Church Is Centered on the Eucharist

Is it theologically correct to hold that one sacrament is greater than the others? It could seem on the surface that each sacrament stands equally in relation to the others. But this is not true. In fact, it is theologically accurate to affirm the superiority of the Eucharist in the life of the Church, and the reasons for making this affirmation are important.

In *Lumen Gentium* (§11) Vatican II speaks of the Eucharist as the "the fount and apex of the whole Christian life." Thomas Aquinas identifies three converging reasons why the Eucharist ought to be considered the greatest sacrament. First, the Eucharist is unique among the sacraments in that "it contains Christ Himself substantially: whereas the other sacraments contain a certain instrumental power which is a

13. *CCC* §1521.

share of Christ's power. . . . Now that which is essentially such is always of more account than that which is such by participation."[14]

The water of Baptism or the oil of Confirmation, for example, cause the spiritual realities associated with those sacraments, but they are not the spiritual realities themselves. In the Eucharist, however, the bread and wine are changed into the substance of Christ's body and blood. The reality signified by the signs of bread and wine is substantially present in the signs. This substantial presence surpasses the mode of presence enjoyed by the other six sacraments.

Second, Aquinas beautifully pinpoints that each of the other sacraments has a certain Eucharistic accent:

the sacrament of order is ordained to the consecration of the Eucharist: and the sacrament of Baptism to the reception of the Eucharist: while a man is perfected by Confirmation, so as not to fear to abstain from this sacrament. By Penance and Extreme Unction man is prepared to receive the Body of Christ worthily. And Matrimony at least in its signification, touches this sacrament; in so far as it signifies the union of Christ with the Church, of which union the Eucharist is a figure: hence the Apostle says (Ephesians 5:32): "This is a great sacrament: but I speak in Christ and in the Church."[15]

Third, Aquinas points out that most of the sacramental rites (Baptism, Ordination, Confirmation, Matrimony, and Anointing of the Sick) are celebrated, whenever possible, within the context of the Eucharistic liturgy, so that they can be consummated by the reception of communion.

For these reasons, the centrality of the Eucharist in the life of the Church is not the product of mere sentiment. There are multiple reasons why the Eucharist stands as the "fount and apex" of life of the Christian life, and these reasons should inform the piety and spirituality of every member of the Church.

Which Sacraments Are Necessary?

Obviously this does not mean that the other sacraments are not important and critical to the organic unfolding of the life of grace in

14. *ST* III, q. 65, a. 3.
15. Ibid.

the soul or its revivification after sin. For example, if the sacraments are considered from the perspective of necessity, Aquinas points out that "Baptism is the greatest of the sacraments," while from the standpoint of perfection "Order comes first; while Confirmation holds a middle place." As remedies for the negative consequences of sin, Aquinas teaches that "Extreme Unction is compared to Penance, as Confirmation to Baptism; in such a way, that Penance is more necessary, whereas Extreme Unction is more perfect."[16] Aquinas points out that in the case of mortal sin committed after Baptism, Penance (and, by extension, Orders) is absolutely necessary.

These reflections indicate the mutual relations between the sacraments established by God in his wisdom. Though Baptism is the most necessary of sacraments, it was never meant to be a stand-alone sacrament sustaining the whole Christian life. The full flowering and perfection of the life begun in Baptism is brought to completion in the other sacraments, especially the Eucharist, which, containing Christ substantially, stands at the center of the Christian spiritual life and the life of the Church.

Fruitful reception and faithful custody of the sacraments preserves and strengthens the bonds of friendship that Christ's followers have with him in the life of grace. Knowledge of the general principles of sacramental theology, with the aid of St. Thomas Aquinas, helps students of theology and Christ's faithful to understand these bonds of friendship. God, in his infinite wisdom, has placed the sacraments at the heart of the life of the Church. Ecclesial renewal and a flourishing sacramental spirituality are inseparable.

May God, in his infinite mercy, awaken in his people the profundity of the sevenfold gift of healing and transformation that is available in the sacramental life of the Catholic Church.

16. Ibid. On the question of Baptism, Confirmation, and Orders, see Robert Christian, "Midway between Baptism and Holy Orders: Saint Thomas' Contribution to a Contemporary Understanding of Confirmation," *Angelicum* 69 (1992): 157–73.

Bibliography

Adams, Marilyn McCord. *Some Later Medieval Theories of the Eucharist: Thomas Aquinas, Giles of Rome, Duns Scotus, and William of Ockham.* Oxford: Oxford University Press, 2010).

Ambrose. *Theological and Dogmatic Works.* Translated by Roy J. Deferrari. The Fathers of the Church 44. Washington, D.C.: The Catholic University of America Press, 1963. Reprint 2002.

Aristotle. *Aristotle's Metaphysics.* Translated by Richard Hope. 26th ed. Ann Arbor: University of Michigan Press, 2007.

Auer, Johann. *A General Doctrine of the Sacraments and the Mystery of the Eucharist.* Translated by Erasmo Leiva-Merikakis. Washington, D.C.: The Catholic University of America Press, 1995.

Augustine. *The City of God against the Pagans.* Edited and translated by R. W. Dyson. Cambridge: Cambridge University Press, 1998.

———. *Teaching Christianity (De Doctrina Christiana).* Translated by Edmund Hill, OP. New York: New City Press, 1996.

———. *The Writings Against the Manicheans, and Against the Donatists.* Edited by Philip Schaff. Nicene and Post-Nicene Fathers 4. Peabody, Mass.: Hendrickson Publishers, 1994.

Bacon, Francis. *The New Organon and Related Writings.* Indianapolis, Ind.: Bobbs-Merrill, 1960.

Bañez, Domingo, OP. *De Sacramentis.* Edited by R. P. MTRO. Vicente Beltran de Heredia, OP. *Comentarios Ineditos a la Tercera Parte de Santo Tomas 2.* Madrid: Imprenta de Aldecoa-Burgos, 1953.

Becker, Sr. Thomas Augustine, OP. "The Role of *Solemnitas* in the Liturgy According to Saint Thomas Aquinas." In *Rediscovering Aquinas and the Sacraments,* ed. Michael Dauphinais and Matthew Levering, 114–35. Chicago: Hillenbrand Books, 2009.

Bianchi, Paolo. *When Is Marriage Null? Guide to the Grounds of Nullity for*

Pastors, Counselors, and Lay Faithful. Translated by Michael Miller. San Francisco: Ignatius Press, 2015.

Biagi, Ruggero, OP. *La Causalità dell' umanità di Cristo e dei Sacramenti nella "Summa Theologie" di S. Tommaso d'Aquino.* Bologna: Edizioni Studio Domenicano, 1985.

Blankenhorn, Bernhard, OP. "The Instrumental Causality of the Sacraments: Thomas Aquinas and Louis Marie Chauvet." *Nova et Vetera,* English Edition, 4, no. 2 (2006): 255–94.

————. "The Place of Romans 6 in Aquinas' Doctrine of Sacramental Causality: A Balance of Scripture and Metaphysics." In *Ressourcement Thomism: Sacred Doctrine, The Sacraments, and the Moral Life,* ed. Hütter and Levering, 136–49.

Bouyer, Louis. *Liturgical Piety.* Notre Dame, Ind.: University of Notre Dame Press, 1955.

Broadbent, Hal St John. *The Call of the Holy: Heidegger — Chauvet — Benedict XVI.* London: T and T Clark, 2012.

Brown, Raymond, SS. *New Testament Essays.* New York: Image Books, 1968.

Burke, Patrick. *Reinterpreting Rahner: A Critical Study of His Major Themes.* New York: Fordham University Press, 2002.

Calvin, John. *Institutes of the Christian Religion.* Vol. 2. Translated by Henry Beveridge. London: James Clarke, 1962.

Casel, Odo, OSB. *The Mystery of Christian Worship and Other Writings.* Westminster, Md.: Newman Press, 1962.

Cessario, Romanus, OP. "'Circa res … aliquid fit' (Summa theologiae II-II, q. 85, a. 3, ad 3): Aquinas on New Law Sacrifice." *Nova et Vetera,* English Edition, 4, no. 2 (2006): 295–312.

————. *The Godly Image: Christ and Salvation in Catholic Thought from Anselm to Aquinas.* Petersham, Mass.: St. Bede's Publications, 1990.

————. "The Sacraments of the Church." In *Vatican II: Renewal Within Tradition,* ed. Matthew Lamb and Matthew Levering (Oxford: Oxford University Press, 2008), 140.

————. *Theology and Sanctity.* Edited by Cajetan Cuddy, OP. Ave Maria, Fla.: Sapientia Press, 2014.

Chauvet, Louis-Marie. *The Sacraments: The Word of God at the Mercy of the Body.* Translated by Madeleine Beaumont. Collegeville, Minn.: Liturgical Press, 2001.

————. *Symbol and Sacrament: A Sacramental Reinterpretation of Christian Existence.* Translated by P. Madigan and M. Beaumont. Collegeville, Minn.: Liturgical Press, 1995.

Christian, Robert. "Midway between Baptism and Holy Orders: Saint Thomas' Contribution to a Contemporary Understanding of Confirmation." *Angelicum* 69 (1992): 157–73.

Congar, Yves. *Tradition and Traditions: The Biblical, Historical, and Theological Evidence for Catholic Teaching on Tradition.* Needham Heights, Mass.: Simon and Schuster,1997.

Congregation for the Doctrine of the Faith. Declaration: *Dominus Iesus, On the Unicity and Salvific Universality of Jesus Christ and the Church.* 2000.

Conley, Kieran, OSB. *A Theology of Wisdom: A Study in St. Thomas.* Dubuque, Iowa: The Priory Press, 1963.

Corbett, John, OP, et al. "Recent Proposals for the Pastoral Care of the Divorced and Remarried: A Theological Assessment." *Nova et Vetera,* English Edition, 12, no. 3 (2014): 601–30.

Cross, Richard. *Duns Scotus.* Oxford: Oxford University Press, 1999.

Daniélou, Jean. *The Bible and the Liturgy.* South Bend, Ind.: University of Notre Dame Press, 1956.

Dauphinais, Michael, and Matthew Levering, eds. *Wisdom and Holiness, Science and Scholarship: Essays in Honor of Matthew L. Lamb.* Ave Maria, Fla.: Sapientia Press, 2007.

———. *Rediscovering Aquinas and the Sacraments: Studies in Sacramental Theology.* Chicago: Hillenbrand Books, 2009.

Deely, John. *Augustine and Poinsot: The Protosemiotic Development.* Scranton, Pa.: University of Scranton Press, 2009.

de la Soujeole, Benoît-Dominique, OP. "The Importance of the Definition of Sacraments as Signs." In *Ressourcement Thomism: Sacred Doctrine, the Sacraments, and the Moral Life,* edited by Reinhard Hütter and Matthew Levering, 127–35. Washington, D.C.: The Catholic University of America Press, 2010.

Denzinger, Heinrich. *Enchiridion symbolorum definitionum et declarationum de rebus fidei et morum: Compendium of Creeds, Definitions, and Declarations on Matters of Faith and Morals.* Edited by Peter Hünermann. Latin/English, 43rd ed. San Francisco: Ignatius Press, 2012.

Descartes, René. *Descartes: Key Philosophical Writings.* Translated by Elizabeth Haldane and G. R. T. Ross. Hertfordshire: Wordsworth Editions, 1997.

Dictionnaire de théologie catholique. Volume 2, part 2. Edited by A. Vacant and E. Mangenot. Paris: Letouzey et Ané, 1905.

———. Volume 14, part 1. Edited by A. Vacant, E. Mangenot, and É. Amann. Paris: Letouzey et Ané, 1939.

Dizionario di spiritualità biblico-patristica. Padua: Libreria del Santo, 1993.

Donahue, John M. "Sacramental Character: The State of the Question." *The Thomist* 31 (1967): 445–64.

Dulles, Avery. *The Assurance of Things Hoped For: A Theology of Christian Faith.* Oxford: Oxford University Press, 1994.

Emery, Gilles, OP. *The Trinity: An Introduction to the Catholic Doctrine of the Triune God.* Translated by Matthew Levering. Washington, D.C.: The Catholic University of America Press, 2011.

———. *Trinity, Church, and the Human Person: Thomistic Essays.* Ave Maria, Fla.: Sapientia Press, 2007.

Fagerberg, David W. *Theologia Prima: What Is Liturgical Theology?* Chicago/Mundelein: Hillenbrand Books, 2004.

Filip, Štěpán Martin, OP. "*Imago Repræsentativa Passionis Christi*: St. Thomas Aquinas on the Essence of the Sacrifice of the Mass." Translated by Roger W. Nutt. *Nova et Vetera*, English Edition, 7 (2009): 405–38.

Gallagher, John F. *Significando Causant: A Study of Sacramental Efficiency.* Fribourg: University Press, 1965.

Garrigan, Siobhan. *Beyond Ritual: Sacramental Theology after Habermas.* Burlington, Vt.: Ashgate Publishing, 2004.

Grillmeier, Aloys, SJ. *From the Apostolic Age to Chalcedon (451).* Vol. 1 of *Christ in the Christian Tradition.* Translated by J. S. Bowden. New York: Sheed and Ward, 1965.

Guerra, Marc, D. "The One, The Many, and the Mystical Body." *The Heythrop Journal* 53 (2012): 904–14.

Haring, Nicholas, S.A.C., "St. Augustine's Use of the Word *Character*." *Mediaeval Studies* 14 (1952): 79–97.

Hofer, Andrew, OP, ed. *Divinization: Becoming Icons of Christ through the Liturgy.* Chicago/Mundelein: Hillenbrand Books, 2015.

Hugh of St. Victor. *Hugh of St. Victor on the Sacraments of the Christian Faith.* Translated by Roy J. Deferrari. Cambridge, Mass.: Mediaeval Academy of America, 1951. Reprint: Eugene, Ore.: Wipf and Stock, 2007.

Hugon, Edouard. *La causalité instrumentale: dans l'ordre surnaturel.* Paris: Pierre Téqui, 1924.

Hütter, Reinhard. *Dust Bound for Heaven: Explorations in the Theology of Thomas Aquinas.* Grand Rapids, Mich.: William B. Eerdmans, 2012.

Hütter, Reinhard, and Matthew Levering, eds. *Ressourcement Thomism: Sacred Doctrine, the Sacraments, and the Moral Life.* Washington, D.C.: The Catholic University of America Press, 2010.

Iturrioz, Daniel. "La definición del Concilio de Trento sobre la causalidad de los sacramentos." *Estudios eclesiásticos* 24 (1950): 291–340.

Janz, Denis. *Luther on Thomas Aquinas: The Angelic Doctor in the Thought of the Reformer.* Stuttgart: Franz Steiner Verlag Wieshaden GMB, 1989.

Jedin, Hubert. *The First Sessions at Trent 1545–47.* Vol. 2 of *A History of the Council of Trent.* Translated by Dom Ernest Graf, OSB. London: Thomas Nelson and Sons, 1961.

John of the Cross. *The Living Flame of Love,* stanza 3, §28. In *The Collected Works of John of the Cross.* Translated by Kieran Kavanaugh, OCD, and Otilio Rodriguez, OCD. Washington, D.C.: ICS Publications, 1991.

John of St. Thomas. *Introduction to the Summa Theologiae of Thomas Aquinas.* Translated by Ralph McInerny. South Bend, Ind.: St. Augustine's Press, 2004.

John Paul II. Apostolic Letter: *Vicesimus Quintus Annus.* 1988.

Journet, Charles. *The Mass: The Presence of the Sacrifice of the Cross.* Translated by Victor Szczurek, OPraem. South Bend, Ind.: St. Augustine's Press, 2008.

———. *Theology of the Church.* Translated by Victor Szczurek, OPraem. San Francisco, Calif.: Ignatius Press, 2004.

———. *The Meaning of Grace.* Translated by A. V. Littledale. Princeton, N.J.: Scepter Publishers, 1996.

Keating, Daniel A. *Deification and Grace.* Ave Maria, Fla: Sapientia Press, 2007.

Keller, Paul Jerome, OP. "Is Spiritual Communion for Everyone?" *Nova et Vetera,* English Edition, 12, no. 3 (2014): 631–55.

Kerr, Fergus. *Twentieth-Century Catholic Theologians: From Neoscholasticism to Nuptial Mysticism.* Oxford: Blackwell Publishing, 2007.

King, Ronald F., CM. "The Origin and Evolution of a Sacramental Formula: *SACRAMENTUM TANTUM, RES ET SACRAMENTUM, RES TANTUM.*" *The Thomist* 31 (1967): 21–82.

Kubicki, Judith, CSSF. "Recognizing the Presence of Christ in the Liturgical Assembly." *Theological Studies* 65 (2007): 817–37.

———. *The Presence of Christ in the Gathered Assembly.* New York: Continuum International, 2006.

Lamb, Matthew, and Matthew Levering, eds. *Vatican II: Renewal Within Tradition.* Oxford: Oxford University Press, 2008.

Langevin, Dominic M., OP. *From Passion to Paschal Mystery: A Recent Magisterial Development Concerning the Christological Foundation of the Sacraments.* Studia Friburgensia. Fribourg, Switzerland: Fribourg Academic Press, 2015.

Leeming, Bernard, SJ. *Principles of Sacramental Theology*. Westminster, Md.: Newman Press, 1956.

———. "Recent Trends in Sacramental Theology." *Irish Theological Quarterly* 23 (1956): 195–217.

Leithart, Peter. "Old Covenant and New in Sacramental Theology New and Old." *Pro Ecclesia* 14, no. 2 (2005): 174–90.

Levering, Matthew. *Christ and the Catholic Priesthood: Ecclesial Hierarchy and the Pattern of the Trinity*. Chicago: Hillenbrand Books, 2010.

———. "Christ the Priest: An Exploration of *Summa Theologiae*, III, Question 22." *The Thomist* 71 (2007): 379–417.

———. *Christ's Fulfillment of Torah and Temple: Salvation according to St. Thomas Aquinas*. Notre Dame: University of Notre Dame Press, 2002.

———. *Scripture and Metaphysics: Aquinas and the Renewal of Trinitarian Theology*. Oxford: Blackwell Publishing, 2004.

———. *The Theology of Augustine*. Grand Rapids, Mich.: Baker Academic, 2013.

Lienhard, Joseph, SJ. "*Sacramentum* and the Eucharist in St. Augustine." *The Thomist* 77 (2013): 173–92.

Luther, Martin. *Martin Luther: Selections from His Writings*. Edited by John Dillenberger. New York: Anchor Books, 1961.

Lynch, Reginald M., OP. "Cajetan's Harp: Sacraments and the Life of Grace in Light of Perfective Instrumental Causality." *The Thomist* 78 (2014): 65–106.

———. "The Sacraments as Causes of Sanctification." *Nova et Vetera*, English Edition, 12, no. 3 (2014): 791–836.

Lynn, G. D. "Christ's Redemptive Merit: The Nature of Its Causality According to St. Thomas." S.T.D. dissertation, Pontifical Gregorian University, 1962.

Mansini, Guy, OSB. "Sacerdotal Character at the Second Vatican Council." *The Thomist* 66 (2002): 369–94.

Maritain, Jacques and Raïssa. *Liturgy and Contemplation*. Translated by Joseph W. Evans. New York: P. J. Kenedy and Sons, 1960 .

Martin, Francis, and William Wright IV. *The Gospel of John*. Grand Rapids, Mich.: Baker Academic, 2015.

Maurer, Armand. *The Philosophy of William of Ockham in the Light of Its Principles*. Toronto: Pontifical Institute of Mediaeval Studies, 1999.

McWhorter, Matthew R. "The Real Distinction of Substance and Quantity: John of St. Thomas in Contrast to Ockham and Descartes." *The Modern Schoolman* 85 (2008): 225–45.

Meehan, Francis. "Efficient Causality in Aristotle and St. Thomas." Ph.D. Dissertation. The Catholic University of America, 1940.

Michelet, Thomas, OP. "Louis-Marie Chauvet et la sacramentalité de la parole entre analogie et paradigme." *Revue Thomiste* 113 (2013): 179–94.

Miralles, Antonio. *I Sacramenti Cristiani: Trattato Generale*. Rome: EDUSC s.r.l, 2008.

Morerod, Charles, OP. *Ecumenism and Philosophy: Philosophical Questions for a Renewal of Dialogue*. Ave Maria, Fla.: Sapientia Press, 2006.

Nietzsche, Friedrich. "Parable of the Madman." In his *The Gay Science*, ed. Walter Kaufmann, 181–82. New York: Vintage, 1974.

Newman, John Henry. *Selected Sermons, Prayers, and Devotions*. Edited by John F. Thornton and Susan B. Varenne. New York: Vintage Spiritual Classics, 1999.

Newton, Isaac. *Principia: The Mathematical Principles of Natural Philosophy*. Translated by Andrew Motte. Whitefish, Mont.: Kessinger Publishing, 2008.

Nicolas, J.-H. *Synthèse dogmatique: De la Trinité à la Trinité*. Editions Universitaires Fribourg Suisse. Paris: Beauchesne, 1985.

———. *The Mystery of God's Grace*. London: Bloomsbury Publishing, 1960.

Nutt, Roger W. "Faith, Metaphysics, and the Contemplation of Christ's Corporeal Presence in the Eucharist: Translation of St. Thomas Aquinas' Seventh Quodlibetal Dispute, Q. 4, A. 1 with an Introductory Essay." *Antiphon: A Journal of Liturgical Renewal* 15, no. 2 (2011): 151–71.

———. "From Within the Mediation of Christ: The Place of Christ in the Christian Moral and Sacramental Life According to St. Thomas Aquinas." *Nova et Vetera*, English Edition, 5 (2007): 817–42.

———. "*Gaudium et Spes* and the Indissolubility of the Sacrament of Matrimony: The Contribution of Cardinal Journet." *Nova et Vetera*, English Edition, 11, no. 3 (2013): 619–26.

———. "An Office in Search of Its Ontology: Mediation and Trinitarian Christology in Jacques Dupuis' Theology of Religious Pluralism." *Louvain Studies* 32 (2008): 383–407.

———. "On Analogy, the Incarnation, and the Sacraments of the Church: Considerations from the *Tertia pars* of the *Summa theologiae*." *Nova et Vetera*, English Edition, 12, no. 3 (2014): 989–1004.

———. "Sacerdotal Character and the *Munera Christi*: Reflections on the Theology of Charles Cardinal Journet in Relation to the Second Vatican Council." *Gregorianum* 90, no. 2 (2009): 237–53.

O'Neill, Colman E., OP. *Sacramental Realism: A General Theory of the Sacraments*. Chicago: Midwest Theological Forum, 1998.

Osborne, Kenan, OFM. *Christian Sacraments in a Postmodern World: A Theology for the Third Millennium*. Mahwah, N.J.: Paulist Press, 1999.

———. *Sacramental Theology: A General Introduction*. New York: Paulist Press, 1988.

Pakaluk, Michael, ed. *Other Selves: Philosophers on Friendship*. Indianapolis, Ind.: Hackett Publishing Company, Inc., 1991.

Perrier, Emmanuel, OP. "Le Pain de Vie chez Louis-Marie Chauvet et saint Thomas d'Aquin. Représentation de l'inconnaissable ou terme de l'union spirituelle?" *Revue Thomiste* 113 (2013): 195–234.

Peter Lombard. *On the Doctrine of Signs*. Book 4 of *The Sentences*. Translated by Giulio Silano. Toronto: Pontifical Institute of Mediaeval Studies, 2010.

Pickstock, Catherine. *After Writing: On the Liturgical Consummation of Philosophy*. Oxford: Blackwell Publishers, 1998.

Poschmann, Bernhard. *Penance and the Anointing of the Sick*. Translated by F. Courtney, SJ. New York: Herder and Herder, 1964.

Pseudo-Dionysius. *The Complete Works*. Translated by Colm Luibheid. New York: Paulist Press, 1987.

Rahner, Karl. *Ecclesiology, Questions in the Church, The Church in the World*. Vol. 14 of *Theological Investigations*. Translated by David Bourke. New York: Seabury Press, 1976.

———. *Inquiries: Questiones Disputatae*. Vol. 9. New York: Herder and Herder, 1964.

———. *Meditations on the Sacraments*. New York: Seabury Press, 1977.

———. *More Recent Writings*. Vol. 4 of *Theological Investigations*. Translated by Kevin Smith. London: Darton, Longman, and Todd, 1966.

Ratzinger, Joseph. *The Spirit of the Liturgy*. Translated by John Saward. San Francisco: Ignatius Press, 2000.

Reid, Alcuin, OSB. *The Organic Development of the Liturgy: The Principles of Liturgical Reform and Their Relation to the Twentieth-Century Liturgical Movement Prior to the Second Vatican Council*. San Francisco, Calif.: Ignatius Press, 2005.

Revel, Jean-Philippe. *Traité des sacrements. I.1 Baptême et sacramentalité. Origine et signification de baptême*. Paris: Les Éditions du Cerf, 2004.

———. *Traité des sacrements: I.2. Baptême et sacramentalité. Don et réception de la grâce baptismale*. Paris: Les Éditions du Cerf, 2005.

Rist, John M. *Augustine*. Cambridge: Cambridge University Press, 1994.

Sala, Giovanni. "What Use Is Kant for Theology?" In *Wisdom and Holiness, Science and Scholarship: Essays in Honor of Matthew L. Lamb*, ed. Michael Dauphinais and Matthew Levering, 293–314. Ave Maria, Fla.: Sapientia Press, 2007.

Schillebeeckx, E. *Christ the Sacrament of the Encounter with God*. Franklin, Wis.: Sheed and Ward, 1963.

————. *The Eucharist*. Translated by N. D. Smith. New York: Sheed and Ward, 1968.

Schwartz, Daniel. *Aquinas on Friendship*. Oxford Philosophical Monographs. Oxford: Oxford University Press, 2007.

Spezzano, Daria. *The Glory of God's Grace: Deification according to St. Thomas Aquinas*. Ave Maria, Fla.: Sapientia Press, 2015.

Surmanski, Sr. Albert Marie, O.P. "Sign and Symbol: Sacramental Experience in Albert's *De corpore domini*." *New Blackfriars* 97 (2016): 479–91.

Sweeney, Conor. *Sacramental Presence After Heidegger: Ontotheology, Sacraments, and a Mother's Smile*. Eugene, Ore.: Cascade Books, 2015.

Thomas Aquinas. *Aquinas's Shorter Summa* [Compendium of Theology]. Translated by Cyril Vollert, SJ. Manchester, N.H.: Sophia Institute Press, 2002.

————. *Commentary on Aristotle's* Metaphysics. Translated by John P. Rowan. Notre Dame, Ind.: Dumb Ox Books, 1995.

————. *Commentary on the Epistle to the Hebrews*. Translated by Chrysostom Baer, O. Praem. South Bend, Ind.: St. Augustine's Press, 2006.

————. *Summa contra gentiles*. Book I. Translated by Anton Pegis. Notre Dame, Ind.: University of Notre Dame Press, 1955.

————. *Summa theologiae*. Complete set, Latin-English. Lander, Wyo.: Aquinas Institute, 2012.

Torrell, Jean-Pierre, OP. *Christ and Spirituality in St. Thomas Aquinas*. Translated by Bernhard Blankenhorn, OP. Washington, D.C.: The Catholic University of America Press, 2011.

Toups, David L. *Reclaiming Our Priestly Character*. Omaha, Neb.: Institute for Priestly Formation, 2008.

Vagaggini, Cyprian. *Theological Dimensions of the Liturgy: A General Treatise on the Theology of the Liturgy*. Translated by Leonard J. Doyle and W. A. Jurgens. Collegeville, Minn.: Liturgical Press, 1976.

Van Roo, William, SJ. *The Christian Sacrament*. Rome: Editrice Pontificia Università Gregoriana, 1992.

————. "Reflections on Karl Rahner's '*Kirche und Sakramente*.'" *Gregorianum* 44 (1963): 465–500.

Vatican Council II: The Conciliar and Post Conciliar Documents. Edited by
A. Flannery. Wilmington, Del.: Scholarly Resources, 1975.

Vorgrimler, Herbert. *Sacramental Theology.* Translated by Linda M. Malo-
ney. Collegeville, Minn.: Liturgical Press, 1992.

Walsh, Liam, OP. "Liturgy in the Theology of St. Thomas." *The Thomist*
38 (1974): 557–83.

———. "Sacraments." In *The Theology of Thomas Aquinas,* edited by Rik
Van Nieuwenhove and Joseph Wawrykow, 327–67. Notre Dame, Ind.:
University of Notre Dame Press, 2005.

———. *Sacraments of Initiation: A Theology of Life, Word, and Rite.* 2nd ed.
Chicago: Hillenbrand Books, 2011.

Weinandy, Thomas G., OFM. *Jesus: Essays in Christology.* Ave Maria, Fla.:
Sapientia Press, 2014.

Welch, Larry. "The Decree on the Ministry and Life of Priests, *Presbyterorum Ordinis.*" In *Vatican II: Renewal Within Tradition*, ed. Matthew Lamb
and Matthew Levering, 205–27. Oxford: Oxford University Press, 2008.

White, Thomas Joseph, OP. *Wisdom in the Face of Modernity: A Study in
Thomistic Natural Theology.* Ave Maria, Fla.: Sapientia Press, 2009.

Wippel, John F. *The Metaphysical Thought of Thomas Aquinas: From Finite
Being to Uncreated Being.* Washington, D.C.: The Catholic University of
America Press, 2000.

Index

General Principles of Sacramental Theology was designed and typeset in Agmena Pro
with Meta Pro display by Kachergis Book Design of Pittsboro, North Carolina.
It was printed on 55-pound Natures Recycled, and bound by Sheridan Books of
Chelsea, Michigan.